The early history of British society presents a recurring theme of conquest and subsequent cultural fusion, a subtle and complex pattern which can only be revealed by using many sources, both historical and archaeological. There is no comprehensive study of these foundations of British culture and society written by experts for a non-specialist audience. This series of books has been designed to meet that need.

There are five volumes in the series, covering the period from Palaeolithic Britain through to the eve of the Norman Conquest; in each volume, the author has sought to bring the often obscure findings of scholarship to a wider interested audience, through the medium of non-technical presentation and carefully selected photographs, maps and plans. Although each volume is complete in itself, the series as a whole forms a complete history of early Britain.

The Author

Born in Mansfield, Nottinghamshire, Stephen Johnson was educated at Christ's Hospital and Wadham College, Oxford, where he took his DPhil. Appointed to the Inspectorate of Ancient Monuments in 1973, he is the author of several articles on the Roman period, and one longer work, *The Roman Forts of the Saxon Shore* (Paul Elek, 1976).

Britain before the Conquest
A Paladin Archaeological History of the British Isles,
c.1500 BC–AD 1066

General Editor: Andrew Wheatcroft

The Origins of Britain Lloyd and Jennifer Laing
Celtic Britain Lloyd Laing
The Coming of Rome John Wacher
Later Roman Britain Stephen Johnson
Anglo-Saxon England Lloyd and Jennifer Laing

STEPHEN JOHNSON

Later Roman Britain

PALADIN
GRAFTON BOOKS
A Division of the Collins Publishing Group

LONDON GLASGOW
TORONTO SYDNEY AUCKLAND

Paladin
Grafton Books
A Division of the Collins Publishing Group
8 Grafton Street, London W1X 3LA

Published in Paladin Books 1982
Reprinted 1986

First published in Great Britain by
Routledge & Kegan Paul Ltd 1980
as a title in the BRITAIN BEFORE THE CONQUEST series

Copyright © Stephen Johnson 1980

ISBN 0-586-08372-3

Printed and bound in Great Britain by
Collins, Glasgow

Set in Palatino

Contents

Acknowledgments

The author gratefully acknowledges the assistance of the following persons and institutions for the provision of illustrative material, and for allowing it to be reproduced: The Ashmolean Museum, Oxford, Plates 9, 33, and 46; P. Barker, Figure 18; The Bodleian Library, Oxford, Plates 1 and 31; The Trustees of the British Museum, Plates 34, 55 and 60; The Cambridge University Committee for Aerial Photography, Plates 3, 4, 8, 19, 23, 24, 29, 43, 49, 52 and 53; The Corinium Museum, Cirencester, Plate 2; The Department of Archaeology, University College, Cardiff, Plate 25; The Department of the Environment, Plates 5, 41, 42 and 54; The Dorchester Excavation Committee and C. J. S. Green, Plate 57 and Figure 19; Paul Elek Ltd, the originals for Figure 15 and Maps 13–16; Fototeca Unione, Rome, Plate 28; Sheila Gibson, Figure 1; The Gwynedd Archaeological Trust Ltd and R. B. White, Plates 26, 27 and 36; The Trustees of the Helms-Museum, Harburg, Hamburg, Plate 14; Kingston-on-Hull Museum, Plate 6; Leicester Museums Service, Plate 59; The Mansell Collection, Plate 12; Mucking Excavation Committee and W. T. Jones, Plates 44 and 47(b); The Museum of London, Plates 47(a) and 48; the National Monuments Record, Plates 7, 40, 50, 51 and 56; The National Museum of Antiquities, Dublin, Plates 22 (a) and (b); The National Museum of Antiquities of Scotland, Plates 20 and 21; Norfolk Museums Service (Norwich Castle Museum), Plates 45 (a) and (b); G. Parnell, Plate 39; Scarborough Borough Council and Londesborough Lodge Museum, Scarborough, Plate 38; Schleswig-Holstein Landesmuseum, Plates 13, 15, and 16; The Scottish Development Department, Plates 17, 18 and 58 (a) and (b); The Society of Antiquaries of London, Plate 37, and the originals for Figures 4, 7, 10, 11, 15 and 20; R. Wilkins, who provided the print for Plate 11; and R. P. Wright and the Clarendon Press, Oxford for Figure 9.

1 The provinces of Britain

Britain, you are indeed fortunate, and now more blessed
than any other land, since you were the first to see Constantine as Emperor. Nature rightly endowed you with every
benefit of land and climate. Your winters are not too cold,
nor your summers too hot: your corn-fields are so produc-
tive they assure you of the gifts not only of Ceres, but of the
Liberi too. No terrible beasts shelter in your woods, no
noxious snakes infest your earth. Far from it! Your domestic
herds are innumerable: their udders bulge with milk, and
their backs are laden with wool. To make life the more
pleasant, the days are of the longest, and no night goes by
without some light, since your flat shoreline throws no
shadow. While the night and its constellations revolve, the
sun himself, who to us appears to go down, in Britain seems
only to go past. [1]

This poetic picture, given in a speech in the year AD 310
before Constantine, who had been acclaimed emperor of
the Roman world some five years earlier at York, sums up
some of the obstacles which block our view of Britain as a
province of the Roman Empire. The passage, like others in
the same vein, forms part of one of the Panegyrics –
speeches delivered by court orators – in which the
achievements and fame of the current emperor were duly
celebrated. The court was at the time at Trier (Augusta
Trevirorum) in present-day Germany, and though this is
not exceptionally far from Britain, the unknown orator
describes something of a cross between prosaic fact and
fictional paradise: Britain, the argument runs, is a fabulous
land of plenty – the most appropriate ` place for the
emperor to have been proclaimed. Had Constantine's
father not died in York, and his son not hurried to his

7

bedside there, any other province would have fitted smoothly into the orator's fulsome summary.

The idea that Britain lay at the edge of the known world, an awkward appendage to Mediterranean culture, was of course a commonplace, even now, after the island had enjoyed 200 and more years of provincial Roman status. Mediterranean authors could still consider Britain, on the fringes of barbarism of a particularly savage kind, as a rather shaky bastion of the civilised world against the increasing pressures from outside. Perhaps there is also a hint that she was ultimately expendable: another panegyrist, giving a speech slightly earlier (in AD 297) labours the many benefits which Britain has brought to the empire – her varied crops and pastures, her flowing rivers of metal, the taxes (!) with which she seethes, her many harbours, her very size![2] This list served to convince the panegyrist that it had been worth bothering to regain for the empire the British provinces which had temporarily fallen under the control of an illegal and officially unrecognised regime.

Clearly, the fact that Britain was an island lying outside the more comfortable confines of the Mediterranean – 'our sea', as Romans called it – was of great psychological importance. Almost certainly the first Roman pioneers on the island, before there was any thought of bringing her into the empire as a province, will have been merchants: their purpose was to tap mineral sources, to gather foodstuffs and livestock and to buy these with Roman luxury goods from the native pre-Roman population. Julius Caesar led the first actual military pioneering sorties across the Dover Straits, and though he gained some success, largely on the diplomatic front, and certainly profited by the propaganda value of his expeditions, it was not until nearly a century later that Roman troops again crossed the Straits, this time properly to annexe the British territory. The aim was to back up with action the foreign policies Rome had been following: one of her allied Celtic chiefs had recently been deposed, and this fact provided a spur to the emperor Claudius, who was relatively new to

8

the throne. He was anxious to show that he, like his more martial and illustrious predecessors Augustus and Tiberius, could contemplate and sustain the annexation of new territory for the Roman Empire. Once the Roman legions and auxiliaries had gained their foothold in the island, the process of Romanisation, though slow, and subject to temporary setbacks, was never seriously halted.

The benefits which Rome brought and imposed upon her subject peoples were many and diverse. In the wake of military domination came the setting up of provincial and local government, political creations in which established native leaders were encouraged to play their part. There followed the organisation of town life, with patterns provided by colonies of retired legionary veterans who in places like Gloucester, Lincoln and Colchester demonstrated a style and a standard of communal living to which native British Celts were scarcely accustomed. Of course, this process was not quickly achieved, but wrongs perpetrated by Roman administrators – and wrongs there certainly were, confiscations, annexations and impositions – were not allowed to rankle too long within the new climate of opportunity and relative peace. Indeed the Roman involvement in Britain seems almost immediately to have given a coherence and a stability to the political balance of the island, which until then had been uneasy, with fragmented Celtic tribal associations and struggles for power between warring or machinating local potentates. Rome used a formula which had been successful with northern Gaul, in many ways at this time similar to Britain: the various tribal units within Britain retained their integrity but as regional portions of a new united Britain, the Roman province of Britannia.

The toughest opposition to the Roman conquest had come from the northern uplands and from Wales. The military assault on Britain came in AD 43, but it was not until the 70s that the Brigantes, most powerful of the northern tribes, were subdued. In that thirty-year space there had been ample time for attitudes to mellow, and for the realisation by the leaders of the Brigantes that the

Roman armies were hardly likely to disappear. The assault, when it did come from the Roman side, was sudden, dramatic and conclusive: having defeated the Brigantes, and taken their stronghold, the Roman armies moved on to consolidate their territorial gain, and to attempt to hold down the less tractable area further north. But both this area of southern Scotland and the northernmost parts of England needed a continuing military presence: neither area ever really ceased to be a frontier zone.

It is surprising that Britain was so effectively united. Roman policies were remarkably sound, for there is no record of concerted action by the British tribes against Rome. The process of Romanisation was one of education and indoctrination, a broadening of society so that each tribal unit became a part not only of its British province, but a small part of the Roman Empire, and thus of the whole world. The benefits which membership of the empire brought were wealth, luxury and a secure if not an enhanced position within this wider scheme of things, though these were only appreciated by a privileged yet politically important minority. There was also official Roman encouragement for the best use of the natural resources of Britain – be it in farming, mining or manufacturing. Thus Britain, accepted within the Roman world, seems to have embraced without undue hesitation, and without later second thoughts, her role as the most northerly province of the Roman Empire.

By the late third century, Britain's name was still ironically a literary commonplace for 'the end of the world', but this is not surprising. Political events of international importance rarely occurred there: annalists mentioned the province's conquests and military vicissitudes only as part of the strategic patchwork of the empire, or for personal motives like those of Tacitus, in his biography of Agricola, one of the greatest of early expansionist generals. References to events in Britain are often chance or incidental remarks within a wider narrative: for 200 years little had happened to reverse the

Romanisation of Britain, which had been a steady process, until by about AD 300 it was as civilised and as cosmopolitan as any other province of the Roman world. 'Romanisation' was no longer an imposition – it was now a traditional way of life. Britannia occasions little comment by historians of the later Roman Empire, for whom the emperor, with his military exploits, his court, his rivals and his travels, is the most important figure.

Source material for the history of Britain in the later years of the Roman Empire comes from a multitude of diverse places. There are factual accounts like itineraries, road-books, lists of dignitaries and their staff, inscriptions, funerary monuments, religious dedications and incidental mentions in historians of greater or lesser value (depending on their motives for writing). Taken on their own, these first-hand written records by contemporary or near-contemporary sources add up to an incomplete picture: a province, or at this later stage a diocese (group of provinces), of the Roman Empire was a complex structure whose organisation can be better understood from fuller sources which give more detail about other portions of the empire.

The ever-growing body of evidence from archaeology supplements this picture. It provides the remains of the buildings, objects of daily use, or in some cases the remains of the people themselves – in short, a whole spectrum of settlement and social history. This, too, has its limitations: it can but rarely pinpoint an historical event within an exact moment in time. Again, by comparing Britain with the rest of the western Roman world as a whole, it is possible to see what her provincial status meant in material terms; to gauge in some measure the wealth and status of some of her inhabitants, and also, from military remains, to assess the areas where her provincial security was threatened by hostile pressures.

By AD 314, the island was subdivided administratively into four Roman provinces forming the diocese of Britanniae, 'The Britains'.[3] Originally a single province with its northern boundary either at Hadrian's Wall

Map 1 Plan of the provinces of fourth-century Britain, showing the administrative divisions within the island

between present-day Carlisle and Newcastle, or at the Antonine Wall (Glasgow–Edinburgh), Britain had been divided into two, Upper and Lower Britain, in AD 197. Under the emperor Diocletian (286–305) the provinces were reorganised: Lower Britain, which lay in the north of England, was further divided and the two halves were renamed Britannia Secunda and Flavia Caesariensis. The capital of one of these provinces was York, the other probably Lincoln. The southern part, formerly Upper Britain, was also subdivided: Cirencester was probably the capital of the western province of Britannia Prima, and London, always the main metropolis of the whole diocese, was the capital of Maxima Caesariensis. Basically this arrangement meant that the old provinces of Upper and Lower Britain were renamed Prima and Secunda, and each subdivided by a province 'Caesariensis', bearing the name Maxima or Flavia. What inspired these names is a matter for debate, but it has been suggested that the names were those of the two Caesars, 'deputy rulers' of the eastern and western empires.[4]

The hub of government of Britain lay in London, at the metropolis. Here the emperor's representative, the *vicarius*, had his staff, his office, and his palace. His chain of command was directly in line with the emperor, through the praetorian prefect, traditionally the commanding officer of the emperor's bodyguard, although now the post had become the emperor's grand vizier. Each of the four British provinces also had a governor (*praeses* or *consularis*), who was responsible for all forms of administration within his province: his department was competent to deal with legal and most financial matters; it maintained law and order and the public post, and also kept a strict oversight of the various forms of local government which went on in the lesser cities. Above these governors, the *vicarius* headed a court of appeal and maintained a further, perhaps somewhat top-heavy, general supervision. There was a distinct tendency in the later Roman Empire towards the proliferation of such provincial governorships, and the post of *vicarius* may well have been an unnecessary

1 The insignia of the *Vicarius Britanniarum* (the Vicar of the Britains) from Chapter 23 of the western portion of the Oxford Codex of the *Notitia Dignitatum*. On a roughly triangular island, the supposed five British provinces are arranged to signify the area which the *vicarius* controlled (Bodleian Library, Oxford, Canon Misc. 378, fol. 150v.)

encumbrance. However, in the upper echelons of the empire there was a massive turnover of men to fill such posts: the average duration in office was less than one year. It is therefore highly probable that the local staffs of civil servants carried on the main running of government, and the rather too elaborate chain of command at provincial diocesan level may have been intended as a

14

2 Inscription from Cirencester (*RIB* 103) recording a dedication to Jupiter by the *Rector Primae Provinciae* – the governor of Britannia Prima. This suggests that Cirencester was capital of this late Roman province

safety check against abuses of the system, which it appears were still all too frequent. Many men who held office as provincial governors regarded their time in office as a chance to make a quick fortune at the expense of their subjects, not so much from extortion of taxes as by receiving payments for court judgments given in a plaintiff's favour, or for public offices which were in their power to farm out. Patronage of this sort was to be found at all levels within the empire, and though the emperors repeatedly tried to stamp it out, the wishes of the central government were ignored at local level, both by the patrons and by those who hoped for jobs, promotions and favours from the relatively influential men above them: no one could afford to fall into disfavour with his immediate superior, whatever the emperor demanded.[5]

If this picture of governmental corruption seems too

black, it must be remembered that it was often only the blackest cases which came in for adverse comment by contemporary writers: the compliment to a good and honest governor's term of office was that he retired from his post 'a poor man', for the burdens of holding office involved him in entertainment and official expenses which he was expected to bear from his own pocket. A governor usually made a comfortable profit from his term of office. The transitory nature of the governor's post may have exacerbated this evil. Of the four or perhaps five British provincial governors or *vicarii* known in the fourth century, two were natives of the Greek-speaking eastern part of the Empire.[6] So, quite apart from any difficulty of communication, a term of office over unknown provincials at the extremity of the empire seems to have been regarded as a fair chance for a quick profit. Provincial governorships were won (or lost), doubtless, by a similar round of payments for patronage among the Emperor's favourites at court. There is little way of telling whether Britain was regarded as one of the richer prizes, but despite the fulsome eloquence of the panegyrists, it is scarcely likely to have ranked high in the bidding for patronage. Thus a governor posted to Britain might be a man who, having paid a large sum, was disappointed with his allocation, and who determined to make good the meagre state salary by ample subsidies from less honest sources.

The full ramifications of the highly centralised system of government were far-reaching. It depended on a highly organised and socially stratified society, on military security, on an efficient bureaucracy, and a meek acceptance of the whole machine on the part of the provincials. Of course, local organisation was much more the arena which held most people's attention than provincial administration. Like that of Gaul, the division of Britain after the initial Roman conquest had been into cantons based on the main pre-Roman Iron Age tribes. Rome therefore encouraged a continuing interest in local affairs, but the organisation into Roman-style towns gave the whole affair a 'Roman' flavour. At the end of the first century,

Britain was divided into some twenty *civitates*, or tribal cantons, and by the fourth century, this number had probably increased to about twenty-eight through the upgrading of some of the smaller settlements.[7] A *civitas* gradually came to mean not just a tribal area but an administrative unit grouped round some important town which itself came to be called the *civitas*. It is by no means easy to be precise about the exact areas covered by the various tribes within Britain: the tribe of the Coritani, for example, had as their territory a large portion of the East Midlands. Their capital was at Ratae Coritanorum (Leicester), but their tribal area included Lindum Colonia (Lincoln), originally an implanted Roman colony of veteran soldiers who would have been independent of the local cantonal organisation. By the later third or fourth century, however, such differences were largely ironed out. Though the term *colonia* was still in use as an honorific title, both Leicester and Lincoln ranked as *civitates* with an administrative area of their own. The area formerly under the control of the Coritani may also have been further subdivided by the promotion of the small town of Chesterton (Durobrivae) to the status of a *civitas*.

These 'country towns' will have had many, if not all, of the trappings associated with Roman city life throughout the empire. By AD 400 a continual process of urban growth will have ensured a roughly equal standard of public amenities, with differences in style and layout resulting as much from the comparative wealth of the local areas as from the original status of the town or city. The *civitas* capitals from the earliest days of organisation were laid out with a regular grid of streets, with *forum* (market), *basilica* (meeting-hall) and baths roughly at the centre. At or near the city centre would be the shops kept by tradesmen who made small-scale metalwork on the premises, or who sold local produce, clothes, or local or imported pottery and glassware; such might either be permanent open-fronted single or double-roomed stores on a street or colonnade, or market stalls within the *forum* area. One of the main functions of the large towns was to act as a market centre,

17

3 Aerial view of the Roman town of Durobrivae, Chesterton, Cambs. The walls enclosed a polygonal area, divided roughly in half by the main Roman road (visible in this plate as a white straight line). From this main street there branch off irregular metalled lanes which similar photographs show to have been bordered by stone-built houses. A courtyard building, possibly the *forum,* lay just north of the town centre

and on this factor the economic viability of the towns in the later empire depended.

The towns would also include more monumental public buildings – baths, temples, theatres – and usually just outside the walled area, an amphitheatre, all catering at various levels for the creative, material and spiritual comforts of the urban population. Perhaps the most important of the public buildings were the city walls and gates which defined the limits of the city. All city walls within the empire had to be built with the emperor's permission, and often with his financial backing or with assistance or technical advice from troops stationed within the province. The date at which cities had been first provided with walls depended greatly on the military emergencies (or perhaps even the local desires for prestige) which may have conditioned their construction. The majority of British *civitas* capitals, however, seem to have followed a roughly parallel development: an early phase of earth and timber defences, constructed in the second half of the second century, was followed in the first half of the third by the addition of a stone wall fronting this earth bank. Britain was unusual in this respect, for city defences were not put up on an empire-wide scale until the latter part of the third century. Only near the western frontiers of the Roman world were city defences constructed earlier than that.

Exactly how the space within these walled areas was used is not always clear. The best evidence for the layout of a Romano-British city which we have is that of Silchester, where excavations in the 1890s revealed the street plan and a number of buildings. These include the *forum* and *basilica*, a temple precinct, a large *mansio* (hotel), and many more houses. The earliest homes and shops were probably timber-framed with wattle-and-daub walls, replaced in stone only during the second century. Most of the *insulae* (housing blocks) enclose open spaces which may have been gardens, yards, or could have contained timber buildings whose remains were not traced. Any city might go through phases of redevelopment, prosperity, or decline, and each block within the walled area needs assessment to distinguish periods of construction and careful use or squalid occupation and decay. Evidence from most Romano-British cities is of a piecemeal nature, and this makes the overall quality of life at different stages within the long period of occupation difficult to assess. We cannot necessarily assume that a town which flourished in the third century did so in the fourth.

Within the territories controlled administratively by these *civitates*, there were a host of smaller settlements. Some might be forts of military origin and purpose, smaller civilian market centres, or official establishments, such as posting-stations where hotels would be maintained and a change of horses would be provided for important official and (at a price) other travellers. Others might be small industrial communities or humbler peasant settlements, often linked with either an official individual concern or the large estate of some local rich man. At the top end of this scale, the smaller settlements may have begun life as spontaneous market centres far enough away from the larger towns to serve a rural population. These were often small civilian communities which had settled round an early military establishment, long since abandoned, and though some were later enclosed with walls, there is no clear indication of an imposed rigorous plan. Those few which were upgraded to the status of *civitas* will have presumably required some specialist administrative buildings, and perhaps a *forum* to bring them into line with their newly improved status, but of such developments there is at present little or no trace in the archaeological record. There are many small Roman settlements in Britain, at road- and river-crossings, or at convenient distances along Roman roads. Some of these were eventually given walls quite late in the fourth century, while others remained as open, straggling settlements throughout their life. The reason for this may be the all-pervading hand of officialdom, which saw a strategic necessity for the defence of important installations at some (corn-stores, official arms or equipment depots or the like) and not at others.

By the fourth century, irrespective of the history which had led up to their formation, there were, then, some twenty-eight administrative units covering all but the specifically military areas of Britain, within which one important town was responsible for any number of smaller settlements. These *civitates* had their own local councils, and in essence had a city organisation which made of each one a 'mini-Rome'. The councils were composed of 100 or so members, and there were strict qualifications of civil status and property for membership, which was for life. The men who comprised this council were *decuriones*, who were natives or residents of the city concerned. The exact qualification for inclusion within the council (or *curia*, which was also the name applied to the Roman senate) varied from city to city, but as there were financial demands as well as benefits placed upon the council members and magistrates, some decurions tried to shirk

20

4 Aerial view of Irchester, Northants., showing the regular circuit of Roman walls round what appears to be a very irregular Roman street pattern

their duties. This was easiest in Italy, where there were opportunities for becoming a senator or of obtaining a post in the central civil service, and by working one's way up gradually to a position of authority. Roman senators and civil servants carried immunity from the demands of being a decurion, as also did military service and ordination as a priest or bishop. The financial obligations which decurions were most keen to avoid were the guarantee to provide the yearly taxation budget for their *civitas*, and the cost of paying for the public entertainments and (even less popu-

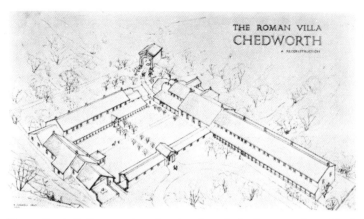

Figure 1 Artist's reconstruction drawing of the Roman villa at Chedworth, showing the extended spacious plan of a prosperous Roman villa by the fourth century

lar) the public works, like road-sweeping, cleaning out the latrines and baths, and heating the public baths.

The local councils were responsible, then, for most aspects of public life. To assist in this, they elected annually two men who presided over the council and acted as local petty magistrates, and further officials (usually junior members of decurions' families) to oversee municipal services and to act as secretaries and accountants for local finances. There were also jobs to farm out – officials to collect taxes for the central government, men to hold the lucrative leases of state corn-stores, depots, mines, factories and the like. In all of these local jobs there was a profit to be made, since tax collectors were not prevented from collecting more than was necessary and only paying the state what it actually demanded: the decurions therefore might expect a handsome reward to ensure that these tasks went into the right hand. Though there was no real reason why tax collectors should get away with extortion, the complicated and expensive methods of redress by appeal were in practice not open to the peasant or to the smaller landowner.

The wealth and prosperity of the cities was largely dependent on the land, its agriculture, and natural

22

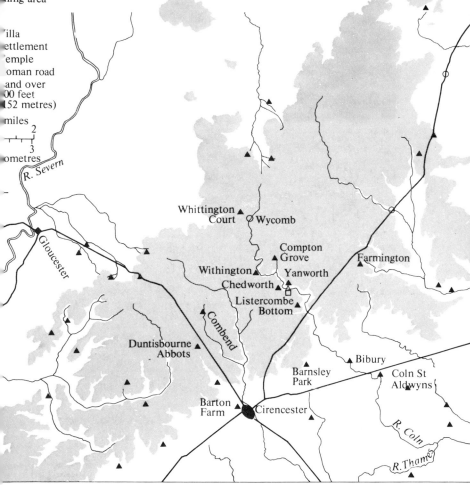

**p 2 The distribution of flourishing villas in the area round Cirencester in the late third and
th century** Within a ten-mile radius of the town over twenty substantial villas are known.
s testifies to the importance of the town as a market centre and to the general prosperity of this
ning area

illa
ettlement
emple
oman road
and over
00 feet
52 metres)

miles

kilometres

R. Severn

Gloucester

Whittington
Court ⭘ Wycomb

Compton
Grove

Farmington

Withington
Chedworth
Yanworth

Listercombe
Bottom

Combend

Duntisbourne
Abbots

Bibury

Barnsley
Park

Coln St
Aldwyns

Barton
Farm
Cirencester

R. Coln

R. Thames

resources in the neighbourhood. One would therefore
expect the decurions in any city to have been landowners
in the surrounding country and it is surprising that despite
their considerable wealth which qualified them for council
membership there is not more evidence of large spacious

23

5 The mosaic of Europa and the Bull from Lullingstone villa, Kent. The verse inscription reads 'If jealous Juno had seen Jupiter do this, she would have had more reason to stir up stormy seas' – a reference linking Virgil's *Aeneid*, where Juno stirs up a storm to prevent Aeneas reaching Italy, and the story in which Jupiter, disguised as a bull, carries Europa off over the seas

housing for rich families within the *civitates*. However, in the countryside surrounding the cities lie the remains of substantial villas, Roman country houses forming the nucleus of large estates. These villa estates almost certainly provide the sort of property qualification which would suit a man for the status of decurion within his *civitas*, and in most cases the villa buildings themselves, which usually comprise main dwellings, barns, courtyards, gardens and enclosures, are a sumptuous indication of the luxurious style of life which might be enjoyed by the privileged of the later Roman Empire. The beginnings and development of the Roman villa in Britain, as so much else, is a subject in itself, but the buildings which date from the third and fourth centuries usually herald a period of occupation of these sites where hypocaust (heating) systems were in operation, and when mosaic floors, some of great beauty and of interest in reflecting the tastes of their owners, were laid in the principal rooms.

Large estates such as these (it is impossible to tell exactly how large, since the boundaries are notoriously difficult to define) may have been farmed by the landowner himself, using slave labour, or peasant tenants who might be housed in more humble accommodation elsewhere: or the

6 The crudely proportioned figures on this mosaic, from Rudston Roman villa in Humberside, show a rustic attempt at Roman imperial culture. Venus, at the centre surprised at her toilet, is surrounded by beasts, including a *taurus omacida* – a (mis-spelt) man-slaying bull

whole estate might be left in the care of a bailiff or an agent who could employ free or slave labour. There is evidence that estates in Britain might belong to families from elsewhere within the empire: the biography of Melania the Younger, who in AD 404 decided to sell her considerable family estates and give the money to the poor, records that she held property throughout the empire, including some in Britain.[8] The British provinces also appear to have been a frequented place of exile for members of the senatorial élite banished from Italy in the fourth century.[9] It is more than likely that such men would live in style at the hub of a villa estate.

The villa buildings themselves portray something of the character and the lifestyle of their owners. The mosaic pavements show scenes from Virgil or from Greek mythology, and a variety of mystic themes, a popular favourite being the depiction of Orpheus playing his music to charm the beasts. Research on these mosaics has distinguished four main schools or firms of mosaicists, based on Cirencester, Dorchester, Brough-on-Humber, and Chesterton (Water Newton).[10] The mosaics exhibit different degrees of

25

7   The Orpheus mosaic from the villa at Woodchester, Glos. The legs and
cloak of the damaged figure of Orpheus with his lyre can be seen at the
lower centre (above the lion and tiger), surrounded by circling animals,
some more mythological than real. The border, composed of panels which
were the stock-in-trade of the Cirencester mosaicists, is of unusual
complexity and richness

competence in workmanship. They range from the picture
of Europa and the Bull at Lullingstone, with its Latin tag
referring to part of Virgil's *Aeneid*,[11] and the finely worked
head, probably of Christ, at the villa of Hinton St Mary in
Dorset, to the rather crude and misproportioned Venus
and the 'man-slaying bull' of the pavement from Rudston
in Yorkshire. But all, whatever the standard of craftsmanship, were composed essentially for a discerning class,
who either appreciated the motifs at their face value, or
saw in them a type of cultured civilisation that was
eminently desirable.

Further down the social scale, but still in the country-

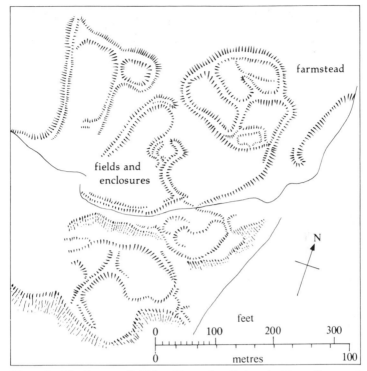

Figure 2 The Romano-British settlement on Butcombe Down, Somerset. This farming settlement, part of which survives as earthworks, was established in the late third century and lasted in use for about a century. The main domestic area was within the roughly circular enclosure in the north-eastern province of the site

side, come so-called 'native farmsteads' or smaller agricultural settlements in which probably the majority of the Romano-British population lived. In essence, such agricultural communities, whether one calls them 'village', 'hamlet' or 'farmstead', were the life-blood of the island's agricultural (and hence economic) prosperity. Many such sites, ranging from a few small huts with associated enclosures to larger conglomerations of 'rectangular-style' buildings, are known throughout the whole of Britain. Despite their number and the regional variations of type which occur, their excavation has not perhaps attracted the attention it deserves. They represent an undercurrent of

27

Map 3 Distribution of fourth-century schools mosaicists in Britain. The four main schools the major identifiable examples of their produ are shown

+ Petuarian School
▲ Durobrivan School
● Corinian School
× Durnovarian School

miles
0   50
0   80
kilometres

Petuaria
Brough-on-Humber

Durobrivae
Chesterton

Corinium
Cirencester

Durnovaria
Dorchester

8 Aerial view of the Roman and native site at Lockington, Leics., one of a series of complex sites on the Trent gravels. This 'native site' with enclosures and hut-circles lies next to the known site of a small Roman villa and may therefore have been occupied simultaneously. If so, it could have housed peasant workmen on the estate

basic subsistence farming, continuing the traditions of the Iron Age throughout the Roman period, often with surprisingly little change of building style from first to last. These sites seem to overlap with villas, and also occupy the areas where villas are not found. They range from sizeable settlements like Kingscote (Glos.) which covers about 200 acres, or smaller, but still village-like settlements such as Catsgore (Somerset) of only ten acres, to the multitude of sites which probably represent a single farmstead. Some areas of Britain have been extensively examined for traces of such settlements, either as earthworks or as crop-marks in cultivated fields, whereas others have not received such attention, or are more heavily built over.

It is a commonplace to say that the whole of the economy of Roman Britain depended on its agriculture. More than half of the population of Britain were small landowners or peasant farmers, tenants, or employees involved in the vital task of production. However, it is difficult if not impossible from the archaeological record itself to be precise about the structure of life in the countryside. The relationship of the two apparently disparate forms of exploitation of the land, the villas and their large estates on the one hand, and the small collections of farmsteads with associated fields on the other, is a problem which has exercised the minds of scholars for many years: is there a tenurial relationship between the small settlements and the villas? Or are they two mutually incompatible forms of exploiting the countryside – the one in the 'Roman', the other in the 'native' tradition?

To some extent, the view that there was a tenurial relationship has an inherent plausibility. The structure of the tribal system in the later Iron Age provided for an élite ruling class to whom the peasant tribesmen owed their allegiance. The Roman concern to preserve the tribal structure probably also ensured the survival of this attitude on the part of the indigenous Romano-Britons, so it may well be that in the later empire the peasant communities still recognised their dependence upon the 'lords of the manor' – the villa owners. But in no case can a direct association between villa estate and native farm or community yet be proved. That they could be contemporaneous and contiguous is known: there are signs in one or two instances of the apparent reorganisation of native-style settlements at the same time as a villa was built in the neighbourhood, as at Butcombe (Somerset) in the later third century. That the one stood in a tenurial relationship to the other, however, can scarcely be established without some documentary evidence. The majority of countryside settlements, then, are likely to be composed of one or more peasant (or slightly grander) smallholdings, adopting to a greater or lesser degree a Roman style of life. The apex of this social pyramid is the villa, with its fully Romanised farming system, possibly even so far in the 'Roman Italian' style as to be worked by slaves under a farm manager. Its buildings are unashamedly Roman in style, though slightly adapted from the Italianate villas for the more rigorous British climate. All shades of wealth and importance are represented as one travels down the social scale to reach the infinitely humble peasant huts (and occasional stone buildings) at the bottom.

One burden which all countryside establishments shared equally was that of taxation. State salaries to civil servants and in particular to the military (for Britain, as a frontier province, contained a substantial army), were paid not wholly in cash, but in rations of food and clothing, all of which had to be collected from the populace. The payment of taxes, therefore, was assessed empire-wide on the basis of the area and value of the property each person held. Each administrative area held a record of all landowners within their purlieu, their holdings and the number of people who worked them reckoned according to a fairly complex tax-unit module. When the central government administrators had worked out their estimates of the amount of supplies to be needed for the coming year, each agricultural producing unit, assessed both in terms of area of land and men to work it, was required to produce an equal share to make up the required total. Thus a villa estate which had staff to farm an area of land equal to three taxable units was responsible for three times more produce for the central fund (the so-called *annona*) than a community of peasant farmers whose combined holdings and work-force amounted only to one tax-unit. Responsibility for collection lay with the decurions of the *civitas*. This system, though ostensibly scrupulously fair, computed the actual tax-demands not in what the land produced in real terms, but as a proportion of what it ought to produce, so that in a good year nothing extra was demanded, and in a bad year no concessions were allowed. The system also failed to allow for the better fertility of some types of soil than others, by demanding from all an equal proportion according to the acreage and man-power of their holding. Most of the documentation which relates to this form of taxation comes from eastern provinces of the empire, notably Egypt. It is not certain, therefore, how applicable this system was to Britain, but there is evidence that, to the Mediterranean mind, used to poor soils and disappointing yields, Britain was a relative powerhouse of food production. In the fourth century, produce from her farms was supporting not only the troops on duty in forts in Britain, but also was being regularly shipped across to provide for some of the troops on the Rhine frontier too.[12]

There were other forms of taxation, but most of these were specialised, like customs dues and sums levied periodically from decurions or *negotiatores* (traders) on their property or on their capital assets. Such sums went into a central treasury, the *thesaurus*, which had its headquarters for the diocese in London.[13] In the *thesaurus*, along with these dues, payable in cash, and usually in bullion, whether gold or silver, went the produce from the mines, and the treasury was also the mint which controlled the issue of coinage. In the later Roman period, there was but a single mint in Britain, at London. This, established by Carausius, a man who in AD 285 set himself up as emperor in Britain in opposition to the 'legitimate' emperor (who had in fact himself become emperor in the same way), surprisingly outlasted his short reign, and was finally closed down only in AD 325–6. Thereafter, though there was still a treasury in London, coin had to be imported into Britain from Italian or Gallic mints. To the same official who controlled the *thesaurus* was given the responsibility for the state armour factories, who decorated troops' panoply with some of the precious metal culled from the taxpayers or the mines; under him also were the weaving and dyeing factories and the state transport supply.

Such a large and elaborately organised system of requirements from the citizens of a *civitas* necessitated close co-operation between local authority, in the person of the decurions, and central government tax offices. The decurions both individually and as a body were financially responsible for the underwriting of the tax assessment of the *civitas*, so they would scarcely fail in their zeal to collect from the local inhabitants. For the repair of roads or bridges, the construction or repair of city walls or more menial tasks like cleaning or heating the public baths, they had the power to organise work gangs and corvées of citizens who had to perform the tasks demanded of them as a public service for nothing, or, at best, for subsistence-level remuneration. Each cantonal area will also have had several official posting-stations to be maintained and run, as well as at least one central state granary (*annona*-store) into which the required produce was gathered, before its conveyance by waggon or ship to its eventual destination.

To assess how onerous or otherwise all these duties were, or were regarded to be, is no easy task. During the course of the fourth century, emperors were continually at pains to make sure that decurions did not shirk their duties, for it was on them that responsibility for the running of much of the system lay. Decurions were forbidden – it was apparently an increasing tendency – from retiring to their country estates and living a life away from the cares of the *civitas*. There was growing concern too, over the number of decurions (this applies particularly to Italy and to the Mediterranean shores) who managed to gain promotion into one of the classes exempted from such duties; additionally, if one became a senator, this achieved exemption for the family in perpetuity. In practice, however, the avenues of escape from such local obligations were limited, and such references as there are to the sons of decurions from Britain are to remarkable men whose fathers' positions in life gave them opportunities they were quick to seize: one of the most famous examples is Pelagius, who was sent away to Italy to study law, and whose controversy with St Augustine about the doctrine of grace gave birth to the 'Pelagian' heresy which gained a great following at least in Britain in the early years of the fifth century. Another example is Patricius, whose father was probably a decurion in some northern *civitas*: at the age of 16, Patricius was captured by Irish raiders, but escaped, and after years of education and training (by bishop Victricius at Rouen?) was eventually consecrated as a bishop. Patricius elected to return as bishop to the Irish, a fact for which he is now principally remembered.

Pelagius and Patrick show that it was possible for the son of a decurion to achieve a status other than that of their fathers, even though the general tenor of legislation throughout the fourth century is against any such change. In general the inheritance of property was enough to compel the heir to take on the financial and public responsibilities which were legally tied to the property. In other areas, too, where it was desirable for the state to keep up the numbers of men available for certain types of work it was made compulsory for sons to take on the trade of their fathers; more especially the military, agricultural workers, the humbler state servants (miners, factory workers, and those in the public post) and also urban craftsmen were thus tied. Faced perhaps with a falling population, lack of enthusiasm for propping up the fabric of society, and with the increasing shirking of duties, the government tried to maintain those services which were essential.

In the face of such a totalitarian regime, but one of uneven efficiency, it is surprising that there was not more protest, either from the decurions themselves or from other classes who might feel oppressed. It was always open to the troops to protest by acclaiming a new leader whom they would follow as emperor. Every time that such a movement began in Britain during the course of the third and fourth centuries (apart from the case of the emperor Constantine I), it was finally quelled in battle by the officially recognised emperor or his representatives. In any case, the troops were not so often complaining about the social system or the inequalities of life in army service, as being egged on by an ambitious officer who saw his chance to seize absolute imperial power. Perhaps the most important of the resistance movements in the later Empire was that of the *Bagaudae*, a term applied to peasant revolts in

Gaul, Spain and Britain from the end of the third century onwards. The exact nature of their complaints is never stated – the accounts given are always those written by the court and its circle – but the resistance offered seems to have been spirited. Following as they did a particularly bad spate of barbarian invasions into Gaul in the later third century, these revolts may have been sparked off by the transfer of portions of land to incoming settlers, and the dispossession of the rightful owners, as much as by any general grievance about the harshness of taxation. A serious revolt seems to have centred on Gaul and Britain in the early years of the fifth century; this may have been more extensive than the Bagaudic uprisings, for a careful reading of the sources indicates that many classes in society were involved in a general feeling against the Roman organisation.

Parallel to this extensive and seemingly all-pervading civil organisation within the British provinces was a large army, supported by the *annona* collected from the local populace. All provincials were expected to rely for protection on this strong arm of the government: indeed civilians were not permitted to bear arms. There had been a trend towards separation of civil and military functions in Britain during the course of the fourth century. Until the end of Diocletian's reign (AD 305) the governor of each province, following the normal tradition, was still in overall charge of all the troops within his own area. Only in the most hard-pressed provinces had Diocletian appointed a separate military commander – usually styled *Dux*, 'Duke', and this had not happened yet in northern Britain.[14] The area of Hadrian's Wall in Britain was still nominally at least under the control of the governor, for an inscription recording repairs to Birdoswald fort in the early years of the fourth century was set up in the name of Aurelius Arpagius, the *praeses*.

Diocletian was responsible for a large-scale reorganisation of the Roman army. The legions, formerly the core of the service, were reorganised to make more units, to which a number of newly formed frontier troops were added:

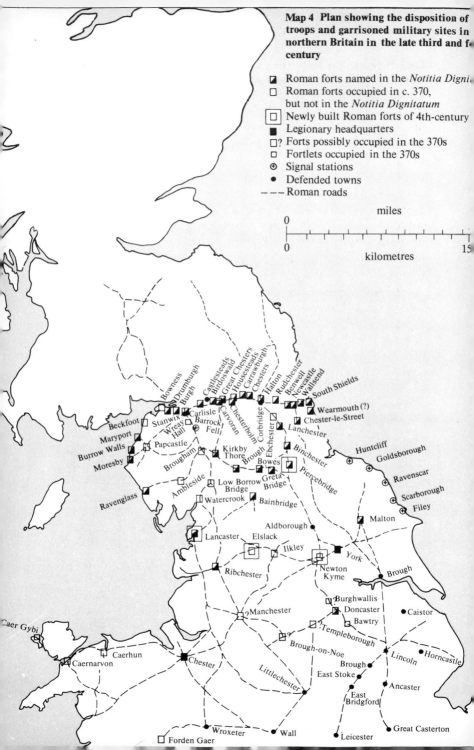

Map 4 Plan showing the disposition of troops and garrisoned military sites in northern Britain in the late third and f[...] century

- ◩ Roman forts named in the *Notitia Digni[...]*
- ☐ Roman forts occupied in c. 370, but not in the *Notitia Dignitatum*
- ⊡ Newly built Roman forts of 4th-century
- ■ Legionary headquarters
- ☐? Forts possibly occupied in the 370s
- ▫ Fortlets occupied in the 370s
- ⊕ Signal stations
- ● Defended towns
- --- Roman roads

miles
0 _____
0 _____ 15
kilometres

Bowness
Drumburgh
Burgh
Castlesteads
Birdoswald
Great Chesters
Housesteads
Carrawburgh
Chesters
Halton
Rudchester
Benwell
Newcastle
Wallsend
South Shields
Wearmouth (?)
Chester-le-Street
Beckfoot
Stanwix
Carlisle
Barrock
Fell
Carvoran
Chesterholm
Corbridge
Ebchester
Lanchester
Huntcliff
Maryport
Wreay
Hall
Papcastle
Brough
Binchester
Goldsborough
Burrow Walls
Kirkby
Thore
Brougham
Brough
Bowes
Greta
Bridge
Piercebridge
Ravenscar
Moresby
Ambleside
Low Borrow
Bridge
Scarborough
Filey
Ravenglass
Watercrook
Bainbridge
Malton
Lancaster
Aldborough
Elslack
Ilkley
York
Ribchester
Newton
Kyme
Brough
?Manchester
Burghwallis
Doncaster
Caistor
Bawtry
?Templeborough
Lincoln
Horncastle
Caer Gybi
Caerhun
Brough-on-Noe
Brough
Caernarvon
Chester
Littlechester
East Stoke
Ancaster
East
Bridgford
Great Casterton
Wroxeter
Wall
Leicester
Forden Gaer

these were styled by the names *equites* or *milites* – simply 'cavalry' or 'infantry' – or *numeri*, which all were equal in status with the legions. Units bearing more traditional names, as for example *alae* – 'wings (of cavalry)' – or *cohortes* – 'cohorts (of infantry)' – were also posted on frontier duty, but ranked below these crack troops. The reason for the creation of such a new force seems to have been to restore some of the Roman army's lost mobility: the old style *alae* and *cohortes* had stayed too long in one place, and had begun to put down roots. By supplementing these garrisons with more highly trained troops as a mobile reserve, Diocletian hoped to restore confidence in the defences of the Roman frontiers which had been breached with startling regularity during the previous thirty years.

These developments were pushed a shade further by Diocletian's successor, Constantine. He continued the separation of civilian from military commands: by the end of his reign in 326 most of the military command of frontier provinces was under the control of Dukes. Britain had two frontiers: in the north, Hadrian's Wall and its associated forts were under the control of the *Dux Britanniarum*; in the south and east, the other frontier was under the control of the *Comes Litoris Saxonici* – 'the Count of the Saxon Shore'. This name and title are probably a later styling for this officer, whose original rank was probably *Dux*. Constantine's second development was to organise mobile troops away from the frontiers, to form field armies as opposed to the static frontier guards, thus emphasising the distinction between these two forms of military service. Constantine also created the rank of *Comes*, 'Count'. This was intended as an order of nobility, given to the highest of the military officials surrounding the court. It could, however, be given to a military commander sent to do a special job and using the crack troops for his purpose. Eventually it came to be given to some of the more important frontier commanders, and the title 'Count' then went with the appointment.

Our knowledge of the military arrangements in Britain comes from the *Notitia Dignitatum*, 'the Notice of Dignities' – a list of civilian and military posts throughout the empire. This is in many ways an enigmatic and puzzling document whose purpose and authorship remains unclear:[15] the copy which has survived may be a record which belonged to the head of the western half of the Roman civil service, and dates probably from the very end of the fourth century. The information within the *Notitia*, however, is not all of one date: within its arrangement in chapters, under the various commanders and officers, there have been several alterations, corrections, changes and updatings. Though they may occur in one chapter, they have not always been followed by consequential changes in another, so the *Notitia* incorporates out-of-date as well as 'current' information. It is also difficult to assess the date of the last revision, but it appears to have been updated in a haphazard fashion as far as 420, a date well past Roman military involvement in Britain; and yet the British chapters are still in the *Notitia*, suggesting that although the information in them was well out of date, it was retained on the official file in case it might ever be useful again. The British material in the *Notitia*, though extremely valuable because it probably dates from about AD 395, is difficult to use, since it may describe a situation several years out of date, or retain items of mutually contradictory information.

The *Notitia* records four officers within Britain, one civilian and three military.[16] The *vicarius* and his staff we have already met. The others are the *Comes Britanniae* (or *Britanniarum*), the 'Count of Britain' or 'the Britains', the *Comes Litoris Saxonici per Britannias*, 'Count of the Saxon Shore in the Britains', and the *Dux Britanniarum*, the 'Duke of the Britains'. The exact relationship between all these military commanders will be discussed in a later chapter, but the important factors are that the *Comes Britanniae* has under him only a relatively small mobile force, while the other two hold sizeable frontier forces in the south-east and the north. Under these officers the *Notitia* records not only the garrisons which patrolled the areas, but also the names of the forts in which they were stationed. It is not realistically possible, however, to estimate the number of troops within Britain during the course of the fourth century; there are surprising omissions from the lists of forts under the frontier commanders – for example the units in Wales do not seem to be mentioned at all, despite evidence to suggest that the area remained in some sense a military zone. Nor is there an adequate field army under the Count of the Britains. The curtailment of his forces may be an *ad hoc* move dating from the very last years of Roman involvement with Britain. The forces in fourth-century Britain could have been considerably larger than those listed in the *Notitia* chapters, and a considerable drain upon the agricultural population, who were committed to supply the *annona* for this large force guarding their frontiers.

On the other hand, the army was a large and available consumer market for all forms of supply. At the lowest level, the necessity for arms and clothing meant that there was always an outlet for the thriving wool and cloth trade. There was an official fulling and dyeing mill in Britain,[17] with, one would presume, a whole ancillary range of buildings devoted to the production of military and civil service uniforms. British cloaks, eminently suitable for keeping out the clammy winter, were renowned throughout the empire, and were regarded as one of the stock luxury items significant enough to warrant individual mention within Diocletian's official price-list published in the early fourth century in an attempt to establish maximum prices and stabilise the economy.[18] Some of the styles of metalwork, too, which were used for belt-buckles and other fitments for equipment turned out from the arms workshops, are particularly notable, and show that even the governmental nature of this work still left room for individual craftsmanship of a high and distinctive order.

Gold, silver and copper mines were developed immediately after the Roman conquest of Britain and there are indications that by the third century they had lost most of their production capacity. If this was so – and the silver ingots which have remained as chance survivals of late

9 Vessels from the hoard of late Roman pewter found at Appleford, Oxon. Metal tableware of this type in silver was a very expensive luxury item: pewter was a slightly cheaper alternative

Roman date bear no official stamp – the mines were probably let out to private enterprise, with a stiff tax in kind on production. Little is known of the methods of lead mining, but Cornish tin was certainly under production in the third century. An industry which thrived on both metals was pewter manufacture, a major centre of which was in the West Country at or near Camerton (Somerset). A range of tablewares were produced, and distributed throughout the British provinces to the homes of those who wanted 'Roman-style' tableware but could not afford silver. There was a flourishing trade in iron objects, with a large range of utilitarian products manufactured at a number of local centres.

More localised industries flourished near sources of

supply: stone quarries, tile and brick works, and the making of objects from shale and jet. Salt production, an important ingredient in food preservation in antiquity, was effected through brine tanks at many places along the East Anglian and the Lincolnshire coastline – some of them now well inland within the present fens. There were natural salt springs at Droitwich, and the Cheshire salt-mines were also in use in Roman times. Added to these of course were the products of the ancient world such as foodstuffs, now all but invisible to the archaeologist, and all manner of animal products, from leather and bone articles to the breeding of hunting dogs, another of her exports for which Britain was famous throughout the empire. Pride of place among such products was the oyster: to cultured Roman taste the name Rutupiae (Richborough) was justly famous as the place where the best oyster-beds were.[19] It is difficult to assess the range of such perishables, but a full range there will have been, including perhaps wine and certainly beer,[20] but whether these were merely for home rather than empire-wide consumption cannot be divined.

Pottery was perhaps the most important British product for the home market, and some also found its way across the Channel. In the wake of the Roman army there followed into Britain a specialist form of red glossy table-ware, developed and mass produced in slightly simplified versions of originally Italian prototypes in Gaul. This *terra sigillata* (often called 'samian ware') was used extensively in Britain for close on two centuries. There were local centres of British pottery at that time, but they had nothing to match the specialised wares produced by the Gaulish centres. Around AD 250, the large central Gaulish factories were forced to close, and since only a limited supply of the similar Gaulish 'samian' was available for import into Britain, centres of British production came into their own. In the early third century the principal kilns were in the Nene Valley, in the Peterborough area, and those round Colchester, which had earlier made some attempt to produce a native British 'samian'. These competed successfully with an influx of pottery from the Rhineland at the same date, and led the way for other centres of production to market their own distinctive wares. Potteries supplying less spectacular cooking and domestic vessels, the so-called black-burnished' ware, had been based at a wide variety of sites, some as far away from the military areas of the north as Dorset. These continued uninterrupted in production, as did midland sites producing specialised pottery such as *mortaria* – mixing bowls. Competitors for the coveted military market soon established themselves, with a priority on producing fine tablewares, often in the same fashion and the same colouring as the now fast disappearing 'samian' forms. Possibly the largest of these was in the region of Oxford, where red-coated wares in a variety of designs, some very reminiscent of samian, were being produced from the mid-third century onwards. Other potteries, for example those based on Farnham (Surrey), or the New Forest (Hants.) had a more restricted market, but still produced a wide variety of wares. Colchester, Much Hadham and Brampton seem to have provided much of the supply for East Anglia, while further sources in Derbyshire catered for the Midlands. The northern area had its own kilns too, the principal one being at Crambeck, some 20 miles northeast of York. It was from here after the disastrous raids of AD 367 that much of the northern frontier area was supplied.[21]

Small-scale craftsmen – smiths, fullers, weavers, basketmakers, carpenters and the like – formed one substratum of urban life. These were the men at whom was aimed the legislation to remain in their occupations and to bring their sons up in the same trade. Inscriptional records are generally lacking from fourth-century Britain, and therefore there is little mention of more professional classes; doctors, schoolmasters, lawyers, architects and surveyors were all essential ingredients of city life. Doctors and schoolmasters – even university professors at the biggest establishments – were paid out of public funds; their existence is known of from other provinces of the empire, and doctors' stamps – as it were, prescription

42

pads – have been found at sites in Britain. Possibly the training required for such specialised occupations needed the kind of money and foreign travel to a more cultured Gallic or Italian city that only a man with the status of a decurion was likely to have at his disposal.[22]

Security within the civilian areas of the provinces was more of a problem. The army was concerned with frontier and border surveillance, and it was no part of its task to interfere with the running of the civilian parts of Britain. It was the responsibility of each city to employ its own police force, though the official title of this is not known. There has been a suggestion recently that items of military panoply found in excavations within towns and cities belong to some fourth-century peace-keeping force of para-military type, but whether such belt-buckles belong in reality to a distinctive group of uniformed military rather than members of the similarly uniformed civil service administration is at present not clear. Evidence for the size and composition of urban police forces, city guards and nightwatchmen is at present not available. Fire-fighting, on the other hand, was an amateur responsibility which was shouldered by the craftsmen's guilds of the city, and fell, like so many of the burdens, as a public duty on the citizens themselves.[23]

In many ways, religion was bound up with city life. The veneration of Rome and Augustus, a cult set up by the first emperor as a focus of provincial loyalties, was now ingrained within the city's religious observances, and the Augustus of the day was a thinly veiled godhead himself while still alive, mysteriously at the centre of this state worship. Bound up with this observance was the whole pantheon of traditional Graeco-Roman Gods, with Jupiter 'the best and greatest' at its summit. How far this type of worship was still relevant in the third and fourth centuries is uncertain: the provincial cities will have maintained temples and priests at public expense, for the pomp of a public religious ceremony, the inspection of the entrails of a sacrificed animal or the divination of some other lucky omen was an essential part of civic dignity. There is

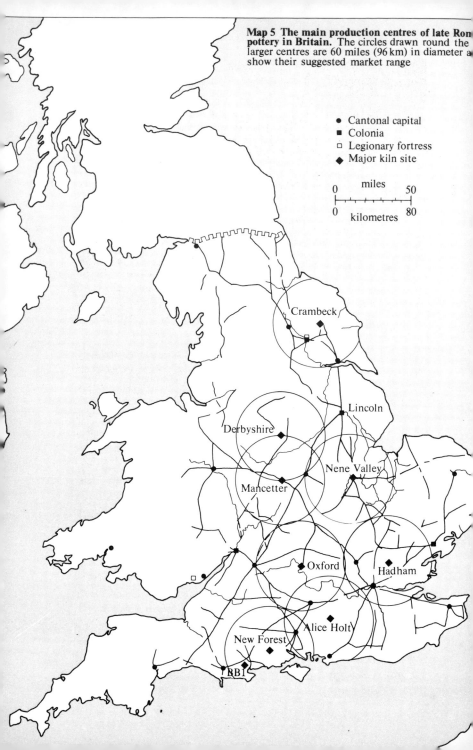

Map 5 The main production centres of late Roman pottery in Britain. The circles drawn round the larger centres are 60 miles (96 km) in diameter and show their suggested market range

- ● Cantonal capital
- ■ Colonia
- □ Legionary fortress
- ◆ Major kiln site

miles
0   50

kilometres
0   80

Crambeck

Lincoln

Derbyshire

Nene Valley

Mancetter

Oxford

Hadham

Alice Holt

New Forest

BB1

10 The *mithraeum* at Carrawburgh, on Hadrian's Wall. The worship of Mithras, a Persian god of light, gained in popularity in the third and fourth centuries. The temple seems to have been deliberately destroyed in the later fourth century by Christians

evidence particularly from this later period of an increasing interest in the more mystic religions of the Greek and Persian east: the cult of Mithras, with its appeal to the military mind, or the cults of Isis, Serapis or Cybele. All these cults will have had their separate temples, and their proliferation in the later Roman period perhaps shows that there was some dissatisfaction with the state religions of the time.

Paramount among the eastern religions which swept the Roman empire from the middle of the fourth century was Christianity. The beginnings of its effect on the empire had of course been felt well before this date. Persecution of Christians, whose extraordinary and cannibalistic rites (for so the eucharist seemed to outsiders) were regarded as unnatural, was carried on with greater or lesser severity according to the seriousness with which the emperor viewed the growing strength of this religion. Early Christians in Britain had not escaped persecution, since several names of martyrs were remembered by the early fifth century, among them that of St Alban, who died at the place which now bears his name in about AD 210. Prior to the last great persecution (in the early fourth century) by Diocletian, however, Christian worship, and some organisation and building of churches had been tolerated, especially in the west. The full brunt of his persecutions fell on the eastern empire, and though the western Caesars paid lip-service to the imperial edicts, they did so without enthusiasm: Constantius contented himself only with demolishing churches in Britain and Gaul between 300 and 305.

The event which gave Christianity its great prominence was Constantine's victory over the eastern claimant to the empire at the battle of the Mulvian Bridge in 312. Constantine's vision of the symbol of the Cross by which he would win, and his success, assured by trust in the Christian God, was sufficient to ensure his conversion. Thereafter, not merely toleration but positive encouragement of Christianity brought into the open much of the church organisation which already existed, and the church's problem now became not the emperor's opposition but his interest and interference in its affairs. That British bishops from York, London and possibly Lincoln (or Colchester?) were present at the Council of Arles in 314, shows the structure which already existed within the province: these bishops will have had churches and a flourishing congregation. At a later council, that of Rimini in 359, more British bishops attended; some were too proud to claim the travelling expenses offered by Constantius, but three of them accepted, saying it was better to rely on state aid than to draw upon the resources of the local community. Not all local churches, therefore, may have been easily able to support their clergy and bishops.

Though Constantine was occupied in building great churches at Constantinople, Jerusalem and Rome, there is no evidence that such work was undertaken in Britain. The best known and identified Christian church has been found at Silchester, but this is a tiny apsidal building which can have held at the most 50 or so worshippers. There may have been a cemetery church at Verulamium, and a small building with an associated cemetery and lead

46

tanks inscribed with the Christian chi-rho symbol at Icklingham (Suffolk) was probably another. Traces of the organised Christianity of the third and fourth centuries are yet to be discovered within the *civitates* of Britain: it may have been strong in some areas, but not in others. A number of buildings with some Christian significance are being progressively identified. The villa at Lullingstone contains what can be described as a 'house-church', a series of rooms with painted frescoes bearing Christian motifs. Other villas in the West Country at Frampton and Hinton St Mary near Dorchester contain mosaics which suggest a religious use for the rooms which they adorned. Indeed, it may be that several of the erstwhile pagan motifs, such as Bellerophon slaying the chimera, or Orpheus himself charming the wild beasts, were endowed, in some minds at least, with new Christian significance at this later period.[24]

The almost overnight transformation of Christianity into an accepted state religion, and its acceptance among the pantheon of Roman religions to be paid lip-service by men anxious to promote their careers, did not immediately give victory in the church's great battle with paganism. There is evidence within Britain for a resurgence of interest in the old pagan Celtic cults of the countryside. A number of Romano-Celtic shrines, many of them established in the ancient places hallowed as the haunts of Celtic forebears, the Iron Age hill-forts, were rebuilt or built new in the fourth century, and, to judge from the quality and quantity of the offerings deposited at their sites, they had a rich and devoted following. One of the most complex of such sites was the temple of Nodens at Lydney, where the cult centre incorporated an elaborate guest house and several temples. Others were established at or near well known hill-forts like Maiden Castle, Jordan's Hill, and Uleybury Hill. The style of such temples owes little to Roman architecture as such. As tall rectangular buildings surrounded by a verandah, they were a distinctively different type of building within the Roman landscape. Such cult ritual as there was would have had to take place in the open air

Figure 3 A lead tank, found at Icklingham, near the building now recognised as a church (see Figure 13 and p. 131). Tanks such as these, now known from many sites, often bear Christian symbols – the chi-rho or alpha-omega – and were probably used for baptism

within the temple-complex – an altogether different style of worship from the secretive mystic cults of the east or the larger temple-cults of Graeco-Roman theism.[25]

It can thus be seen that in religion, as in many other walks of life, the society of late Roman Britain was as mixed a population as any other part of the Roman empire. At the head of the civil service it was possible to have a governor whose native language was Greek, and there are inscriptions and dedications to show that Gauls and other provincials lived within British *civitates*.[26] Traders and businessmen from all over the empire will have thronged into the British provinces. Products and produce from all over the empire will have been imported in exchange for sought-after British goods. Though this sort of exchange can hardly have reached below the luxury market, yet the demand was there, and there were fortunes to be made through such merchandise. The story of the brother of Ausonius the poet, by no means a poor man, who died in Britain on one of his business trips, offers an example.[27]

As well as this influx into Britain of empire-wide expertise for the top executive jobs in the civil service and positions of command within the army, there was a host of foreign military recruits bringing with them their own styles

11 Drawing of a mosaic from Frampton villa, Dorset, made at the time of its discovery in 1796. It is a product of the same school of mosaicists, based on Dorchester, who laid the Hinton St Mary pavement (see Plate 56, p. 168), and contains several elements of Christian symbolism, notably the chi-rho symbol, the *cantharus* (the communion cup) and the dolphins. Despite these Christian associations, the main themes of the pavement are still steeped in the traditions of Classical mythology – Bellerophon and Neptune – but the early Christians apparently saw nothing strange in the juxtaposition

of life, devotions and tastes. Such men, though usually perhaps on short-term posting to Britain, might settle there in retirement and by inter-marriage add a mixed element to the predominantly Celtic native population. During the third and fourth centuries, troops who were stationed permanently in Britain, wherever their place of origin, tended to gain an interest in the land surrounding

49

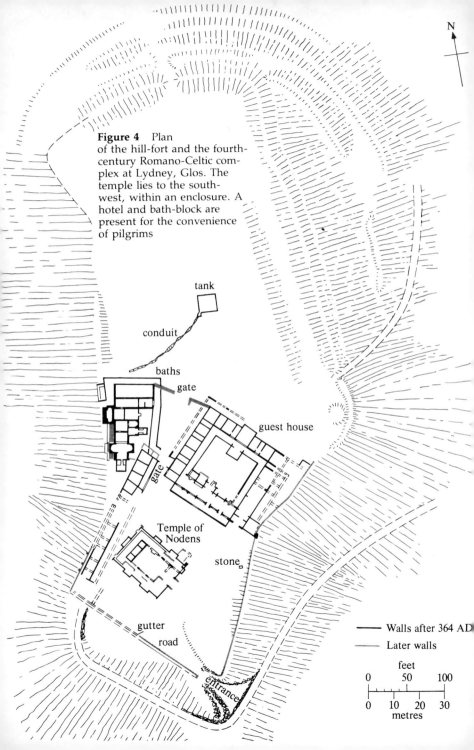

Figure 4 Plan of the hill-fort and the fourth-century Romano-Celtic complex at Lydney, Glos. The temple lies to the south-west, within an enclosure. A hotel and bath-block are present for the convenience of pilgrims

N

tank

conduit

baths

gate

guest house

gate

Temple of Nodens

stone

gutter

road

entrance

—— Walls after 364 AD

—— Later walls

feet
0   50   100

0   10   20   30
metres

Figure 5 Reconstruction drawing of a Romano-Celtic temple

their forts. Moreover the stricter rules of military service were relaxed so that men could actually marry while in service.[28]

An increasing element within the Roman army was provided by Germans – the sons of those who in the third century had been invading the vacant lands of the Roman empire seeking land on which to settle. To such men, service in the Roman army gave an honourable and well rewarded method of gaining Roman citizenship, while from the Roman point of view it channelled their sometimes quixotic spirit in a controllable direction. By the end of the fourth century, many of the most prominent of Roman generals, and the closest confidants among the emperor's bodyguards, were Germans – men such as Stilicho, thrice consul and one of the most powerful men in the Roman world of his day. As a corollary of this step of employing the German youth in the army, often under their distinctive federate bands and possibly with their own distinctive uniforms, came the policy of settling groups of barbarians inside the empire.

Rome's relationship with her immediate neighbours has a long and rather murky history. For many years she seems to have used a mixture of diplomacy and ruthlessness, jealously guarding the boundaries of her empire against any contamination from outside, particularly from the large, fair-skinned northern Europeans.[29] On occasion it was necessary to pay to keep the peace on the frontiers, but a combination of events in the third century changed these conditions. A plague which seems to have been fairly widespread in the empire decimated parts of the population, rendering areas under-cultivated. Military security was weakened because army commanders at the head of their troops marched against other imperial contenders from elsewhere within the empire. Consequently invaders pressed forward to seize unpopulated areas within the empire at a time when the frontier was not fully guarded. At first Rome withstood, but finally developed a policy of settling tribes or groups of tribes in the frontier zones to act both as farmers of these otherwise under-used areas, and as an effective buffer zone to cushion the effects of further raids from outside the boundaries. Scant record exists of such tribes being settled in Britain from the end of the third century onwards, but settlers might be expected quickly to assume the cultural benefits of their new province, so the areas where they settled are still not easily discerned. There is specific record, however, of Burgundians, Vandals and Alemanni within Britain.[30] It is notable also that in 306 at York, when Constantius died and Constantine was urged to make his bid for imperial power, a man called Crocus, described as 'king of the Alemanni', was among his most insistent advisers for positive action.[31]

The undercurrent of indigenous traditions was strong enough, however, to combat all such foreign influences and to preserve, with only a slight veneer of Romanisation, Celtic art styles and native religious cults. Probably there were other, now irrecoverable, aspects of Roman life in Britain which had a Celtic antecedent. Much of the provincial legal system, at least in the private sector where it had little to do with administrative life, will have been in origin Celtic, and will itself have formed a basis for medieval Welsh codes.[32] Specialists in the Celtic law therefore may well have been needed to plead a case before a British court. One of the most crucial questions concerns the language of Britain in the Roman empire. Was it Latin or Celtic?

12 Ivory diptych (commemorative tablet) showing Stilicho and his family, issued to commemorate his consulship at Rome. His dress is that of a late Roman military official attired for civilian life, and, despite his barbarian origins, he has adopted the pose and conventions of polite Roman society

There is a considerable body of evidence now for the point of view that Latin was a current spoken language within Britain.[33] The corpus of inscriptions, admittedly, are a formalised group of specialist 'Roman' monuments, gravestones, official commemorations, building plaques and dedications to various gods, all of them in the strictest sense part of the Roman tradition. In the same category come even more obviously 'Roman' items – the official stamps on tiles, leather, coins and the like. Graffiti on materials which have survived show the widespread non-Roman native use of Latin, often with colloquial mis-spellings which suggest it was spoken first and written second. These relics range from the odd word dashed off on a tile before firing to the complicated and often almost unreadable *defixiones* – curse tablets dedicated to the gods and deposited usually by someone with a particularly virulent grudge.

Against the vast body of Roman Latin material there is little written material to set on the Celtic side, though the language of Britain before the Romans arrived must have been a Celtic one. To some extent British Celtic was the language of spoken communication, the language in which places were named, and in which the everyday details of family or market life were transacted. Latin was the formalised language of the administration, the language of education and of an imposed cultured class of society. A number of aspects of the contact between Roman civilisation and Celtic native are illuminated by the 'loan-words' which the British language gained from Latin. This includes such clear benefits as 'fenestra', window, and 'pont', bridge, but also a wide range of other less immediately striking words which may derive from administrative or official contact.

To some degree, the Roman message failed to get through to the lowest rung of the population. Citizenship within the Roman state gave them little besides the responsibility of propping up an imposed social order, essentially the same social order as already existed within the Iron Age Celtic framework, but given an enhanced appearance by the attractiveness of Roman civilisation. This sketch of Roman life in Britain in the fourth century is one of two separate worlds: that of the administrators, soldiery and the decurions, whose lot might be hard at times, but for whom in general the comforts, security and opportunities of life outweighed the demands which the state imposed upon them. Against this we must set the lot of the peasants, who had probably always been content with a simple life, and for whom freedom from actual slavery meant at best the serfdom of agricultural production to satisfy the demands of the taxman. It is hard to believe that such men and families were ever politically significant within the terms of reference of Roman planners. They might depend for protection upon a patron big enough to shield them from the power of authority but they would not expect him to champion any political claim they might make. They might cling forcefully to long-cherished customs; they might embrace a religion which proclaimed all men as equal before the True God in the next world if not in this with all zeal and fervent belief; or they might regard with apparent unconcern events of political moment around them, preferring passively to proceed with the business of ekeing out a living whatever befell.

It is with the upper social class, the *decuriones*, that most of the political activity of late Roman Britain lies. The men who wrote histories and poems, celebrated the emperor's campaigns, exchanged letters, all saw the world from the Roman point of view. It is difficult for the modern historian not to do the same; not only written sources but the majority of archaeological material is the product of such Romans for a Roman market. After several centuries of Roman occupation of Britain, was the Roman face of the island still a veneer which might be removed and rejected fairly simply in a crisis, or was the Roman way of life so deeply engrained that all sections of the populace would cling to it and not hanker after some new order? In short, how much of a national identity did the late Roman provinces of Britain have? And was any such identity Roman or British?

Questions like these, to which the answer must lie in the sum total of small scraps of evidence culled from here and there around the archaeological and literary record, will underlie this book. It must be emphasised that it is from Roman sources that most of the material comes with which we construct the picture of this awkward, formative and ultimately (from the Roman viewpoint) catastrophic period of British life. Any assessment of it must commence with an almost inescapable bias towards seeing the identity of Roman Britain as something essentially imposed by four hundred years of Roman presence, rather than as something peculiarly individual to Britain herself. Despite the uniformity of the later Roman world and its cosmopolitan nature, each province or group of provinces will have been subtly different from the others. This is perhaps why after so long, Britain's name was still linked in the literary mind with the horror of the 'end of the world' so perpetrated by poets and speechifiers. Yet the quality of Roman civilisation within Britain is not that of the Italian Mediterranean – it is a conglomerate of cultures, art-styles, languages and beliefs which earn it the distinctive title 'Romano-British'.

2 The enemies of Roman Britain

Britain faced the barbarian on several fronts. Early attempts to extend the domination of Rome into the lowlands and even the highland areas of Scotland had had to be abandoned: the Antonine Wall, a turf-built rampart reinforced by military forts, was not occupied after the middle of the second century AD. The northern frontier of the Roman province was now along the line of Hadrian's Wall, with outpost forts in the Cheviots and Scottish lowlands manned by Roman garrisons. Hadrian's Wall acted more as a control line than a barrier to separate Roman from barbarian. Those who lived north of Hadrian's Wall were probably as dependent, for trading purposes, on the presence of Roman troops as their counterparts south of the barrier. As an indication of this, there is no succinct and visible difference between native farmstead settlements south and north of Hadrian's Wall.

To the west, there lay the hilly regions of Wales – an area which was technically within Britannia, but which, partly because of its very inaccessibility, was not altogether receptive to Roman influence. Portions of southern Wales, occupied by the Celtic tribes of the Silures and the Morini, were eventually organised on the Roman pattern, but the central areas and Snowdonia were continually policed by a military garrison of varying proportions. By the fourth century, the indications are that a great many of the Welsh forts were no longer occupied by Roman troops, and that small nucleated settlements or farms were beginning to spring up within the northern uplands – particularly on Anglesey and in the Caernarvonshire plains, while villa-style farming was confined to the southern tip, around the well established centres of Venta (Caerwent, the Silures' capital) and Moridunum (Carmarthen, probably the capital of the Morini). This suggests that whatever problems Wales had formerly held for the Roman military authorities, all that was now thought necessary was some patrolling of those areas most difficult to control.

Sea-borne raiders increasingly descended upon Britain from Ireland, where the Celtic tribes preserved their native Iron Age styles of life and traditions, and from the European coastline north of the Rhine, whence a number of Germanic seafaring peoples were beginning to invade exposed portions of the Roman empire, in particular parts of Britain and northern Gaul. Such attacks were not unique to Britain in the later years of the third and the fourth century. Outside the frontiers of the Roman empire, many barbarians looked with envy upon the rich land inside. Large-scale migrations of tribes deep within Europe, occasioned by the search for better land, a better climate, or simply food to live on, produced a chain reaction, in which those peoples whose territory was near the Roman frontier were pushed towards it. At this time, Rome's European frontier consisted in the main of the two great rivers Rhine and Danube, both visible and defensible barriers which were connected by a short, heavily guarded land-frontier line. Despite this, there were constant inroads from Germanic tribes, the most troublesome of which were the Franks and the Alemanni in Gaul, and the Sarmatians and Goths in the Danube area.

Of the nations threatening Britain during this period, the most feared by Roman historians and writers were the Saxons, a seafaring nation from the base of the Danish peninsula. Their stealth and speed on the attack earned them grudging admiration but their bloodthirstiness and lack of compassion for a vanquished foe filled Roman writers with dread and horror. It was their boats which gave such great mobility to the Saxons and other tribes from the same regions, Angles and Jutes, who may have been identified in the Roman mind with 'Saxons'. In the 1860s remains of two longboats full of weapons were found at Nydam,[1] on the border between Germany and Denmark at the base of the

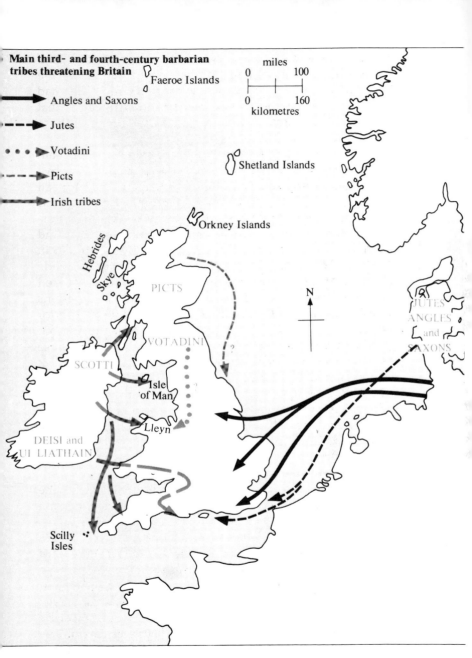

Main third- and fourth-century barbarian tribes threatening Britain

→ Angles and Saxons

⇢ Jutes

•••► Votadini

⇠ Picts

⇒ Irish tribes

Faeroe Islands

miles
0   100

0   160
kilometres

Shetland Islands

Orkney Islands

Hebrides

Skye

PICTS

VOTADINI

N

JUTES
ANGLES
and
SAXONS

SCOTTI

Isle
of Man

Lleyn

DEISI and
UI LIATHAIN

Scilly
Isles

59

13 The Nydam ship, a large Saxon rowing boat of the fourth century AD, found in Jutland. This was possibly only used for short sea-trips, though it may have been the sort of boat in which raiders reached Britain. It had been deliberately sunk in the Nydam marshes, probably as a ritual offering

Danish peninsula. One, built of softwood, was badly preserved; the other was clinker-built of oak planks. Because of distortion, it has not been possible to reconstruct the exact shape of the boat, but it was about 50 feet (15 m) long, and was powered by oars only, with high stem and stern posts – indeed it seems to have been fitted with a steering-oar socket at both stem and stern, making it reversible. It is remarkable that such a boat had no mast, and it may be that these examples from Nydam were ritual offerings of captured warships and captured weapons (some of them Roman) pushed out and sunk into the marsh. They are scarcely appropriate for long-distance raiding parties, since there was no available space for booty or for sleeping.

The Saxons belonged to a group of Germanic peoples whose distinctive type of settlements and artefacts are found in the coastal areas of northern Germany and Denmark. The best known of the inhabited sites in this area of Germany between the Elbe and the Weser is Feddersen Wierde,[2] which lies on the coastal marshland. At the beginning of the first century AD, the village centre comprised some seven or eight long-houses – rectangular timber buildings with partitioning inside for living accommodation, stabling for animals and storage of equipment. A

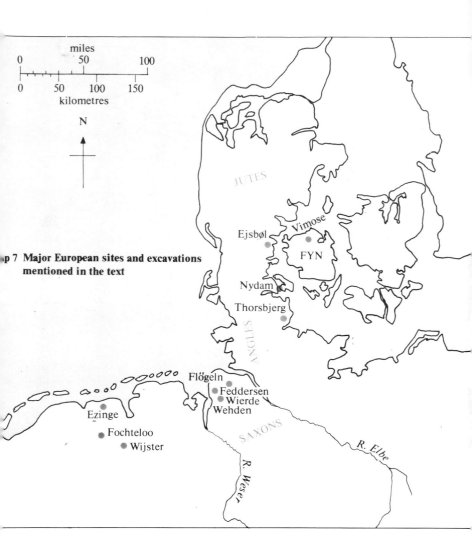

miles

0   50   100

0   50   100   150
kilometres

N

Map 7 **Major European sites and excavations mentioned in the text**

JUTES

Ejsbøl

Vimose

FYN

Nydam

Thorsbjerg

ANGLES

Flögeln

Feddersen

Wierde

Wehden

Ezinge

Fochteloo

Wijster

SAXONS

R. Elbe

R. Weser

phase of growth in the second century led to a new radial plan covering the whole of the 'terp' – the mound of occupation debris which continually raised and defined the settlement area. During the course of this period, one large long-house with barns and buildings devoted to craftsmen's use was separated from the rest of the village within

61

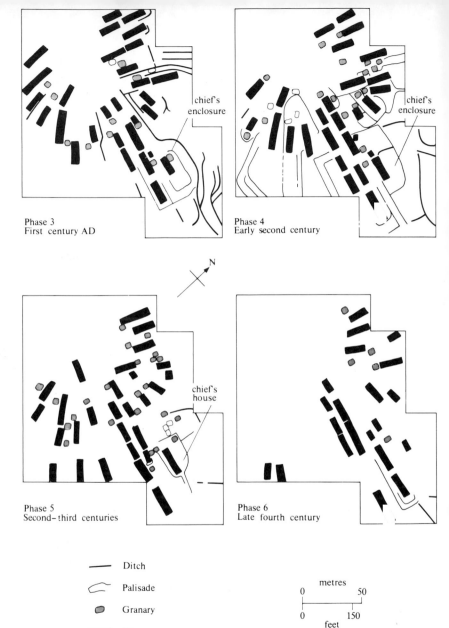

Figure 6 Plans of four phases of the settlement at Feddersen Wierde. In its earliest phases, no single house dominates, and the plan of radially orientated dwellings is not disturbed. By the early years of the second century, one house in the south-eastern area was marked out from the rest by its enclosing palisade and ditch. The domination of the settlement by this house and its associated buildings lasted until the abandonment *c.* AD 450

a special enclosure. A number of changes of plan followed, but throughout them all the large long-house within its palisaded enclosure was a dominant feature. It is hard to escape the conclusion that one family within the village somehow gained a raised status in about AD 100, and maintained a superior position until the fourth century.

The similar development of a village from a single farmstead, though without obvious dominance by one family, can be seen at the coastal settlement of Wijster,[3] further south and west. Around AD 100, within the portion excavated, there was one substantial farmstead and by AD 225 this had been replaced by three long-house dwellings, presumably the home of no more than a single extended family. During the next 75 years, new buildings replaced the small nucleus, and lines of long-houses were added. The regular layout was continued until the end of the settlement in about 425, and though there was clearly some period of decline before its final abandonment, there were still some five or six families on the site. If there was one particular house reserved as the headman's quarters, this has not been located within the excavated area. At Wijster there are two types of building: post-built long-houses are often supplemented by smaller huts with sunken floors – the so-called *Grubenhäuser* – which seem to have been used for a variety of purposes.

At Fochteloo, a large long-house with further enclosures nearby and a settlement not far away perhaps shows some form of tenurial relationship in the fourth century.[4] A number of settlements in the area between the Elbe and Weser were of a more transitory nature. Some farmsteads were continually on the move after every few generations, whereas in other places, as at Flögeln, the whole settlement shifted once or twice, occupying the same site during the late second and early third century, and the late fourth and fifth.[5] If one family group retained its prominence within a village for over two centuries, giving encouragement to craftsmen, the community must have been economically independent, the farming successful, and the settlement continuous. Feddersen Wierde and Wijster show to good advantage the permanency of sites with a continued process of building and rebuilding.

Not all 'terp' sites managed a parallel development. Some failed to progress beyond the earliest stages and others were abandoned in the third and fourth centuries as the sea flooded into parts of Holland and Germany;[6] but it is clear that this development of the 'terp' into a small village comprising long-houses and sunken-floored huts was a natural growth. At Ezinge,[7] on the Netherlands coastal plain, a long-house settlement which had been inhabited up to the end of the fourth century was then replaced by a large number of sunken-floored huts in a startlingly different style. Until recently this had been regarded as an invasion by a tribe using the sunken-floored hut. Since it has now been established that sunken-floored huts were in use on other sites at the same time as long-houses, this explanation no longer seems to be the only one possible.

Pottery styles of the various Germanic areas are also of significance in defining tribal groups: much of the most distinctive pottery comes from cremation cemeteries. In the area between the rivers Elbe and Weser lie several cemeteries where cremations in urns were being deposited between about AD 200 and 500.[8] Most characteristic of the coastal area is the open-mouthed bowl with a carinated body and a narrow (sometimes a pedestal) base. This continues as a pre-Roman Iron Age form until well into the fifth century AD, when bowls of this type are among the earlier signs of Germanic presence at several English sites. Another of the most important forms was the handled jar, which, with its sagging profile and everted rim, was to turn into one of the most typical of Anglo-Saxon vessels, the *Buckelurne*. By the fourth century, these types of pottery were being decorated with incised geometric decorations on the shoulder, or with features which became steadily more common towards the end of the century – stamped decoration and semicircular incised curves.

A little further north, in Jutland itself, another group of pottery, a globular type with a wide mouth and zig-zag incised decoration, signifies a slightly different tradition.

14 Pottery typical of the Lower Elbe region in the second to fourth centuries AD from the sites of Hamburg-Marmstorf and Putensen (Kr. Harburg). The funnel-shaped urn with its footstand and incised linear ornament is perhaps the most characteristic vessel of this period, and its derivatives are found among the earliest Saxon pottery in Britain (see Plate 47)

Many of the pots have a single lugged handle, rather like a beaker, and one or two begin to show forms of pressed-out bosses. The Danish peninsula, and in particular the island of Fyn, from which some of the most distinctive of this type of pottery comes, were the homelands of the Angles, and these pottery types are consequently labelled 'Anglian'.[9] At the beginning of the third century, groups of pottery bearing decorations in distinctive Anglian styles are found infiltrating the areas south and east of the Danish peninsula, and, to judge from the styles of pottery decoration, this influence increased throughout the succeeding centuries. This is not to suggest that there was an 'Anglian' takeover in this area, but an acceptance and use of the distinctive decoration perhaps shows that there was some rapprochement between the Frisians or Saxons on the coast and Angles in Jutland, leading to the consolidation of the strong Anglo-Saxon people of the later fourth century.

Though there are few excavated settlements in this central 'Anglian' area of Jutland, some continuity of habitation in the area is shown by the use of a number of sacred sites within the peat bogs where votive deposits were left. The ships of Nydam have already been mentioned. Here, the first offerings seem to have been made in the second century, and the cult grew more popular 200 years later. At another site, Thorsbjerg,[10] a great hoard of weapons, both Roman and German, and many personal objects and coins

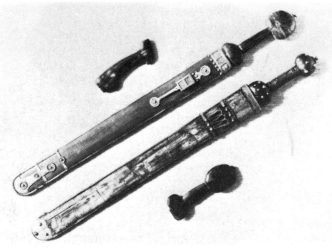

15 Swords and sword-grips from the votive deposits at Thorsbjerg. Although much of the material recovered from these deposits is of Roman origin, these pieces are of Germanic type, and show the sort of 'native' weapons in use during the period AD 100–300

were discovered. A surprising proportion of them were Roman, including parade helmets, shields, spears and swords, most of which had been deliberately broken. Not all this material had been deposited at the same time: there are items of pottery dating from the first centuries BC and AD, and many brooches and much of the Roman equipment from the second and the third centuries. From this and other votive deposits of similar types at Vimose and at Ejsbøl [11] the continuity of religious sites at which there were offerings of captured material can clearly be seen to have lasted several centuries. Thus in Anglian as well as in Saxon areas there was some stability of population and tradition for much of the 'Roman' Iron Age.

Contact with Rome was of course maintained through trade, and the presence of Roman luxury and quality goods will have been an ever-present stimulus to these Germanic peoples. During the second century AD, the somewhat stagnant crafts of metalworking in bronze, gold and silver began once more to flourish, providing metalwork decorations of the highest order. Prime examples of this are two

16 The better preserved of two *phalerae* from the Thorsbjerg deposits. These discs were part of the decorative panoply of Roman armour, and the workmanship is that of expert Roman craftsmen. Of particular interest however are the small animal figures flanking the lower part of the four roundels in the outer band which have been added by Germanic craftsmen. Of the original eight, only four (three horses and one fish) survive (see the rivet holes in the right-hand field where two figures have been lost)

phalerae from the Thorsbjerg deposit. These are bronze discs covered with ornamented gilded silver, decorated with animals in Germanic style, of which one has a central figure of Mars imitating a classic form. These discs, whether the product of home-trained German craftsmen or a man who learned his trade in Roman workshops, are indicative of the skill which Germanic smiths could now achieve, and provide a pointer towards later gold- and silver-work which is so lasting a feature of Germanic craftsmanship of the fifth and sixth centuries.

The first mention of Franks and Saxons threatening the coasts of Britain comes at the end of the third century, when the situation was so serious that a new Roman commander had to be appointed with a fleet to clear the seas of them. Exactly what these raiders wanted is not clear: the historical accounts show that they were definitely collecting plunder. At best perhaps, such raiders and arrivals wanted acceptance within the Roman world, with all the benefits this would bring. If this was not possible, they would gladly seize the wealth of the empire for booty to take back to their homelands. Many of the Germanic tribes in due course won recognition from Rome and a place within the empire, enjoying special status as federates or *Laeti*. Once inside the empire, their intention was not to bring it to its knees, for they became as economically dependent upon its survival as any provincial Roman. The barbarian's aim was to become as civilised a 'Roman' as he was allowed. This was a culmination of a long process during the first three centuries AD when the German barbarians learnt new skills and rediscovered techniques which could make them equal, in terms of material culture and manufacture, with the standards of the Roman Empire. By the end of the fourth century, such German tribesmen had already proved their worth to the army and to the civilian administration, for many of the army units were composed of Germans. There is no specific mention, however, in any Roman source of Saxon or Anglian settlement within the Roman Empire. The culture and occupation of the German coastal homelands appears to tail off towards the end of the fourth century and into the fifth, and the cultural sequence is apparently continued in the Anglo-Saxon areas of Britain, showing that the pressure of these seaborne tribes eventually resulted in their gaining land within the Roman world.

The aims of the other tribes threatening Britain are less clear. Of the northern and western raiders, Picti, Attacotti and Scotti, the Picts are perhaps the most enigmatic. Their name means 'the painted ones', and is a Latin name given to them: we know little of their racial history or of what they called themselves. The Picts are best known for a series of carved stones – probably grave-stones – mainly dating from the seventh century AD, and found in the central and eastern areas of Scotland. These stones, executed in a high degree of craftsmanship, are the only visible memorial which the Picts have left. They show a series of decorative themes which are always in combination – animals, figures, V- and Z-shaped bars, discs and other symbols. The exact meaning of these carvings is not known, but they probably date from a time when the Picts were Christian. It was the pagan ancestors of these men, or proto-Picts as they are sometimes called – who were assaulting the northern frontier of Roman Britain.

It is notoriously difficult to tie down a tribal group, even supposing that we know its name, to the area from which it came. As with the tribes in Germany, where the distinctions between the various areas have given rise to much speculation about which tribes belonged where (and therefore which area is more truly 'German'), it is difficult within Scotland to be precise about which of the Iron Age tribes was the Picts. The identification of tribal areas in Germany is helped by Roman historians' descriptions of the tribes and the rough areas they lived in, and also by the loosely defined cultural affinities of one area as against another: this enables us to define with greater or lesser accuracy where the Frisians, Franks or Saxons came from. There is a general lack, however, of precise Roman source material of the same sort for Scotland, and the archaeological picture provided by pottery and settlement studies allows of no clearer definition of where the Picts were to be found in the late Roman period. In the earlier Roman period, central Scotland was divided between two main tribal groups, the Caledonii and a loose confederacy of probably originally distinct tribal groups called the Maeatae. A fourth-century Roman historian, Ammianus Marcellinus, describes the Picts as composed of the Dicalydones and the Verturiones, and the Pictish homelands were later defined closely as Fife, Strathmore, Athol and Fortrenn.[12] This comprises a large bloc in central Scotland, a region where the archaeological record shows no particular distinctive features which might be individualistic signs of an emerging Pictish nation. The most distinctive

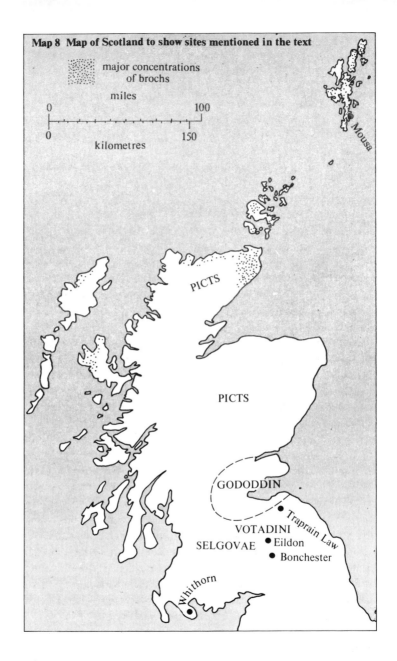

Map 8 Map of Scotland to show sites mentioned in the text

major concentrations
of brochs

miles

0   100

0   150

kilometres

Mousa

PICTS

PICTS

GODODDIN

VOTADINI

SELGOVAE

Traprain Law

● Eildon

● Bonchester

Whithorn

17 The Pictish symbol-stone from Dunnichen. This stone has several of the typical Pictish symbols, for example the double-discs and the Z-rod. At the bottom are the two symbols thought to represent a mirror and comb

element during the Roman Iron Age period is the so-called Caledonian tradition of metalwork which flourished particularly between 50 and 200 AD.

In the northernmost parts of Scotland and in the Shetlands and Orkneys are traces of a separate people, far removed from the farming communities further south. This society, again of the later Iron Age, succeeded earlier settlers, who lived in small stone-built oval huts, with the constructions of duns and brochs. Both of these were Iron Age predecessors of a type of castle. The dun was a small stone-walled enclosure, sometimes with a galleried passageway running through it, and the broch was a tower, with a cellular wall-structure, possibly containing a gallery or a hearth. These types of settlement were normally in use in the first two centuries AD, and are clearly heavily fortified houses, emphasising the isolation of each family or kinship group within its small farming area of the Scottish highlands. By the second century AD, some of these brochs were beginning to be replaced by the wheelhouse, a round hut with its roof supported on radial pillars like the spokes of a wheel. To these northern peoples, the sea was all-important, and their isolation within the most inaccessible portion of Scotland meant that contact between them and

18 View of the broch at Mousa, Shetland, from the south

the remainder of the Iron Age Scottish tribes of more lowland areas was kept to a minimum. Despite their dependence on the seas, and their consequent mobility, it is
unlikely that these distinctive peoples will have been
among those actively engaged in infiltrating the frontiers of
the Roman Empire. It is as well to notice, however, that
brochs have been discovered as far south as the Galloway
peninsula. [13]

In the southern portion of Scotland, where the landscape
is less harsh, the development of Iron Age tribes as they
came into contact with Rome seems to have been largely
peaceable. There were four main Iron Age tribes recorded
by Roman writers in the area, of which the Selgovae and the
Votadini seem to have been the most important. In the
period before Roman contact, these tribes were based on
hill-forts, together with an assortment of other habita-
tions – including souterrains (underground dwellings) and
crannogs – settlements on wooden platforms built out over
a lake. With the arrival of Roman troops in the late first
century, and the consolidation of their positions over the
succeeding 150 years, these tribes were brought out from
their hill-fort environment either by force or by example.
Few hill-forts are known to have survived, and of these

19 Aerial view of the Romano-British settlement site at Jenny's Lantern, Titlington, Northumberland. One can clearly see the earthworks of the main ditched enclosure at the top of the picture, with the outline of irregular fields and hut-circles scattered below it

Eildon Hill North and Traprain Law were probably the tribal centres of the Selgovae and of the Votadini respectively. [14]

All over northern Britain, both inside and outside the 'Roman' world – a distinction culturally false, for Rome's influence extended far beyond the mere physical defended limits of the Roman Empire – there sprang up in place of the hill-forts small homestead farm settlements and groups of huts within enclosures. It was possibly with the encouragement and from the example of the Romans that such buildings were put up, for in Roman forts the Iron Age

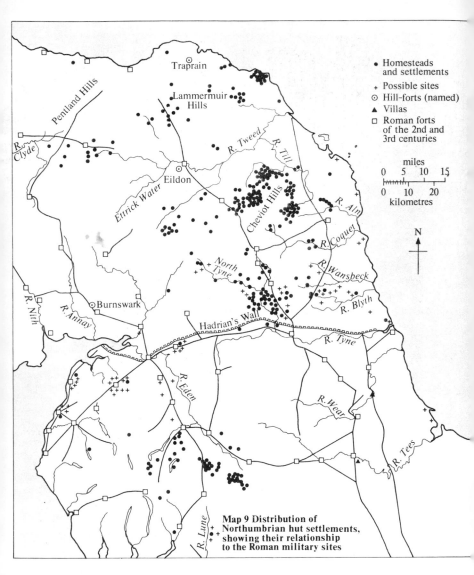

Homesteads and settlements ●
Possible sites +
Hill-forts (named) ⊙
Villas ▲
Roman forts of the 2nd and 3rd centuries □

miles
0 5 10 15
0 10 20
kilometres

N

Traprain
Lammermuir Hills
R. Tweed
R. Till
Pentland Hills
R. Clyde
Eildon
Ettrick Water
Cheviot Hills
R. Aln
R. Coquet
North Tyne
R. Wansbeck
Burnswark
R. Nith
R. Annay
R. Blyth
Hadrian's Wall
R. Tyne
R. Eden
R. Wear
R. Tees
R. Lune

Map 9 Distribution of Northumbrian hut settlements, showing their relationship to the Roman military sites

populace could see how stone could be put to use as building material. Their farming too may have been encouraged by the Roman authorities, who saw any surplus which these peoples might produce as a welcome addition to the *annona* supplies from the interior of Britain. Some of the

74

20 The treasure from Traprain Law, as found. Almost all the pieces were damaged or had been snipped up ready for melting down. Only the triangular bowl (at the top of the pile, *left*) was complete

farming settlements are so remarkably regular in shape – their rectangular form has in some cases led to their being initially mistaken for Roman forts – that it is difficult not to believe that the Roman influence over them must have been considerable. A number of them were built over former hill-forts, and their main concentration appears to have been within the eastern half of lowland Scotland, in the territory belonging to the Votadini, whose contacts with Rome were better organised than those of their western neighbours. [15]

This is no better shown than at Traprain Law. [16] This, if not the actual 'capital' of the Votadini, was a most important centre, and an exceedingly large settlement. In the first century AD it extended over 30 acres, and by the third century, apparently the time of its greatest prosperity, it covered about 40 acres. The variety and number of Roman objects found at Traprain mark it out as an exceptional trading centre. The majority of the Roman finds were rather more elaborate or luxurious items – there was very little coarse Roman pottery, and the most surprising collection of material was a series of button-and-loop dress fasteners. The most spectacular of the finds, however, dated from the late fourth or fifth century and was a collection of Roman silverware. [17] Among the 160 pieces all but the most robust had been cut up, bent, folded or otherwise mangled. The

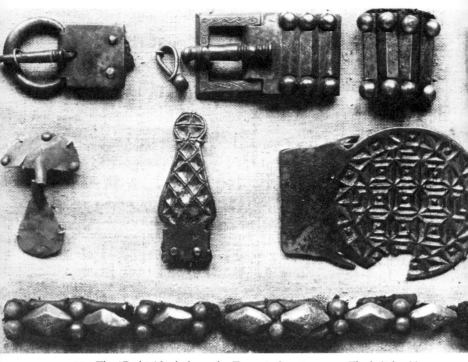

21 The 'Gothic' finds from the Traprain Law treasure. The belt-buckles are of continental, not British, origin. All are of silver. There is an alpha-omega punched on the plate of the buckle (*top centre*)

majority were late Roman silver vessels, many of them bearing figured scenes with punched or graffito inscriptions, including Christian symbols. Very few were complete examples, and most seemed to have been crudely snipped up and were to be melted down – the hoard had been summarily shared out with no regard for the quality of the vessels represented. Together with the hoard were four late Roman coins, and also a series of silver ornaments which appear to be of Gothic or Germanic character – belt fittings and buckles (one bearing the alpha-omega Christian symbol) which were sufficiently rich to have formed part of the parade armour of one of the Germanic chiefs of staff on the Roman frontier. The silver tableware is an astonishingly rich array: part of it is a table-service of bowls and dishes, cups and plates, but other pieces seem rather to be for religious use, either pagan or Christian. The whole assemblage was clearly treated by its possessor as bullion silver, ready for the melting pot, and it may have been either the product of raiding or a lump sum payment in late Roman times to preserve the peace.

No such pattern easily explains other Roman finds in Scotland. It has been claimed that Roman material from contemporary Iron Age settlements within Scotland (including some in the very far north, among the duns and brochs) came from raids or from abandoned Roman forts. It is more likely, however, that the scatter of Roman material which is increasingly coming to light [18] represents the contact established through normal trading activities first among people who came to dwell near Roman forts to service them, and then through continued Roman and native presence at markets which were held by tradition both north and south of the border. Though the pattern of Roman finds is continually being filled in, there is no other site yet known with such a varied assemblage of Roman material as Traprain. The hill-forts of the Selgovae, as, for example, Bonchester or North Eildon, have produced little, or at best only a slight scatter of Roman material. The western Scottish tribes were not so evidently involved in day-to-day commerce with the Romans. Roman coins, however, are to be found in the west, including a number of late second-century coin hoards found in the area between Edinburgh and Glasgow, which may have been part of the payment made by the Romans to the Maeatae to keep the peace.

The view that the Votadini were Roman sympathisers, and that by the fourth century they were no more than a friendly state with whom Rome maintained diplomatic and trading relations, is born mainly from the story of Cunedda's transference of the tribe to Wales (see below p. 86). In reality, peace may have been harder and more expensive to achieve. From the Maeatae, the Caledonians and the tribes of south-western Scotland, there was more pressure, both in the early period, when the Hadrian's Wall

Map 10 Map of Ireland to show sites mentioned in the text

N

Coleraine

● Balline

ULSTER

Navan Fort

CONNACHT

MEATH

Tara ●
Lagore ●

LEINSTER

Dun Ailinne ●
(Knockaulin)

●
Freestone
Hill

MUNSTER

miles
0   20   40   60

0   50   100
kilometres

defence system was extended westwards down the Cumberland coast, and also later, for the distribution of Roman
finds in Scotland shows that although there was contact
with these people, it was by no means as continued or as
friendly as perhaps the northern Roman military authorities
would have wished. This is not to say, however, that the
Roman army could not recruit barbarian tribesmen from the
area into its ranks. Three units listed within the *Notitia
Dignitatum* are called Attacotti, and one of these units was
attached to the imperial bodyguard, the *auxilia Palatina*.[19]

The other direction from which Britannia faced barbarians was from Ireland. The tribes who lived here were known to the Romans as Scotti, a name which seems to have meant 'the plunderers', and it is as raiders that the Scotti of Ireland are most frequently mentioned in classical sources. The discovery of two silver hoards within Ireland, neither containing material as extensive or as varied as that from Traprain, but still containing large amounts of Roman silver coin and bullion, gives substance to this impression. One hoard, found at Coleraine in the nineteenth century, contained 1,506 Roman coins, comprising issues from 337–423, seven silver ingots of the type which were regularly given out as a cash donation to soldiers and civil servants on significant anniversaries of the emperor's rule, and several pieces of other Roman silver, in a bent or broken state. The hoard from Balline was similar, but smaller, with only four ingots and three pieces of chopped-up silver plate.[20] All these hoards, including that found at Traprain Law, and others from areas of Europe outside the Roman Empire, as at Gross Bodingen in Germany, or Høstentorp in Denmark,[21] are most obviously to be interpreted as barbarian 'loot', but the presence of these silver currency ingots, most of them bearing the official moneyer's stamp, suggest that they may be more plausibly seen as a late Roman payment or subsidy to keep the peace.

It is not known exactly when the Celts arrived in Ireland, but the Iron Age within Ireland is a period of Celtic culture, influenced by imports from the Continent and Britain, but developed in its own insular Irish fashion. There is no spectacular break between the Bronze Age and Iron Age cultures, and many settlement types were used at many periods during this time. The commonest type of habitation is the ring-fort – a misnomer since it is not really a fort but an enclosed farmstead – which was current from the late Neolithic period onwards, and in places used until the late seventeenth century.[22] Although there are over 30,000 of these enclosures – earthen 'raths', stone built 'cashels' – very few have been excavated, and there is a general difficulty in dating such settlements without Roman

(a)

(b)

22 (a) and (b) Finds from the Balline Hoard. The silver ingots are stamped with the official Roman moneyer's mark

imported objects to provide a guide. Other centres of habitation are similar to those in southern Scotland – crannogs, souterrains and promontory forts.

Rarest of the settlement sites are the hill-forts – again not easily dated. One of the most recently examined was Freestone Hill, near Kilkenny, where a large irregular fort with rampart and rock-cut ditch was built round the site of a Bronze Age cairn.[23] A number of dwellings lay inside the

80

23 Aerial view of the rath, north-west of Tulsk (Co. Roscommon, Ireland). There are about 30,000 of such enclosures known in Ireland, their periods of use ranging from prehistoric to the nineteenth century. Most of them seem to have been enclosures round a single farmstead

ramparts, and the associated bronze objects found formed a reasonably concise group dating to the fourth century AD, a conclusion suggested by the presence of a Roman coin and contemporary Roman objects. One of the most interesting of the finds was a bronze open-work mount of late Roman type bearing typically Irish Celtic scroll decoration, symbolic of the cultural interplay between the Roman world and the Irish Celts. The fourth century AD date for occupation at the hill-fort of Freestone Hill was surprising but fits in well with the fragmentary knowledge of other Irish hill-fort sites, most of them of better pedigree. The majority of Irish hill-forts are traditionally the royal strongholds of family groups of Irish kings, for example those at Dun Aillinne (near Kincullen, County Kildare), the seat of the kings of Leinster, or that at Emain Macha, Navan fort, the seat of the kings of Ulster.[24]

The most famous of these sites is the royal capital at Tara, where a series of monuments represents the royal seat of Cormac Mac Airt, who was probably alive in the third century AD. [25] The few Roman finds from Tara confirm that the site was in occupation during the Roman period, but not all the very varied elements of the site have been dated. The main hill-fort, a large oval enclosure with bank and ditch, called the Rath na Riogh – 'Royal Enclosure' – incorporates an older burial mound, the so-called 'Mound of the Hostages', as well as two more normal rath-type enclosures, one of which contains traces of a rectangular building, and is traditionally the royal seat. Outside the main 'hill-fort' enclosure to the north lies the Rath of the Synods, misguidedly ruined by excavation in the last century, but re-excavation of which has produced some evidence of Roman date. Further enclosures lie to north and south, adding to an extremely large and complex centre, the final element of which is the 'Banqueting Hall', a pair of mounds running parallel for 700 feet, and traditionally the site of the great hall. The identifications of all these elements come from the Middle Ages, by which time the site at Tara had been imbued with legends. Although some of the features, including the Bronze Age Mound of the Hostages, date certainly from the second millennium BC, the foundation of the fortress came to be associated with Cormac Mac Airt. The greatest of the Irish kings, Niall of the Nine Hostages, ruled a unified Ireland from Tara in the fifth century, and later divided the northern and southern parts of his kingdom between his sons. According to tradition, the site at Tara was not occupied after AD 554. About that time another site, a crannog at Lagore some miles to the southeast, was first used. From the quality of its finds, Lagore has also been supposed to be a royal seat, and it is possible that it took the place of Tara as the king's capital. [26]

The period immediately around the end of the Roman administration of Britain was for the whole of Europe a period of great migrations of peoples. Indeed, the process had been happening intermittently for a century or more before the greatest phase began, with pressure on the Roman frontiers from Franks, Saxons, Alemanni, and other barbarian peoples. The Scotti were one of the most persistent of the potential settlers, and yet one of the most difficult

24 View of Tara, Co. Meath, from the air. The two enclosures in the foreground, 'Cormac's House' and 'The Royal Seat', and the smaller 'Mound of the Hostages' all lie within a larger ditched enclosure, the 'Rath na Riogh'. Immediately outside this (near the clump of trees) lies the Rath of the Synods, whose earthworks have been somewhat obliterated. The 'Banqueting Hall' and a further enclosure can be seen in the middle distance

for us to recognise since their Irish Iron Age culture was in many respects similar to the only slightly 'Romanised' Iron Age culture of those parts of the west country, Wales and Scotland to which they moved. Irish Annals record an early settlement of a southern Irish tribe, called the Deisi (or Desi) in south Wales, and it was once thought that a class of monument very similar to the Irish raths, and found in Pembrokeshire and Carmarthenshire, was the archaeological trace of these people. In fact the Irish sources are unreliable for dating the move of the Deisi into south Wales, and

25 The Stone of Vortepor. It bears an inscription MEMORIA/ VOTEPORIGIS PROTECTORIS – 'the memorial stone of Vortepor, the protector'. Around the top the name VOTECORIGAS is chiselled in Ogam script

the 'raths' of the area have been shown to date at the latest from the first century AD and to have been in use for much of the Roman period.[27] The Irish tale which records this move gives a genealogy of the tribe, partly confirmed and added to by a separate Welsh genealogy of the kings of Dyfed. Both sources give the fifth generation king of the Deisi as Vortepor, mentioned also by one of our more reliable very early sixth-century historical writers, Gildas. At Castell Dwyran, near the ancient capital of the kings of Dyfed, was found a grave-stone marked MEMORIA VO-TEPORIGIS PROTECTORIS, 'the memorial of Vortepor the protector'. Around the edge of the stone was carved, in the notched ogam script which is considered to be of Irish origin, the letters VOTECORIGAS. Here is confirmation that this area of Wales is the correct one, a deduction supported by the further distribution of ogam-inscribed memorial stones, and by the scatter within a confined area of Cardiganshire and Pembrokeshire of place-names with an Irish element in them, for example *meidr*, a lane, or *cnwc*, a hillock.[28]

The same sorts of evidence can be used in other areas to suggest the presence of Irish settlers in different parts of the western sea-coasts. There is a tradition that as well as the Deisi, a tribe called the 'sons of Liathain' (Ui-Liathain) also crossed to southern Wales, and there is even evidence in a ninth-century compilation for their presence at some earlier date at a site by the same name, 'Liathain', somewhere in the West Country, perhaps in west Devon or the Cornish borders. Here, too, there is a small distribution of ogam stones which can be tentatively dated to the late fifth century. Further west in Cornwall, and on the evidence of excavated Cornish sites, slightly later, there was another group of Irish settlers who, judging from the pottery and objects found, had more affinities and connection with the Irish of the northern part of the Island.[29]

Movements of the northern Irish are also attested. One group, a surprisingly small band of only 150 men, if we are to believe Adomnan's *Life of St Columba*, arrived in the mid to late fifth century on the coasts of Argyll, from Dal Riata in Antrim, and carved out for themselves a new kingdom of Dalriada from Pictland. This area, too, is identified from the distribution of Irish names for familiar elements of the landscape, such as *sliabh*, cliff. A further area which can be so distinguished, even though there is no historical evidence for Irish settlement there, is the Galloway peninsula. The last area of Irish settlement, again given by place-name evidence only, was in northern Wales, in Anglesey and the Lleyn peninsula, the name of which is traditionally derived from the Irish name for Leinster, *Lagin* or *Laigin*.[30] There is a tradition here that the migration of another tribe from Manau Gododdin, under their leader Cunedda, displaced Irishmen and founded their own dynasty, later to become the kings of Gwynedd. This needs examining in more detail, for there are elements of this story which suggest that there may have been Roman control of the settlement of Cunedda, and of the consequent curbing of the Irish expansion into north Wales. The whole episode, too, is an example of the difficulty of trying to reconcile historical sources among themselves and harmonising them with the archaeological evidence.

There can be no doubt about Cunedda's origins: he was a

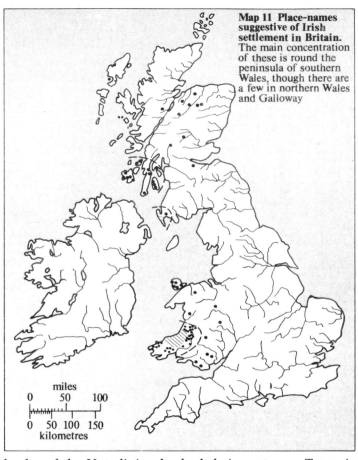

Map 11 Place-names suggestive of Irish settlement in Britain. The main concentration of these is round the peninsula of southern Wales, though there are a few in northern Wales and Galloway

miles
0   50   100
0   50 100 150
kilometres

leader of the Votadini, who had their centre on Traprain Law. In earlier days, they were friendly to the Romans, and had built up a flourishing trade relationship. 'Manau Gododdin', the area from which the settlers came, lies on the Firth of Forth. According to a ninth-century source (Nennius' *Historia Brittonum*), Cunedda and eight of his sons, some of whom seem to have had names similar to elements of the native Welsh landscape, arrived in the area 146 years before Maelgwyn's reign, and expelled the Scots with great slaughter, so that they never again returned. Normal historical writing of this date relies not so much on

26 (a) and (b) (*below*) The two inscribed faces of the 'Cantioris' stone from Penmachno, Gwynedd. The original inscription, 'Cantioris lies here' (CANTIORI HIC IACIT) is on the top line of plate (a). The remainder of the inscription has been added to the stone, and is in a different style

accurate dating by years, but by 'generations', leaving a problem for modern-day historians to guess how many years there might be in a generation.[31] Thus Nennius' precision of dating has always been regarded as slightly suspicious, but the story itself might seem plausible within some context of late Roman or sub-Roman Britain.

There are hints in the story that suggest Roman influence in the transfer. According to his genealogy, Cunedda's father and grandfather have the names Uetern, Patern Pesrut and Tacitus, the first of which might conceal the Latin names Aeternus and Paternus 'pesrut' – 'of the red cloak'. These Roman names, and the nickname 'red-cloak' (possibly referring to that worn by a Roman army officer), have led to the belief that Roman influence on this tribe was considerable, since Roman names are rare (except later, in Christian times) among peoples on the fringe of the Roman

Empire. They tended to stick more assiduously to their own native names. Thus, under a strong Roman influence the move of Cunedda to north Wales would have been in line with Roman practice, to give land inside the empire to a friendly client kingdom.

It is far more likely, however, that the whole story is a myth perpetrated by ninth-century Welsh scholarship to justify the contemporary positions of the north Welsh kingdoms, and to provide a welcome historical parallel to recent events which had seen a new ruling dynasty within Gwynedd established by outsiders.[32] By working back from the accepted date of Maelgwyn's accession in 534, the ninth-century historian has calculated 146 years from the magic date of 388, the death of the established Welsh hero who usurped a position as emperor of the Roman world, Magnus Maximus. This idea has received renewed support from the re-examination of the inscribed stone from north Wales which records the last resting-place of Cantioris in the late fifth or early sixth century. The stone reads 'CANTIORI HIC IACIT/VENEDOTIS CIVE FUIT/C]ONSOBRINO/MAGLI/E]T MAGISTRATI' – 'Cantioris lies here: he was a Venedotian (= of the Votadini) citizen, and kinsman of Maglus and a Magistrate'. This would be fine confirmatory evidence for the presence of the Votadini in north Wales, were it not for the fact that it is now established that originally it read 'Cantioris lies here' only. All the rest is added by a different hand. Could this be a ninth-century forgery to ensure that the story of Venedotian origins reached a wider audience, and to strengthen the north Welsh claim to ancestry from the hero Cunedda?[33]

There is very little evidence on the ground to define where either the Irish or Venedotian settlement may have taken place. Some enclosed hut-groups peculiar to the lowland slopes of north-west Wales have been tentatively suggested to have been of Irish origin, but there is little in Ireland to which they can be seen closely to relate. These sites, single homestead farms with round stone-terraced fields, were mainly set up and used during the latter part of the third century and the whole of the fourth. Possibly this

27 View of the farmstead of Cefn Graeanog, Clynnog, Gwynedd, under excavation. The latest phase of use of this settlement dated from the third to the fifth century AD. Three corners of a roughly rectangular enclosure were occupied by domestic circular buildings, and entrance to the yard was gained through the short axis of a rectangular barn (*to left, centre*). The remainder of the interior of the enclosure was taken up by yards and cultivated plots or paddocks

dating is too restricted, for although a fourth-century date has been established for some of the better known settlements, as for example Din Llygwy, or Ty-mawr on Anglesey, some are being shown to belong to an earlier period, as, for example, Caerau and Cors-y-gedol, which may have been in use in the first half of the second century. Finds from the large hill-forts of the area, Tre'r Ceiri and Brach-y-Dinas, show that similar hutments were apparently in occupation from AD 100 onwards until about 400. Instead of being dominated by one particular group, whether Irish or Venedotian, at any particular period, it now looks as if this area was slowly settling down under the *pax Romana* in its own individual style.[34]

There are thus good reasons to disbelieve the story of the migration of Cunedda and the Votadini to north Wales. The arrival of an Irish tribe, the Deisi, into south Wales is, if anything, better established. Here at least is conclusive evidence of a concentration of Irish settlement in Dyfed, both from ogam-stones and place-names.[35] It is interesting to note that in the dynasty of their kingdom too, there appear men with Roman names: Vortepor's father was Aircol, a name that looks a little like the Latin Agricola, and his grandfather was Triphun (*tribunus*?). The beginnings of the Welsh form of the genealogy are garbled, but contain striking confirmation of the words on Vortepor's memorial stone: the founder of the line is regarded as *Maxim Guletic map Protec map Protector*.[36] Magnus Maximus, British usurper of Roman power, who in 383 set himself up as Roman emperor, is a figure much commemorated in ancient Welsh annals. If there is indeed a connection here with Magnus Maximus, perhaps he was responsible for bringing the Deisi under their leader Eochaid Mac Artchorp into south Wales, and for conferring somehow the name *protector* upon his family, and possibly also the title (now somewhat outdated) of *tribunus*.

Apart from these two cases, the Votadini and the Deisi, there are no further examples of the Roman policy of settlement of native tribes from within Britain in underdeveloped areas, or in territory in need of protection, which can be argued. The historical records of this happening come from a variety of authors – the emperor Probus (276–82) is reputed to have settled Burgundians and Vandals in Britain,[37] and Valentinian transferred a whole tribe – the Bucinobantes – to Britain (364–78).[38] The presence of an Alemannic king with Constantine when he decided to attempt to become emperor has led to a search for an area of Alemannic habitation round York or in west Yorkshire: this has so far failed through lack of a sufficient amount of convincing evidence.[39]

The importance which the Roman military authorities appeared to attach to maintaining a friendly buffer-zone between the empire and potentially dangerous tribes outside it ought similarly to be revealed in the treatment of the threat from Franks and Saxons in the east. Before this can be done, however, it would be as well to view the military and political history of Britain for the last 150 years of Roman rule in the way that Roman historians record it, and to supplement this by noting such material as finds and sites of the period within Britain can afford.

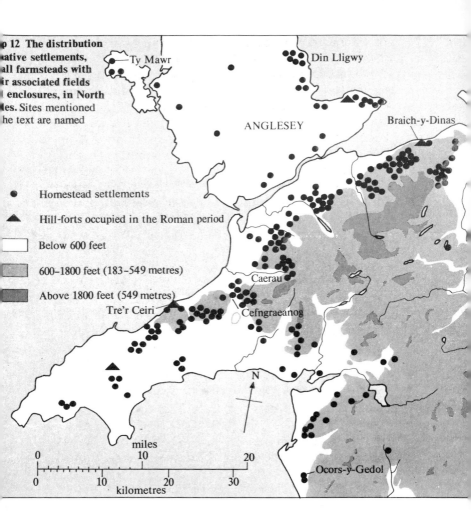

Map 12 The distribution of native settlements, small farmsteads with their associated fields and enclosures, in North Wales. Sites mentioned in the text are named

Ty Mawr

Din Lligwy

Braich-y-Dinas

ANGLESEY

- Homestead settlements

▲ Hill-forts occupied in the Roman period

☐ Below 600 feet

Ⓖ 600–1800 feet (183–549 metres)

Ⓖ Above 1800 feet (549 metres)

Caerau

Tre'r Ceiri

Cefngraeanog

N

miles
| 0 | 10 | 20 |

| 0 | 10 | 20 | 30 |
kilometres

Ocors-y-Gedol

3 Defence against the barbarians

The last decades of the third century were a time of considerable crisis for the Roman Empire on a number of fronts, with a series of symptoms which were not altogether unconnected. Between the death of the emperor Gordien III in 244 and the establishment of Diocletian and Maximian as co-emperors of the two halves of the Roman world in 285, so many men had been proclaimed as rival usurping emperors that there was a situation similar to anarchy. Frontier armies repeatedly championed their own commanding officers as candidates for imperial power, so that the soldiers of both the east and west were prepared to engage in civil war to press the claims of their own favourites.

Such forceful political moves on the part of the army emphasised the disunity of the empire, because usurpers would claim imperial power within their own half of it, while hardly expecting to extend their authority over the whole Roman world. Desertion of frontier duty while assisting an imperial candidate also led to undermanning of the defences, giving tribes from outside a chance of entry which they were not slow to seize. During the half century up to 280, barbarians from many different tribes forced their way into many parts of the empire, although the archaeological trace of these incursions is slight. It is often assumed that the location of coin-hoards buried for safety at this date (the date comes from the latest coin in the hoard) ought to reveal the waves of panic set up by the threat or the actuality of these invasions. The distribution patterns of coin-hoards of dates within this range shows that the unease reached deep into Gaul, Spain and Britain. Many of our recovered hoards within Britain were buried particularly in the 270s, as is shown by hoards ending with the coins of the Tetrici (270–3). [1]

In addition to this pressure, and possibly in part adding to disaffection with present policies among the troops, monetary inflation was rampant, and it was one of the major tasks of successive emperors to attempt to find a financial policy which would stem this upward trend. [2] The exact reasons for the financial crisis are difficult to explain, but a contributory factor was the loss of the bullion mines of Dacia, when that Roman province (now modern Romania) proved untenable in the 270s. After that, there was less precious metal in the common coinage – a debasement which led to money finding its natural rather than its artificial value. Inflation undoubtedly worsened during the late third and fourth centuries, though some of the emperors desperately tried to improve the standard of coinage.

These empire-wide trends were bound to have some effect on Britain, although the island provinces appear to have been less troubled than mainland Europe by either barbarian incursion or military disaffection. The northern frontier of Britain had been extensively restored under the Severan emperors in the early third century, and towns on the whole by now had stone-built defences, in contrast to their Gallic counterparts which were mostly still open and extensive. Although Britain was technically part of the separatist 'Gallic Empire', established by the usurper Postumus in 259, this interlude seems to have been a time of comparative peace during which the normal run of official business continued unabated. The frontiers were still held, troops were paid, and, as inscriptions show, military buildings were kept in good repair and roads were mended. The 'Gallic Empire' had gained such acceptance that even after its suppression in 273 by one of the more competent of the legitimate Roman emperors, Aurelian, two further attempts were made to re-establish it. Revolts led by Proculus and then Bonosus, who had a British father, were both summarily dealt with by the emperor Probus (276–82), who, in energy and military zeal, took upon himself a positive role as the successor of Aurelian, and earned himself a reputa-

93

28 A portion of the walls of Rome, built in the years 270–6 as a protection for the city against possible barbarian onslaught. The gate is the Porta Tiburtina, and the rectangular towers, one of which shows a blocked window at rampart-walk height, are typical of this phase of Rome's defences

tion as a martinet among soldiery and provincials alike.[3]

One of Aurelian's projects which Probus completed was the construction of defensive walls round the city of Rome itself – the first time the full extent of the capital city had been so protected.[4] The provision of this massive new circuit of walls for a city so far from the frontiers of the empire is indicative of the seriousness of the challenge which the invasions of barbarian tribes had caused. This was brought home most clearly to the cities of Gaul in 276, when Franks and Alemanni crossed into the empire and devastated as many as seventy of the provincial cities.[5] This appalling object-lesson brought quick remedial action. Not only were the raiders summarily expelled, but a comprehensive campaign of walling the Gallic cities was begun. The three strong military emperors of the later third century, Aurelian, Probus and Diocletian, had all come to power at the head of eastern armies, and it was from the advanced

29 Aerial view of the fort of Housesteads, on Hadrian's Wall. The plan of the fort, though not fully understood, is a typical original layout of the early second century. The headquarters lay in the centre, and the remainder of the middle range was taken up by the hospital, commandant's house and granaries. Long, narrow barrack blocks occupied the majority of the remainder

types of military construction to be found in the Roman provinces of the east that many of the techniques now employed in the west were derived. These included massively thick free-standing walls, projecting rectangular or D-shaped towers, and heavily defended single gateways and posterns.[6]

There are indications that Britain did not altogether escape the brunt of barbarian raiding. Many of the coin-hoards deposited in the late 260s and 270s were in coastal areas of the south and east; so there was some trouble in that

95

30 The late Roman walls of Le Mans. These walls, with projecting towers, are typical of defences built in the later third century to protect the Gallic cities from barbarian raiding

region, probably caused by the increasing advent of Saxon raiders, whose ships enabled them to strike suddenly from the sea and to penetrate deep inland along river estuaries and creeks. The date at which these raids first became a nuisance cannot easily be determined, but it may have been as early as the beginning of the third century, when a number of places, including Colchester, Chelmsford and other coastal sites in Essex suffered some destruction. Roman measures for defence from this unexpected attack appear to have come in at least two phases, first with the mobilisation and defence of some of the more vulnerable ports in East Anglia and Kent, followed later by a full-scale organisation of new forts to combat the more serious threat.[7]

A number of defended Roman harbour-bases lay round the southern and eastern coastline, and results from excavation or from chance finds suggest that they belong to the late third and fourth centuries. From the mid-first century onwards within Britain, the Roman military fort was built to a standard pattern – a rectangular plan with rounded corners, and a layout of buildings within the fort if not instantly

Figure 7 The Reculver inscription. The text runs 'the shrine and the hall of this headquarters were built in the governorship of . . . Rufinus, of consular rank'

recognisable in every case, at least fairly well understood in main outline. This design, at first executed in earth and timber, was soon translated into stone: the early earthen rampart was reinforced by a stone front, and the central *principia* (headquarters building), the granaries, officers' quarters, and the mens' barracks were now solidly built. This design satisfied the British military command for at least two centuries. When the southeastern harbour bases came to be built, however, only two were constructed in this old-fashioned style. The others, like the Gallic city walls of the 270s and 280s, were built with thick, free-standing walls, projecting towers, and many of the refinements of late Roman defensive architecture. [8]

The dating of these forts is crucial. On the basis of parts of an inscription found at the fort of Reculver (Kent), recording the dedication of the shrine of the headquarters building, the construction date there can be assigned to the governor-

97

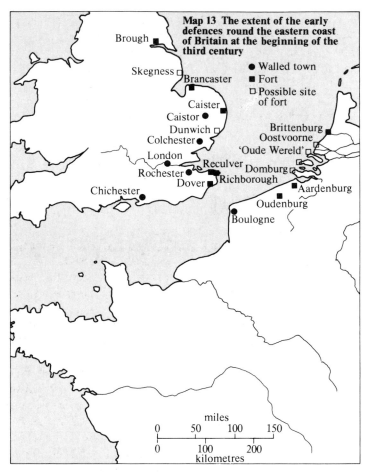

Map 13 The extent of the early defences round the eastern coast of Britain at the beginning of the third century

Brough

Skegness

Brancaster

● Walled town
■ Fort
□ Possible site of fort

Caister

Caistor

Dunwich

Colchester

Brittenburg

Oostvoorne

'Oude Wereld'

London

Reculver

Domburg

Rochester

Dover

Richborough

Aardenburg

Chichester

Oudenburg

Boulogne

miles
0   50   100   150
0   100   200
kilometres

ship in Britain of a man called Rufinus, a name common enough in the third and fourth centuries. There is no proof that either of the two possible men of this name who are known to have been qualified for the post as governor of Britain by holding consulships at Rome is the Rufinus mentioned at Reculver.[9] The fort is one of those built in the 'old' style, and a construction date in the first half of the third century would correspond well both with the date that two men named Rufinus are known to have held consulships at Rome, and also with typological arguments based on the

98

fort's ground plan and layout. Excavations there have revealed that it had an initial phase of construction and use, followed by a later reorganisation of some of the layout of buildings within the fort. These might provisionally be dated respectively to the early and later third century.

The other fort built in what appears to be a traditional military style lies at Brancaster, Norfolk. Examination of the site suggests that the fort was imposed on a settlement possibly associated with an earlier harbour-base at the creek-edge. Excavations within this settlement have revealed that the Roman occupation was mainly of second and third-century date, and such work as has been done on the fort itself suggests that it was in occupation from about 260 or 270 onwards.

Even though the forts built in the typical military style cannot themselves be dated accurately, there are indications that a number of other sites round the southern and eastern coasts were mobilised in the third century. Paramount among them was Dover, where a second-century fort built as the base for the British Fleet was probably still in use in the early third century; later this was abandoned and a completely new fort, partly overlapping the site of the old one, constructed. The ports which may have supported some Roman patrolling, if not a counter-offensive against raiders, in the third century will have included the walled towns of Caister-on-Sea, Colchester, London, Rochester, and probably Richborough and Lympne. The fleet which patrolled the coast will have been divided between Dover and Boulogne, which was the headquarters for a similar series of harbours on the continental side of the Channel.

These preliminary precautions such as they were, were inadequate by the end of the third century, for by then our sources record that Franks and Saxons were infesting the seas. [10] At about this time, the Roman military authorities began to develop a number of the existing harbours into full-scale defended bases, positioning strongly walled forts on the larger river estuaries and on the exposed coasts, to protect the anchorages and by their presence to block Frankish and Saxon access to the interior of the province. These

31 The insignia of the *Comes Litoris Saxonici* (the 'Count of the Saxon Shore') from the *Notitia Dignitatum*. The Count has under his control the garrisons of nine posts 'throughout Britain', and these are shown on the island of Britain as little walled forts, their names super-inscribed. A parallel text on the facing page gives the garrisons of each of the named posts. As far as the names can be related to surviving Roman remains, they are all the sites of heavily defended Roman forts in the south-east of Britain, and there seems to be little or no relationship between their actual disposition round the coast and their representation on the *Notitia* picture (Bodleian Library, Oxford, Canon Misc. 378, fol. 154v.)

forts, clearly intended to hold a military garrison of both soldiery and sailors, were later to be known as the 'Saxon Shore' frontier, protecting Britain from assault in an area she had little expected to be at risk. The Roman name 'Litus Saxonicum' ('Saxon Shore') is preserved only in the *Notitia Dignitatum*,[11] and its inclusion within that list of late Roman military and civil postings can therefore be dated to about AD 395. How much earlier than this the name was applied is uncertain, but there are in the *Notitia* named garrisons on the continental coast which also belong 'on the Saxon Shore', suggesting that the command may originally have covered both sides of the Channel, only at a later date (but

32 The Roman 'Saxon Shore' fort of Richborough, Kent. The walls, enclosing a quadrilateral shape, are of Kentish ragstone and tile-courses. They have projecting rectangular towers, the site of one of which is shown by the ruined masonry and joist-holes which would have supported the tower floor

pre-395) being subdivided into its British and Continental components. The Gallic forts, Marcis and Grannona (neither name has been proved yet to belong to an identified archaeological site) appear in the *Notitia* under two separate commanders with coastal responsibilities which span the continental shoreline from the Rhine mouth round as far as the river Garronne. [12]

There is growing evidence that shore defence at this period was not confined to Britain alone. The area between the mouth of the Rhine and the Channel Straits was most at risk from raids, and here too there were Roman military establishments. The most important fort at present known is that of Aardenburg in Holland. It had stone-built towers, walls and headquarters building, and is one of a chain of sites known or assumed to have existed from fragmentary records and indications. In the later third century Aardenburg was abandoned for reasons not yet clear, and the site of Oudenburg, some distance to the south-west in Belgium, was fortified with a large four-square fort of a type similar to those built in Britain. There is thus a strong case for considering the two sides of the Channel as one in the minds of Roman defensive planners. This had traditionally been the case with the British Fleet, and there was little point in altering the tactical arrangement now. It follows that measures taken to protect the cities of Gaul have their logical extension in a series of coastal forts as a frontier against penetration by seafaring tribes into areas where they were not welcome. Seen in this light, therefore, it comes as little surprise that the British and Continental defences built in the late third century were in a style new to Britain, using the same military constructional techniques as near-contemporary city walls in the hinterland of Gaul built as a response to the barbarian raids of the 270s. The 'Saxon Shore' forts protected the whole north-east portion of the empire, not just Britain. To do this, their command had to span the dioceses of Britannia and Belgica, and their scope was the whole of the northern seas.

The straightforwardness of this conclusion is, however, bedevilled by the one historical episode of the later third century within Britain for which we have good source material.[13] The Roman Caesar, Maximian, shortly to become co-emperor with Diocletian, had been involved in 284–5 in the process of mopping up resistance to Roman rule in northern Gaul. Men described as *Bagaudae* had staged a rebellion. Prominent among the officers who were involved in the quelling of this disturbance was a man named Carausius, coming by birth from the Belgian coastline, and something of a sailor as well as soldier. When casting around, therefore, to find someone to command the newly revitalised Channel fleet in its campaign against Franks and Saxons, Maximian selected Carausius. In 285, he became the first fleet-commander, based at Boulogne, with a commission to 'bring peace to the seas in the area of Belgica and Armorica' (all along the Gallic Channel coastline).

The story goes that Carausius was rather too elated by his promotion. His success against the barbarian pirates was phenomenal: he captured many of them, but although recovering the booty they had plundered, he was accused of returning it neither to the rightful owner nor to the imperial treasury. This action was seen by Maximian, now elevated to imperial status, as treasonable, and orders were issued for Carausius' arrest and execution as a rebel. Forced therefore into revolt, and following a precedent set several times in the recent past, Carausius relied on the fidelity of his troops and declared himself emperor, in effect claiming equality with Maximian and Diocletian. He still held his base of command at Boulogne, and since the only serviceable fleet in the Channel was at his disposal, he could claim to be holding Britain as a separate empire.

There is little to add to this bare outline. It is possible that the charges levelled against Carausius were trumped up, or that Maximian had received a biased account of the methods which Carausius used to trap and capture the pirates. Maximian may have been jealous of Carausius, and regarded him as a dangerous rival who was best removed. Historical accounts seem to preclude the idea that Carausius was always greedy for power, or that he had been aiming at a position as co-emperor for some time. His elevation to the Channel command was perhaps Maximian's way of removing him from the main arena of political action, and giving him a responsibility which would be rough, dangerous and unrewarding, ending possibly in a political backwater.

Whatever the personal or political motivation for these events, Carausius had clearly won some British support, and the merchants who plied their trade between the Channel ports were doubtless grateful to him for the safety which his policing of those waters brought to their livelihood. Carausius never relinquished the idea to which he laid claim, that he might actually achieve equality with the emperors. His first priority was to issue coinage, both to pay the troops who were loyal to him, and to steady the economy. Britain's mineral resources were no longer sent away to the central imperial treasury, so the new money was of higher standard, with a considerable precious metal content. The legends which his coinage bore were aimed in part at crediting his faithful troops for his success, in part at reassuring the British provincials that this was to be a time of peace and plenty, and in part at conciliatory gestures to Diocletian and Maximian.

Such courtesy was not returned, and panegyrics which survive show how Maximian was preparing a fleet of his

(a)

(b)

33 Coin portraits of (a) Carausius and (b) Allectus

own with which he could challenge Carausius' superiority over the Channel seas. By 289 it had been built, and was sailing down the Rhine ready to do battle. The outcome is nowhere stated, and for some reason the attempt ended in failure. If Carausius had scored a signal victory, the panegyrists of all people would have been the first to obscure the fact. There is some vague mention in a later speech of bad weather which prevented this fleet from achieving its objective. The panegyrists never mention Carausius by name – to them he is always a public enemy – and the hostile pressure clearly did not abate, for despite the setback of 289, Maximian seems never to have intended to recognise the 'British' empire. Other affairs on the frontier in Europe for the moment claimed his attention, and Carausius was therefore able with impunity to celebrate five years of separatist rule.

In 293 Maximian and Diocletian decided to appoint deputies in each half of the empire. Maximian's Caesar of the western half was Constantius, a forthright military tactician, whose first task was to attack and demolish the empire built up by Carausius and by Allectus, his adviser. Constantius was not slow in moving to the attack. Since the seaborne assault was not really possible in the face of Carausius' naval superiority (his fleet by now had had at least seven years of training and active experience in combat against the Saxons), Constantius moved overland against Boulogne, still Carausius' principal base on the Continent. With a sharp attack, the construction of a mole across the

34 Commemorative gold medallion found near Arras in France, showing the citizens of London on their knees welcoming Constantius Caesar's arrival. Clearly it was struck to celebrate the delivery of London in AD 296 from the ten years of rule by Carausius and Allectus

harbour to cut off all relief from the sea, and a short siege Boulogne fell. Carausius had suffered his first defeat, and was now isolated within Britain.

With his political credit at a low ebb, Carausius became the victim of treachery on the part of his closest supporter. An assassination was arranged (so Roman sources relate) and in 293 Allectus, once Carausius' *rationalis* (finance minister), seized control. What Britain now needed, however, was a military tactician, not an economist; and three years later, in the face of a two-pronged attack with a newly prepared fleet from Boulogne and from the Seine, Allectus' empire fell. One force eluded the British fleet on the south coast near the Isle of Wight, and, landing, burned their boats and marched towards London. Allectus, caught in indecision, hastened to meet them with a force largely composed of Germanic mercenaries, and was soundly defeated. Remnants of his beaten army, with no thought but to claim some retribution for their effort now that their paymaster was dead, turned back to the city, probably intending rape and pillage before being driven out. Constantius himself, leading the second army of the expedition, arrived up-river in London in time to prevent a disaster, and to receive the grateful thanks of its citizens.

If this breakaway empire of Carausius and Allectus, the

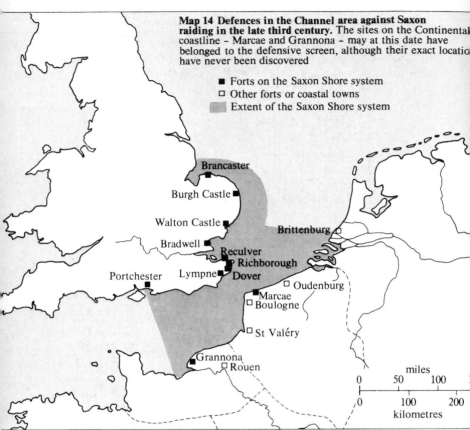

Map 14 Defences in the Channel area against Saxon raiding in the late third century. The sites on the Continental coastline – Marcae and Grannona – may at this date have belonged to the defensive screen, although their exact location have never been discovered

- ■ Forts on the Saxon Shore system
- □ Other forts or coastal towns
- ▨ Extent of the Saxon Shore system

Brancaster

Burgh Castle

Walton Castle

Bradwell

Brittenburg

Reculver

Richborough

Portchester

Lympne Dover

Oudenburg

Marcae

Boulogne

St Valéry

Grannona

Rouen

miles

0   50   100

0   100   200

kilometres

latest in the long line of attempts to form a separate state of a portion of the Roman world, succeeded at all, it was by the acceptance of the provincials who lived within it. There is nothing to show that military defence was in any way endangered by the establishment of this empire; there are indications that Carausian coinage was welcomed for its value, and could hold its own with the new coinage now issued by Diocletian. As before, under the Gallic empire of Postumus, roads were kept in repair, and there is every reason to believe that life was maintained more or less as normal.

This already rather romantic story has been seen by some historians, ancient and modern, as a foundation for more fanciful tales. In some medieval accounts, the more way-out being those of Nennius, Giraldus Cambrensis and Geoffrey of Monmouth, fragments of other legends were woven into the tale to make the Carausian career more picturesque. Modern debate has centred round Carausius' relationship with the 'Saxon Shore' forts. These impressive defences might not be seen simply as the extension of an overall Roman imperial defensive screen. It is thought Carausius may have built the forts himself, not so much as a defence against Saxon piracy, but as a British defence against the avenging power of Maximian and Rome. It is possible, however, on the basis of coin evidence, to argue that Richborough, a key site within the shore defensive system, was under construction before Carausian coins had become at all widely current. The evidence from other sites does not admit of such close dating: the first occupation layers within the fort at Portchester have produced coins of Carausius and suggest that its first use, if not its actual construction (or completion), was his responsibility. His commission to stamp out piracy would make better sense if it were to have sprung from the establishment of modern bases recently purpose-built to the same standards as Gallic city walls. If Carausius had to build these forts from scratch, he did so remarkably quickly considering the early success which he achieved against the pirates from their use. If he built them when he knew of the threat of reprisals from Maximian, it is curious that none of his coins are found within the constructional layers. In any case, the value of such forts against the Roman army was small. They were vulnerable to a siege, and Carausius' defence lay in ships, as the events of 293 and 296 were to show. These bases, on both the British and the Gallic coastline, were a secondary factor in the decision to create a separate empire; they were an encouragement to Carausius who might think, with some reason, that by their use he could mount counter-offensives against Saxons or against Roman seafarers.[14]

Events in other areas of Britain at this time are harder to follow. As far as military installations themselves are concerned, there was little new building on the northern British

35 The aspect of a late Roman fort. The surrounding enclosure of Cardiff Castle, an early twentieth-century reconstruction of the Roman walls of the Cardiff fort which were discovered there in excavation at the turn of the century

frontier or its hinterland. Unlike other areas of Britain, where the 'continental style' of defences came into service, the forts on Hadrian's Wall were never adapted to receive externally projecting corner-towers, as happened on other frontiers of the empire. Even new forts built in the north at this later period – Piercebridge, Co. Durham, and possibly sites such as Newton Kyme and Elslack (North Yorks.) – were still constructed in the traditional style, although the interior buildings at Piercebridge showed considerable variation from earlier layouts.[15]

There are some indications that the Roman military hold on the Pennine areas was being relaxed. A number of forts holding this region may have been abandoned in the later third century. Inscriptional evidence for rebuilding (in the 240s) comes only from Lanchester, and the formation of new *civitas* units at Carlisle (Civitas Carvetiorum) may have taken place in the 260s. Corbridge, originally a fort but turned into a supply depot, may have had a similar development.[16]

On Hadrian's Wall itself, archaeological evidence sug-

108

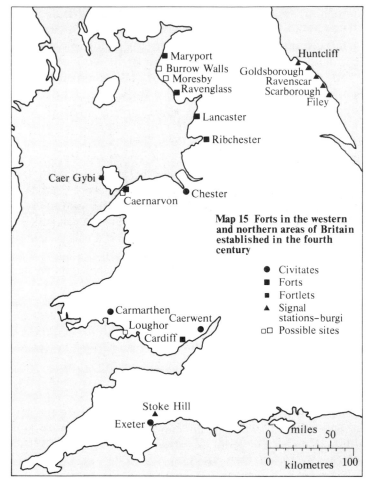

Map 15 Forts in the western and northern areas of Britain established in the fourth century

Maryport
Burrow Walls
Moresby
Ravenglass

Goldsborough
Ravenscar
Scarborough
Filey

Huntcliff

Lancaster

Ribchester

Caer Gybi
Caernarvon

Chester

● Civitates
■ Forts
▪ Fortlets
▲ Signal stations–burgi
□□ Possible sites

Carmarthen
Caerwent
Loughor
Cardiff

Stoke Hill
Exeter

0 miles 50
0 kilometres 100

gests a certain amount of decay towards the late third century. There are burnt layers in some of the excavated fort-buildings, and rubble and debris was packed in under later laid floors in some of the milecastles and turrets along the wall. It is questionable, however, how far such destruction can be attributable to barbarian incursion into the frontier areas. The list of Wall and outpost forts which suffered damage is impressive: it includes Benwell, Haltonchesters, Greatchesters, Housesteads, Birdoswald, High Rochester,

109

Risingham and Bewcastle, but even so it is difficult to be certain about the perpetrators of the damage. Destruction by fire is more likely to be due to enemy action or accident, but mere dismantling is more probably the work of Roman troops themselves prior to some fairly radical replanning of the interior accommodation of the forts at a slightly later date.[17]

The very last years of the third century bring with them the first historical mention of the Picts. This is no more than a passing aside in a speech by one of the panegyrists, but it shows that some trouble was to be expected from the unified tribes north of the border.[18] The emperor Constantius, newly elevated to the post in 305 after the retirement of Diocletian and Maximian, had as one of his first tasks a visit to Britain to campaign against the Picts, and it was probably due to his presence and influence that a number of northern forts were refurbished at or around this date. His earlier visit, in 296, had perhaps begun to pin-point a number of defensive improvements which should be carried out on the northern frontier. The fort of Birdoswald, for example, had suffered considerably from neglect, for its commandant's house, *principia* and baths were restored (the inscription records that they had been covered in earth!).[19] A fragmentary inscription on which the reading is very dubious may have recorded the same sort of thing at Housesteads.[20] A collection of the archaeological evidence for early fourth-century reconstruction of the northern forts shows that although there are problems over exact dating, at Chesterholm and Risingham the *principia* buildings were completely redesigned, with a consequent reorientation of the whole fort layout. At Housesteads not only was the *principia* altered, but the barrack blocks were adapted to changed circumstances, possibly a reduction in the garrison. Traces of similar alterations of layout can be seen at other Wall forts.[21]

Coupled perhaps with Constantius' campaigns in 305–6, which the panegyrist with his usual fulsomeness celebrated as a resounding success, came the reinstatement of some of the forts south of Hadrian's Wall to add depth to the line of defence. At Bainbridge, for example, excavation has suggested that there was a Constantian phase of construction, though later alterations have all but eradicated it, and there are similar findings at Brough-on-Noe, Ilkley and Malton.[22] It was not that fort defences came in for wholesale reconstruction. At Manchester and Templeborough recent reinterpretation has suggested reconstruction of the walls and ditches,[23] but only at Binchester and Lanchester[24] is there clear sign of rebuilding of the defence systems.

Military arrangements of this period in northern Britain, however, are reflected within the *Notitia Dignitatum*.[25] Despite the late date of the compilation of the list, it has been demonstrated that the majority of the garrisons which are listed on the line of the Wall under the command of the Duke of Britain are those known from independent epigraphic evidence to have been present at the forts in the third century. There are difficulties not only over the original *Notitia* text of this passage on the Wall forts themselves, which are adequately documented in other places, but also over the identification of other forts under the command of the Duke. The *Notitia* entry records a section *'per lineam valli'*, and links garrisons with some of the names familiar to us from other sources as those of Wall-forts, Segedunum (Wallsend), Pons Aeli (Newcastle), Condercum (Benwell) and so on. Under the Duke's command, a further twenty-two garrisons are listed in the *Notitia* linked with Roman names which are not always with certainty assignable to an archaeological fort site in the north. From itineraries some tentative evidence exists for the identification of a name with a fort, but the problem is that on current interpretations, not all the forts known to have been occupied at some period in the fourth century seem to be listed in the *Notitia*. Most surprising is the fact that Ambleside (Galava), Lowborough Bridge and Kirby Lonsdale forts have all produced abundant evidence of their use and occupation in the fourth century, yet none of these is identified by a *Notitia* name. Conversely, Bravoniacum, with a *Notitia* garrison, is identified as Kirkby Thore, where there is as yet no evidence for late occupation at all. It is possible that new studies such as

111

that which has recently sought to reinterpret old evidence from Manchester and Templeborough forts (places where the recorded material is all the more precious because of the present inaccessibility of the sites) may show renewed occupation in the fourth century at more of the northern forts, but at present the evidence in the main consists of a few pieces of pottery or coins picked up by chance on the surface of the site.

A scatter of late Roman pottery and coins itself gives no indication of who was using a site, nor the use to which it was put. The possibility must always be considered that some former fort sites may have become civilian communities rather than military bases. This explanation has been suggested for the fort of Templeborough. A stone-built *principia* (of Constantinian date?) was unfinished, but ill-assorted timber buildings of fourth-century date occupied the site of the former fort.[26] Caution must again be exercised, however, in the interpretation of such material, for work at Wallsend, the easternmost fort on Hadrian's Wall, has revealed the existence of ungainly fourth-century timber buildings there which may still have fulfilled a military purpose.[27]

There are clear examples, however, of civilian centres which grew out of military sites in the area. Catterick, for example, was a fully fledged town in the Roman period, and, like Corbridge, occupied the site of a former fort.[28] The fourth-century *vicus* at Chesterholm had also perhaps acquired something of a separate status from the nearby fort,[29] and the *vici* of several of the forts on the wall had spread in the fourth century to cover a quite disproportionate area by comparison with the forts to which they belonged. The growth of such civilian centres, including the larger units such as Carlisle and Corbridge, was due not so much to the spread northwards at this period of peaceable conditions, but to the increasing transformation of military establishments into mixed or fully civilian centres because of the mollifying influence of a long period of static duty on the frontier. This tendency was not unique to Britain, and military authorities all over the empire had to face it.[30]

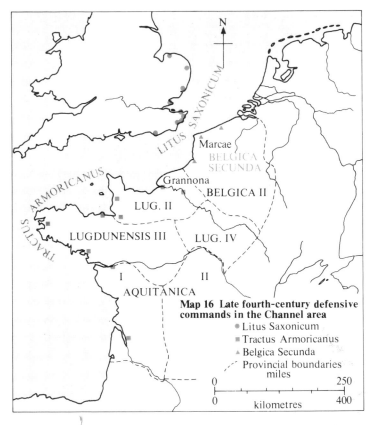

N

LITUS SAXONICUM

ARMORICANUS

TRACTUS

Marcae

BELGICA SECUNDA

Grannona

BELGICA II

LUG. II

LUGDUNENSIS III

LUG. IV

I

II

AQUITANICA

Map 16 Late fourth-century defensive commands in the Channel area

● Litus Saxonicum
■ Tractus Armoricanus
▲ Belgica Secunda
--- Provincial boundaries

miles

0   250

0   400

kilometres

The recognition of this fact led Diocletian to changes in army organisation, which saw the separation of frontier duties from active campaigning. Thus when Constantius came to Britain in 305–6, he brought with him a force capable of carrying the battle to the Pictish enemy – the so-called 'field army' whose task was to be in reserve and be ready for action should the need arise. The emperor, of course, maintained a troop of men ready for such duties, and his deputies too had similar forces: such men will have been those who ousted Carausius from Boulogne in 293, and destroyed Allectus in 296. The immediate problem within Britain was the policing of the two frontier areas. There was probably no specific *Dux* appointed to the north-

113

ern area until after Diocletian's reign, and his appointment may have come in 306 as a result of the campaigns of Constantius.[31]

Despite the episode of Carausius' usurpation, there is every reason to suppose that the Channel coastal command in the south-east continued in operation. It might have seemed sensible to separate the British from the continental portions of this command, and not to run the risk of similar bids for power in the future. But the Channel coasts must have still been afforded protection. The way in which the known forts are spaced out suggests that control of both sides of the coast was vital to the scheme's early operation. Pirates passing through the Dover Straits from their northern homelands were likely to be caught either on their inward or their homeward run if effective surveillance was maintained from both sides of the Channel. The chain of forts would need to have been linked by signal stations, of which one has been identified at Corton, on the Suffolk coast, and another discovered not far from the city walls of London at Shadwell. If the system remained under the command of a *Dux* after the Carausian episode, it must have been subject to considerable safeguards – not least those mirrored in the *Notitia*, where the administrative staffs of most of the military commanders contain members appointed from the staff of their superiors to keep a strict watch on loyalty. In addition, in Britain's case at this time, there were now four provincial governors rather than the original two, and possibly other army commanders of equal or nearly equal rank, to act as extra safeguards.

It was after his Pictish campaign that Constantius died in 306. This was the occasion for the hurried journey of Constantine, his son, from Rome to be by his father's deathbed at York, and to claim the imperial title at the instigation of his father's troops gathered there. After the accession of Constantine, and his gradual assumption of sole imperial power by a combination of intrigue and warlike action against his rivals, military affairs in Britain became somewhat quieter. This may have been a time for consolidation rather than spectacular success. Constantine, however,

took the title *Britannicus Maximus* in 315, signifying some
achievement or victory within the island, and the troops
which the *Notitia* records at Danum (Doncaster) bear the
name *Crispiani* after the Caesar Crispus who ruled as one of
Constantine's juniors from 317–26. This suggests that garrisoning of these back-up forts was continuing apace during
these years,[32] a policy which is strikingly borne out by
contemporary historians who criticised Constantine for, as
they saw it, weakening the frontiers by over-emphasising
defence in depth.[33] Constantine's biographer records that
this refers to trouble in Wales and the west.[34]

Documentation of attacks on Britain from the direction of
Ireland is not easy, and apart from the above reference to
Constantine's western victory there are no records of
attacks from the Scotti until about the 360s.[35] Nevertheless it
has been claimed that the coastal defence of Wales and
western Britain was every bit as important as that of the
south-east, and that there was a western coastal command
under another military official, possibly the other one
recorded in the *Notitia*, the *Comes Britanniae*.[36] The more
normal interpretation of this post, however, is that it
belongs late in the history of Britain, and represents that of a
permanent Count in charge of an established British field
army. This is unlikely to have been set up much before the
end of the fourth century.[37]

A series of late Roman defended sites round the western
British coastline adds some substance to the view that some
form of protection was necessary here also. The western
topography, however, is nothing like as conducive as the
eastern to warding off serious inroads: the best that a
Roman strategist could achieve was to police most of the
obvious estuaries along which Irish raiders might travel.[38]
Thus not only for forts which were established now, such as
those at Cardiff and Lancaster, but also for Carmarthen,
Caerwent, Chester, Caernarvon and, to a lesser extent
Gloucester, the later Roman period brought a new importance and a distinct defensive role. Parts of the Welsh coastline may have been as well defended as the 'Saxon Shore'.
Carmarthen, itself a walled town, was linked to the sea

115

36 Caer Gybi, a fortified landing base at Holyhead on Anglesey. It is late Roman in date, but its purpose is by no means clear. A substantial portion of the walls if of Roman workmanship, but the circular tower (*left*) and the gate (*centre*) are of medieval date

along its river by a series of signal stations; coin finds at Loughor and at Pembroke – both key sites later occupied by Norman castles – suggest that there were late Roman bases here too. The fort at Cardiff is difficult to date precisely: its original design had an interior earthen rampart and rounded corners, features which link it with forts of earlier date; yet its polygonal projecting towers, obvious elements of the present modern reconstruction, and clearly a very early adaptation of the original plan, should date it at least to the closing years of the third century.

As a whole, however, there is little evidence for military occupation during the fourth century at many of the Welsh forts. Two legionary fortresses, Caerleon and Chester, had controlled Wales in earlier centuries. Caerleon was abandoned in the last quarter of the third century, for the mere trickle of finds thereafter hardly suggests a grand scale of occupation.[39] Chester, with repairs to its walls attested about this period,[40] was clearly still in occupation, but it is more likely to have begun by now to combine both civilian and military functions within its walls. Here a western command may have been based, but Chester, like other legionary fortresses at the same date in other parts of the empire, had probably become a *civitas*. The fort at Caernar-

37 Fourth-century mosaic from Lydney (Glos.) Roman temple and its precinct. The inscription records that it was given by a man whose rank was PR.REL – possibly fleet quartermaster

von was occupied in the fourth century, and nearby is an enigmatic stone-walled enclosure probably of late Roman date; it was possibly a base for stores, or even for protecting the harbour from some considerable height above the estuary. A small fortified harbour at Holyhead on Anglesey completes the picture of late Roman coastal fortification in Wales.

A link with a line of outpost forts down the Cumberland coast from the western end of Hadrian's Wall is provided by the fort at Lancaster. Here, on the hill now occupied by the castle, where Roman military establishments of all periods once stood, a soundly built wall of typical late Roman construction is part of a fort built in the 330s.[41] A connection between the Bristol Channel and a Roman fleet is suggested by a pavement from the great temple complex at Lydney dedicated by a man whose official title was shortened to PR.REL, which is interpreted as *praefectus reliquationis Classis* ('in charge of the fleet's supply depot'). Such a base probably lay nearby. Thus though there are indications of defences along the western coastline, it is impossible to describe them as a comprehensive and coherent series like those on the northern frontier or the Saxon Shore.

Fourth century Britain contained a number of smaller settlements enclosed by walls, a feature unparalleled in the remainder of the Roman world except in those areas contiguous to the imperial frontiers. It is true in a sense to say

117

that Britain was composed of four frontier provinces, threatened as she was by enemies from three sides. A list of Roman provinces prepared in 312–14 (known as the 'Verona List') has as a strange appendix a list of the hostile tribes which repeatedly battered at the gates of the empire.[42] As far as Britain was concerned, these included Scotti from Ireland, Picts and Caledonii from Scotland, besides Franks and Saxons. The proliferation of strongly walled posts in areas within Britain which had always been civilian rather than military is therefore a natural progression. All over the empire, local people were finding that the frontiers were no longer far-off, but were being brought by the depth, frequency, and even the very alarm of barbarian attacks to their very doorsteps. In provinces with one clearly defined frontier – Germania for example – the late third and fourth centuries saw the construction of small posts at key points along routes, providing safe places for supplies, troops, local men and beasts, against the onslaught of an invader. Most of these are no more than a solid and unsurmountable barrier which would discourage a raider who was keen to grab what he could as quickly as possible.

Among the small walled fourth-century posts in Britain, there are undoubtedly several categories. One of the most obvious is the posting-station, and a chain of these along the line of Watling Street has been distinguished.[43] The characteristics of these posts differ considerably: some seem to have had stone walls and ramparts, some ramparts and ditches only, but they are nearly all of small dimensions. Defences for these posts were probably provided in the early fourth century, but to date them all to a single building campaign may be misleading. Watling Street is not the only Roman road in Britain which has posts of similar type evenly spaced along it: the Fosse Way, for example, has an equally impressive run, as do other roads in the Midlands and south-west. Not all the posts on these roads are of the same diminutive size as those of Watling Street; some were fully fledged 'towns'. A series of posts in many ways similar to these in Britain has been identified along the line of the main Roman road from Bavai to Cologne (in northern

118

France, Belgium and Germany), but here, excavation is beginning to show that various sites were occupied at different periods within the third and fourth centuries, and also that, as elsewhere, an apparent similarity of shape from initial reconnaissance does not on closer examination necessarily imply that the sites were built or occupied contemporaneously.[44]

The division of Britain into four rather than two provinces, with the creation of more government officials who needed protection, may have added to the proliferation of such small posts.[45] The addition of a few *civitates* to the original number, suggesting some slight fragmentation of administration at this later period, indicates that the whole process of law and order and taxation was already adequately decentralised through the administration of the *civitates*. It is difficult to divine any overall pattern within which some smaller settlements were provided with defences. Archaeological evidence suggests that some town walls date from the end of the third century, others from various dates within the fourth. There is in all a studied lack of standardisation: some have integral projecting towers, for example, others have them added, still others have none at all.

The minor walled settlements have a singular lack of imposing buildings. Scarcely any have recognisable features of larger *civitates* – a *forum* or public buildings. Inside Margidunum, for example, lying astride the Fosse Way north of Leicester, only two stone buildings are known, despite wide-scale sampling.[46] Such open spaces within the polygonal walled area as were found by excavation may have been occupied by timber buildings which have left no trace, but it is surprising that at Margidunum there are more stone buildings attested by excavation outside than have been found inside the defences. Though shops, houses and perhaps temples are usually to be found within the walls, *mansiones* (hotels) which one could associate with the official postal system have strangely escaped identification except in one or two cases. Some of the settlements will have had local functions as industrial communities, others may have been no more than fortified villas. Some of them housed police posts for *beneficiarii*: an inscription from Dorchester (Oxon.) records the commander of such a unit there.[47]

Though it is difficult through lack of evidence to find any single satisfactory explanation for the growth of small towns ('fortified villages') in Britain, prime among their uses was probably the provision of refuges to which the scattered local population could retreat in times of greatest danger and threat. In areas of the empire threatened by invasion, and where no walled centres lay nearby, some hill-top sites, the positions of former Iron Age hill-forts, were reoccupied (and sometimes refortified after a very rudimentary fashion) from time to time throughout the fourth century. There is little trace of this happening in Britain, although a scatter of late Roman material has been found at several hill-forts in the south-west and in Wales.[48] Elsewhere in the empire, the provision of such sites, and in some cases their refortification, was due to the public-spiritedness of a local patron, who would arrange and pay for this form of protection for his workers and dependents. To what extent the provision and preparation of such refuges (or even the construction of walls round a small town itself) might be the product of pressure from local people rather than some overall military design is not really clear, for in theory no defences should have been built without imperial permission.

It becomes relatively easier to chart the quickening pace of military emergencies within Britain after the death of Constantine in 337. An imperial visit at dead of winter (a time normally considered most inappropriate for sailing) was made in 342–3 by Constans, his successor.[49] The reason for the visit is not clear, for the book in which Ammianus Marcellinus, our prime source for this period, told of his visit, is lost. However, he did refer to the episode in two other places within his surviving work, and both passages give some clue as to what emergency the emperor had to face. In one passage, Ammianus refers to the 'ebb and fall' of the ocean, which may suggest that he was describing some feature of the Channel defensive system. There is some archaeological evidence which leads to the belief that the fort of Pevensey, one of the more irregular-shaped and better defended of the 'Saxon Shore' forts, was added to the defensive screen at that time. A coin of Constans discovered in one of the constructional beam-holes underneath the wall (the beam itself had rotted) gives a firm date after which the fort must have been built. Thus Constans may have been instituting some tightening of the Channel system – a view which is given support by the diagnosis of a curious structure at Aleth near St Malo in France as another late Roman fort dated to the same period. [50] More research on other Gallic coastal sites may chart more developments on this coast at a similar date: in particular the fort at Brest may also have been built then.

The other mention of Constans' business in Britain is enigmatic. His presence was in some way connected with a group of men called *areani*, whose task, in Ammianus' own words, was to 'hurry around here and there over long distances, giving news of trouble among neighbouring peoples to our military leaders'. [51] Despite some confusion over their correct name these men clearly were undercover agents who could report on trouble from a hostile quarter and enable preparations to be made to meet it. Some thirty years later the Roman general Theodosius, answering a similar emergency, was to disband this intelligence system because it was becoming corrupt, and feeding its military secrets both ways. The service had been set up before Constans' visit, and this sort of operation was probably a vital part of any Roman frontier defence. The only area of Britain where such undercover tactics could usefully be employed was in the southern fringes of Pictland, and this was surely the main concern of Constans during this brief visit to Britain.

From the increasing frequency of alarms on the northern frontier, it is evident that the unity of Picts, Caledonians, Attacotti and Scotti was causing problems in the north. It was at about this time that Gratian, the father of the later emperor Valentinian, was posted to Britain with a special command and a status as *Comes*: he must have been in command of a relief force to answer another emergency.[52] During the campaigns of the Caesar Julian in Gaul (AD 360), word came from Britain that the Picts had broken the terms of the peace treaty which prevailed – maybe an agreement made by Constans or Gratian – and that they had ravaged areas near the frontiers.[53] Julian, occupied in combat with the Alemanni, did not like to go himself, but sent his commander Lupicinus, who took some time to restore the situation, and therefore missed the potentially explosive events later in the same year when Julian was proclaimed emperor by his devoted troops in opposition to the jealous Constantius II.

An emergency of 367 is more fully reported by Ammianus possibly because the emperor Theodosius at his time of writing was the son of the general who was sent to restore the British frontiers.[54] While he was engaged in northern Gaul, a message came to Valentinian that the barbarians had conspired to launch a concerted attack on Britain. Nectaridus, who was Count of the maritime area (?'Saxon Shore') had been killed, and Fullofaudes, who was a *Dux*, had been captured. After sending two of his staff to reconnoitre and to put matters right, if at all possible, it finally became necessary to send Theodosius with a force of rapidly gathered troops. He landed at Richborough and marched quickly on London. Once in the neighbourhood of the city, he split up his forces and mopped up bands of invaders who had taken booty from the provincials. He restored as much as he could to its owners.

It seems from Ammianus' account that not only was there a problem of invaders who had overwhelmed the frontier defences, but much of the regular army had deserted or was on leave. Theodosius issued a proclamation of pardon and reinstatement for deserters, and after his first year's campaign had the situation so well under control that he was able to ask for a civilian governor to be sent to take control of the province. In the campaign of 368, he carried the fight to the invaders, and 'restored the cities and forts'. At this moment, revolt broke out led by a man named Valentinus, a Pannonian who had been banished to Britain. He was an ambitious character who was possibly rich enough to promise to troops attractive rewards for their support. Although Ammianus' account makes the 'barbarian conspiracy' of 367 separate from Valentinus' revolt of 368, they may have been linked more closely, for it was a common enough pattern for serious barbarian inroads in the Roman provinces to follow the summoning of army units away from the frontier to the help of a commander aspiring to personal power. Valentinus' revolt may have left the way open for Picts and Scots to enter north Britain. The plot was nipped in the bud, however, and Valentinus executed. Theodosius' leniency in dealing with the revolt's supporters (as outlined by Ammianus) compares well with his proclamation of pardon to deserters, who are far more likely to have deserted to an aspiring imperial candidate than to join the Picts and Scots.

How serious was the barbarian conspiracy and the revolt of 367–8? They tend in modern eyes to become great events of fourth-century Britain because of the full coverage given by Ammianus. Normally as far as we are aware he was the most objective of historians, but perhaps he was indulging in some glorification of the father of his own contemporary emperor. If so, then the achievements of Theodosius are probably little different from those of other generals who led relief forces to Britain to answer similar emergencies. Therefore the date 367 is not necessarily a correct one on which to hang, for example, the abandonment of forts north of Hadrian's Wall, or the construction of defensive bastions round city walls, or indeed the beginnings of the break-up of the Roman hold on Britain. The ineffectiveness of Roman defensive arrangements was exposed not by a single disastrous raid such as this one, but by the cumulative effect of a series of such raids.

Theodosius, in Ammianus' phrase, 'restored the cities and forts'. It has been suggested that as a result of the experiences of 367, a reorganisation of city defences in Britain was undertaken. Ditches were widened and external towers were added to city walls to provide projecting fighting platforms for military flanking fire. [55] That a great many of the British *civitates* had such towers added to their

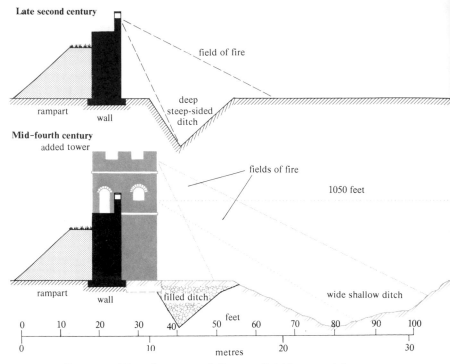

Late second century

field of fire

rampart

wall

deep steep-sided ditch

Mid-fourth century
added tower

fields of fire

1050 feet

rampart

wall

filled ditch

wide shallow ditch

feet

| 0 | 10 | 20 | 30 | 40 | 50 | 60 | 70 | 80 | 90 | 100 |

| 0 | | 10 | | 20 | | 30 |

metres

Figure 8 The adaptation of Romano-British town defences to meet fourth-century requirements. The ditches were deepened and widened, and towers were added to the exterior of the walls. This considerably increased the protection which could be afforded to the walls. From the tower top and its windows, comprehensive fire-cover could be given to the wide and irregular ditch

defences during the course of the fourth century is clear from excavation, but they cannot be dated with confidence to a sudden rash of 'restoration' after 367–8. Cumulative evidence is beginning to show that some of these external towers were in use by about 360: a coin-hoard buried in the floor of a tower at Caerwent seems to have been deposited in the 350s, and it is quite possible therefore that external towers were added to city walls at various times during the fourth century.[56] Fragmentary scraps of evidence like coins buried in layers sealed by the construction of these towers, for example, suggest that the major period of strengthening the defences in this way came just at the time (340–70) when we have documentary evidence that security in Britain was under severe and possibly constant threat.

The building of towers and widening of ditches indicates a more positive military outlook by the British *civitates* and suggests an extended range for defensive weaponry. The towers were capable of supporting *ballistae* – arrow- or dart-firing machines working on the principle of the cross-bow but on a larger scale. This augmentation of fire-power might therefore be seen as part of a more general defensive move which gave each city its own militia, independent of the army. Such a force, often called *laeti* because of lists in the *Notitia* which show barbarian mercenary troops billeted on (and therefore intended to protect) threatened areas of Gaul, are not directly attested in Britain. However, the presence of a distinctive style of metalwork – buckles, belts and other fittings – which seems to have strong associations with French and Belgian finds from places where *laeti* may have been stationed suggests that such men were present in Britain as well. This would be a natural corollary to the authorisation of the construction of external towers. If the text of the *Notitia* were not defective at this point, it might have given us a complete list of irregular troops, showing where they were stationed within the British provinces.[57]

It is difficult, however, to argue from a particular type of equipment exactly who wore it, and it is not unlikely that these belt-fittings belonged to regular units of the Roman army, not necessarily to *laeti* alone. That *laeti* were listed under their prefects in the *Notitia* suggests that they were something more than an irregular mercenary force, and possibly on the official payroll of the Roman army. State arms manufacturers in various depots and factories round the empire seem to have produced their own variations on a standard theme for the design of belt-buckles: a distinctive Pannonian style, for example (made in the area of modern Hungary) is quite different from some of the buckles and fittings apparently made in Britain. In one of the cemeteries recently excavated near Winchester, a group of graves, unusual in the context of the rest of the cemetery, containing bodies buried in full uniform together with such belt-equipment, cannot be taken to mean that around 350 a group of *laeti* moved into the city to protect it.[58] These few graves are military in nature, but the style of their equipment would suggest a Pannonian rather than German origin, and they may therefore be a group of regular troops stationed at or near the town at the time.

The sites of several towns, *civitates* and forts have now produced this sort of military metalwork, but the occasional find of a belt-buckle or a strap-end does not necessarily give sufficient evidence to postulate a complete garrison. Increasing numbers of finds of this type on sites which are unlikely to have been other than civilian, including some villas, suggest that the wearing of such equipment was not necessarily the privilege of the military. It is known to have been the uniform, not only of late Roman troops, but also of officers of the civil service, so its presence in towns can be explained in terms of the normal run of civilian duties.[59]

In 367–8, as we have seen, Theodosius probably did no more than continue the strengthening process which had been going on over some years previously. It is difficult to recognise rebuilding of 'Theodosian' date at military sites, but there were late improvements to the interior buildings of the forts at Bainbridge (North Yorks.), Ilkley (West Yorks.) and Bowes (Co. Durham).[60] The defences of forts in the north do not at this time seem to have come in for wholesale reconstruction and they were never strengthened by the addition of external towers – a point which militates against the view that Theodosius was responsible for such towers round cities. If this had been his restoration programme, it is surprising that the northern forts (which Ammianus also mentions) were left out.

Two factors emphasise the achievement of Theodosius and help to show that the emergency which he answered was one of Britain's most serious. The first is the renaming of London, which after 368 was known as 'Augusta', an honorific title perhaps given in recognition of loyalty during Valentinus' uprising.[61] The second is the mention of the province Valentia, often thought to have been a fifth pro-

38 Model showing a reconstruction of Scarborough Roman signal station. A central large watch-tower stands in a courtyard defended by a circuit of walls with corner-towers. The site, one of five known on the Yorkshire coastline, stands at the cliff edge within the promontary occupied by Scarborough Castle

vince of Britain swamped by the enemy and recovered from their clutches by Theodosius. This fifth province has been located by modern scholars in various parts of Britain, the preference being for Wales or the north. It would make better historical sense, however, to accept what Ammianus seems to be telling us, that because of Theodosius' complete recovery of Britain, the whole group of four provinces was now renamed Valentia – an honorific title linked to that of the current imperial household. Examples of such titles given to provinces had been relatively common within recent history, and would accord well with the grateful thanks of the populace to the emperor for his protection.[62]

The position now on the northern frontier was one of retrenchment.[63] Because of their infidelity the *areani* (see p. 93), who perhaps had been the link between Valentinus and the Picts, were now disbanded, and by now there was no Roman presence in any of the forts to the north of Hadrian's Wall. This process of withdrawal was probably begun about 340, for the loss of contact between the tribes north of the wall and the Roman military is shown by the small amount

Figure 9 The inscription from the *burgus* at Ravenscar, probably a signal station of the same type as at Scarborough. The text is a little doubtful, but it seems to show (in rather illiterate fashion) that the *burgus* (tower) was constructed by Justinianus the commander, and Vindicianus the *magister*

of distinctive late Roman pottery to be found on 'native settlement' sites north of the wall despite its abundance in Wall forts and sites in the hinterland. This situation helps to explain the Traprain Law hoard of silver treasure (see p. 75) which is harder to understand if there was a continual friendly relationship between the Romans and these buffer states to the north. New measures for defence, almost certainly against Pictish raiding, involved the construction of a series of towers along the north-eastern coastline.[64] We know of such buildings, comprising a central tower surrounded by a wall with projecting corner towers and a ditch. These look-out posts, on the more prominent of the Yorkshire headlands from Goldsborough to Filey, must have been of limited use, because it is impossible, except in exceptionally clear weather conditions, to see from one to another along the coast. They were probably part of a communications system which stretched inland to Malton or York to give advance warning about Pictish movements. The site at Ravenscar has produced a rather illiterate inscription datable to the Valentinianic period, which records the construction of the *castrum* by a man called Justinianus between 367 and 395.[65] A number of the forts down the Cumbrian coastline have also produced evidence for late

128

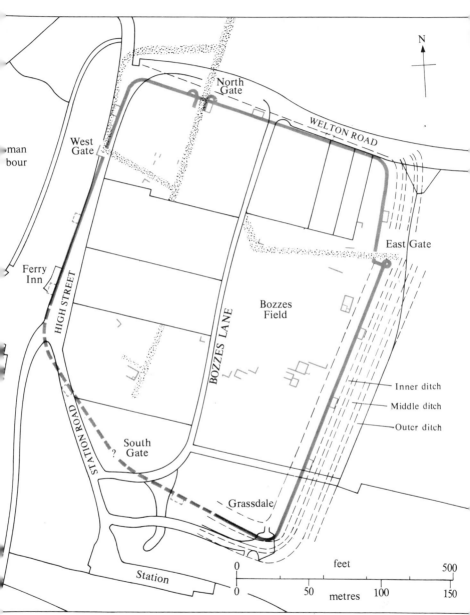

Figure 10 The plan of the stone walls of Brough-on-Humber. They date from the late third or fourth century

Roman occupation, and at least one of the small mile-fortlets, Cardurnock, has a rampart rebuilt in the fourth century.[66] The two systems of defence along eastern and western coastlines extended the protective screen against sea-borne raiders – Scots, Picts or Caledonians from either side.

Study of the coastlines in Roman times in East Anglia and the Lincolnshire fenlands reveals the proximity of many of the walled sites, not only those traditionally designated 'Saxon Shore' forts, to rivers and waterways. Prominent among these is the fort or town of Brough-on-Humber, with its ambivalent status as *civitas*, central focus of the tribe of the Parisii. There is nothing in such a status at this late period which precludes the site from containing also a naval base, in the same way that Gallic coastal *civitates* seem to have done on the Armorican coastline.[67] Other sites now well inland which probably had some bearing on coastal defence along this eastern coast are the small walled towns of Caistor and Horncastle. Caistor lies near the river Ancholme which was probably navigable thus far in the late Roman period, and Horncastle is at present on the river Bain, but was accessible to shipping in Roman times through the system of waterways which connected Lincoln with the sea. A much larger area of Lincolnshire fenland was then salt marsh pierced by creeks, with the principal outlet of the river Witham forming a navigable route into the heart of the province and therefore in need of protection.

No further alarms are recorded until the 380s, though the threat of more trouble must always have been in the background. In 382 there is mention of another campaign against the Picts and Scots in the north, led this time by Magnus Maximus. He was a Spanish soldier who had been with Theodosius in Britain in 367–8,[68] and who, on the accession in 379 of Flavius Theodosius (son of the hero of 367), had probably been sent to Britain to organise the defences there. The exact date of his commission is not known, nor is it certain whether he was known as *Dux Britanniarum*, or as a special commander with rank as a *Comes*. His popularity in Britain was such that he was persuaded in 383 to declare himself emperor, and to challenge the rather weaker intellectual emperor of the west, Gratian, still in his early twenties. This rebellion, which involved the withdrawal of British troops from the island, was aimed at uniting Britain and Gaul under a strong military command, thereby ensuring the safety not just of Britain but of Europe too. After collecting his army, Magnus Maximus crossed to Gaul, and within a matter of months had met the opposition mounted by Gratian, swept it aside and killed the young emperor. He maintained Gaul as the base of his operations, and for five years held his empire against the avenging wrath of Valentian and also against serious inroad from barbarians. He seems to have been able to negotiate with the Germanic tribes, and although there is no sign that he ever again returned to Britain after 383 his rule was one of positive importance for the area. The tradition that he was the founder of the dynasty of the Welsh kings of Dyfed is often linked with steps taken to control Irish infiltration of the Welsh coastlines by the establishment in the southern part of Wales of tribal protectorates of the Deisi, possibly a friendly tribe from Ireland (see p. 83).

Despite the withdrawal of Roman troops from Britain to support Maximus' European campaigns, there is no indication yet of a complete breakdown either of the Hadrian's Wall frontier or of the 'Saxon Shore'. Coin finds from the northern line suggest that it was still held, and the same is true of the 'Saxon Shore' forts, though arrangements for the garrisoning of these coastal defences are imperfectly known. By 395, the coastal command, originally a simple unit covering both shores, British and Gallic, had been split up. The Count of the Saxon Shore was now limited to Britain, according to the *Notitia* lists, and two continental Dukes (of the Armorican tracts, and of Belgica Secunda) had taken over responsibility for the Gallic side. This is a significant step, for it heralds a military view which saw the defence of Gaul as separate from that of Britain. It is likely that the commissioning of the *civitates* along the Armorican coastline belongs to the years after the final defeat of Maximus at Arles in 388.[69]

39 The riverside wall of Roman London, dating to the very end of the fourth century, found in excavation in the Tower of London

There is at present no unequivocal evidence to support the view that there were late Roman protectorates in eastern Britain to compare with Wales. The name 'Saxon Shore' itself is ambiguous: it could be interpreted as 'the shore settled by Saxöns' rather than as the shore 'attacked by Saxons'. In 395 the name was used to describe a system of bases on what was clearly called a *limes* or frontier.[70] It would be special pleading to insist that these bases were set up to watch over an untrustworthy protectorate of settling Saxons. It is easier to assume that they had a defensive military function associated with harbours and a fleet with which they were designed to liaise. That such a fleet existed in Britain, on patrol against invasion, is shown by the Roman military writer Vegetius, who mentions camouflaged ships of the late Romano-British navy.[71] Finds from the 'Saxon Shore' forts themselves suggest neither that they were garrisoned by troops other than units of the regular Roman army, nor that they were surrounded by communities of Saxons occupying settlements like those of their homelands.

The closing years of the fourth century saw yet another breach of the northern defences: again Rome sent one of her better generals, Stilicho, himself by origin a barbarian. From the accounts of Stilicho's activities given by the Roman court poet Claudian, it appears most likely that the invasion occurred in 398, and that Stilicho had the situation covered by the end of 399.[72] It is to this date that the last of Britain's fortifications may well belong, for the riverside wall of London was now repaired or newly built. The campaign was in all probability the last in which a Roman general in command of a mobile force was sent specifically to meet an emergency. From now on, such security was to be in the hands of the *Comes Britanniae*, a recently created post as the commander of the field army within Britain. Claudian records that a legion was withdrawn from northern Britain in 401 or 402,[73] so Britain's defensive resources were dwindling; but there was no sign yet that Britain was shortly to be abandoned by the Roman military or administrative advisers and severed from the Roman Empire.

4 History of the Anglo-Saxon invasion

For the five years from AD 406 to 410, we have more historical documentation for events in Britain than for any time
since the episode of Carausius and Allectus more than a
century earlier.[1] This, in itself, amounts to little more than a
few sentences in the writings of a Greek historian named
Zosimus, but his account, patchy though it is, derives from
more reliable authors who were near contemporaries of the
events described and whose works have survived only at
best in very fragmentary form. The sequence of related
events leads up to Roman loss of administrative control over
Britain. Zosimus' historical writing is such that, despite his
relatively good documentation of what actually happened,
many of the reasons for the various events are shrouded in
mystery.

During 406, the troops in Britain, under some disenchantment with the rule of the legitimate emperor Honorius, had once again elected their own emperor, a man
named Marcus. By early 407, he had been deposed and
killed, and Gratian, described as a town-councillor,
appointed in his place.[2] Our knowledge of the reasons
either for the appointment of a British emperor at this time
or for his deposition and replacement is scant, and the
interpretations of the reasons for these events are modern
speculation. In the meantime, at the very end of 406, a
large-scale invasion of the Gallic provinces by Germanic
tribesmen from across the Rhine had begun with a crossing
of the river somewhere near Mainz.[3] By the beginning of
summer 407 there was concern in Britain over the direction
of this invasion, and the troops there feared that it might
affect Britain. They accordingly deposed Gratian, and ele-

vated a soldier named Constantine to imperial power.[4]

To combat the barbarian threat, perhaps to head off the invasion, or with the idea of re-establishing contact with Rome (and thus paying his army) in the face of this threat to cut off communications, Constantine crossed to Boulogne with much of the remaining garrison of Britain – possibly all but the static frontier guard troops. There is no record of a serious confrontation between Constantine's army and the barbarians, and he seems to have spent much of 407 and 408 strengthening the defences along the Rhine to prevent recurrence of the trouble.[5] The barbarians were in the meantime making for south-western Gaul, and Constantine sent part of his army off to Spain under his lieutenant Gerontius to contest their arrival there. Gerontius, however, soon rebelled from Constantine and encouraged the barbarians still in Gaul to turn on him, a move which was so successful that Constantine was left powerless to defend either Gaul or Britain.

It is at this point in Zosimus' narrative of these events that he records a remarkable revival. The British, overwhelmed by a barbarian onslaught (Zosimus does not say who these were), were forced to accept the necessity of rebelling from the Roman Empire: they therefore took up arms and freed the cities from the barbarians who were harassing them. The whole of Armorica (western Gaul) and other Gallic provinces imitated the Britons, and freed themselves in the same way, by expelling Roman officials and establishing a sovereign constitution on their own authority.[6] From its position within Zosimus' narrative, this occurred in 408, before the barbarians (in Gaul) had again turned south and reached Spain, which they did in 409. Confirmation that there was a barbarian raid on Britain in 408 comes from a near contemporary Gallic chronicler, who under that year records that the British provinces were devastated by an incursion of Saxons.[7] At all events, Constantine survived the attack on him by the Gallic barbarians, and was even recognised as a legitimate emperor by Honorius in Italy. As a consequence of the revolt and rebellion of his Spanish forces under Gerontius, however, he was soon discredited, and after an attempt to invade Italy in 411, he was attacked and captured by Honorius and executed.

The traditional date for the end of Roman involvement with Britain is 410, the date at which the final fragment of this rather puzzling five years belongs. The emperor Honorius, occupied with other matters, wrote to the cities of Britain instructing them to look after their own defence.[8] The natural assumption is that this was a reply to an unrecorded letter to the emperor from the cities of Britain asking for help against some emergency. Help was not forthcoming: the Roman emperor was not able to give any assistance, and thus the British provinces lapsed from Roman control. By Zosimus' account, however, the Britons had already risen up and rejected the Roman administrators in 408. Clearly the whole episode was complex, perhaps too complex for us to disentangle fully.

The elevation of British emperors is clear enough up to the time that Constantine himself took control, and his involvement with affairs on the continent of Europe is understandable both in the light of the concern felt in Britain about the threat posed to the island by this latest German invasion and also in the feeling of British troops whose pay was locked up in Italy. From here onwards, however, if we assume that Zosimus' overall picture of events records each episode in its chronological order, things start to go haywire. No reason is given for Constantine's involvement with Spain, nor are his later actions of setting up his own capital at Arles, and challenging Honorius for legitimate power given sufficient explanation. It is possible, however, to speculate a little about the extraordinary events in Britain in 408, when, despairing of the help from central Roman authority which had been forthcoming so many times in the past, the Britons themselves combined to beat back Saxon barbarians and free the cities, an action which at the same time sparked off a rebellion from the Roman Empire.

The only dissident groups of which we know in the later Roman Empire of the west were the *Bagaudae*, whose aim seems indeed to have been the rejection and overthrow of Roman power.[9] Such men, however, seem largely to have been composed of the lowest classes of society whose main grudge was against those who held power, wealth and land. The rebellion in Armorica and other Gallic provinces which Zosimus mentions as a copy of the British one was certainly a rebellion of *Bagaudae*, for other independent sources say so.[10] It might be natural to assume, therefore, that such was the case with the British one of 408. But this rising of 408 had as its first aim the overthrow of the Saxons, and then the liberation of the cities, both very unlikely targets for men with a grudge against the powerful élite. If Britain's rebellion was really a Bagaudic one, then the *Bagaudae* ought to have joined with the Saxons to overthrow the cities, and not assisted in their liberation. Despite Zosimus' assertion that this British rising of 408 was similar to that in Armorica, it is hard to reconcile his account with what is known of other Bagaudic uprisings. The events of 408, however, were remarkable if only for the spirit shown by the British provinces in response to an emergency. By taking their own defence into their own hands, and by organising as a province rather than waiting for military help from Rome, they had already shown their readiness to face the future independently. Thus Britain, through necessity, had already broken out of the rather depressed passivity characteristic of the Roman world as it faced the barbarian invasions of the fifth century.[11]

The appeal to Honorius, however, and the response it elicited, suggests that someone within the cities was still prepared to remain in contact with the emperor. Thus it may be surmised that there were two opposed political camps within Britain at the time – broadly the pro-Rome and anti-Rome factions. Disenchantment with Rome could be born from the failure of central government to offer help in this latest crisis, with the general burdensome level of public dues, and with the established success of those who believed Britain could go it alone. On the other hand, there must have been those who saw a return to legitimacy (Britain was technically in revolt from Rome since the appointment of her own emperor, Marcus, in 406) as the only way to restore the situation. The way to receive further financial and military support from Rome was once again to declare allegiance to the emperor and ask him for assistance. Honorius' reply of 410 was to the cities of Britain, and, we may assume, in answer to a request from a delegation of city councils, or, perhaps more likely, the provincial council itself. The exact nature of the request cannot be known – it could have been for help, apparently rejected by the emperor in this rather offhand manner. It is not quite clear, however, what help was at that moment necessary, for Britain had just liberated the cities from their barbarian attackers. It is perhaps better to see the approach to Honorius as a diplomatic one, reporting on the events which had taken place, and inviting imperial comment on a course of action already undertaken. Honorius' reply, a brief mention sandwiched among other more pressing business which affected the safety of Rome, Ravenna (now Honorius' capital) and Italy, was tacitly to accept what had happened in Britain, to approve the cities' own defence of themselves, but to ignore the wider question of Rome's present claims over Britain and the expulsion of Roman officials, which Zosimus tells us had happened two years earlier. In effect, Honorius washed his hands of Britain with a temporising reply.

The political climate within Britain at this time may have been affected by a set of religious views then current, promoted by a man named Pelagius, himself a Briton, who had been sent in the 380s by his parents to study law at Rome. Once there, he had been converted to Christianity and took holy orders, remaining in the capital as a religious teacher from 394 until 410. There was during the latter part of these years a lively theological debate between Pelagius and Augustine, who disagreed violently over the problem of the sinfulness of man. Augustine in his *Confessions* maintained the view that man was always sinful in the sight of God, and was therefore entirely dependent upon God's forgiveness and mercy. Pelagius believed that God had given man freewill, by the correct exercise of which it was possible for a man to lead a life free from sin and thus to gain justification in the sight of God by his own efforts. The debate was

138

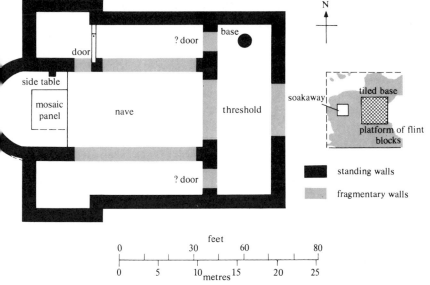

Figure 11 Plan of the church at Silchester. Very few buildings in Roman towns have been identified as Christian churches, and although the heat of the Pelagian controversy shows that Christian communities were active, the only churches known are small buildings which can only have housed a relatively small congregation. The stand outside the west door may well have been for an outside font for baptisms

keenly fought, and Pelagius' views, which clearly gained some currency, were denounced by Augustine and others in the years after the sack of Rome by Alaric in 410, and only finally declared heretical in 418.[12]

Despite this, Pelagianism was clearly an issue in the British church as late as the year 429, when envoys came to the Gallic Bishop Germanus of Auxerre with a report that the heresy was gaining converts, and a request for his intervention. It is not certain, however, at what date the Pelagian views would have first arrived in Britain, but some of the religious tracts written to support the Pelagian cause appear to have been written in Britain in the years immediately following 410, one of them (*De Vita Christiana*, 'On the Christian Life') by a British bishop named Fastidius, suggesting that the doctrine of man's ultimate salvation through his own sinless efforts was at least known in Britain

139

during the chaotic years around 410.[13] The reason for the acceptance of this view is not clear, but it has been suggested that the theological doctrine provided at least some justification for the militant and self-assertive course of action which the British people had recently undertaken for their own safety against the barbarians.[14] It is stretching credibility, however, to regard the ultimately pacific view of individual salvation propounded by Pelagius as having any material effect on the decision to take up arms against a barbarian attack, or even, on a wider scale, for Britain to believe that she could work out her own salvation independently of Rome.[15] Elsewhere in the Roman world at a similar time, some city dwellers were finding that the bishops were the only leaders who would lead an active fight against the encroachment of barbarians. This happens certainly now in parts of Africa, but there is no record of British bishops leading the resistance to invaders.[16]

By 410, then, Britain had rejected the Roman administrators, and at least one 'party' had decided that control of her own affairs was best left to those within Britain itself. This did not mean, however, a complete rejection of Roman lifestyles, nor the expulsion of large numbers of 'Romans' who were still 'occupying' Britain. After so long as part of the Roman world, most Britons would additionally have regarded themselves as 'Roman'. The refusal to accept central Roman authority will have meant the expulsion of only those men, probably themselves foreigners, who were in positions of authority and appointed by the central government. Such men would be the provincial governors, perhaps the topmost civil servants, and maybe also the army commanders. Much of the Roman army within Britain had already been withdrawn for various purposes over the last decades: Magnus Maximus, for example, took troops with him when fighting in Gaul in 383–4; Stilicho had withdrawn 'a legion' from Britain at the turn of the fifth century; and Constantine had taken yet more of the island's force on his continental escapades of 407 and 408. Such troops as were left in Britain were probably mainly recruited locally. They will also have formed the less mobile frontier forces

40 St Alban's Cathedral, formerly a Norman abbey church on the site of an eighth-century Benedictine abbey founded here to commemorate the death, in about AD 200, of the first British Martyr, Alban. The martyr's shrine, then less grandiose, was one of the most famous of British shrines in the fifth century, and was visited by St Germanus in the 440s

who probably had made their posting into their homes, and had nowhere else to go. The men who would be least prepared to throw in their lot with an independent Britain were those who had their homes elsewhere, or who still saw the prospects of a career in the service of Rome. In any case, the majority of such men would probably already have left as soon as Britain declared her independence from Rome in 406: indeed, the necessity of disassociating themselves from Rome's rule may have been as clear for the Britons in 406 as

141

Zosimus says it was in 408, and may have resulted therefore in the choice of Marcus as British emperor.

As to the form of government which replaced the Roman administration, we are poorly informed. Historical sources for events in the years after 400 are scanty in the extreme, but when bishop Germanus visited the island in 428–9 and again in the 440s, he met civic leaders, church dignitaries, and much of the outward trappings of normal Roman life, at least in that portion of Britain (probably the south-east) to which he was invited.[17] Some indication of the principal actors in the political arena of the portions of Britain which had formerly been Roman can be gained from fragmentary mentions of half-remembered tales in later writers, but the main participants were those to whom some measure of political power had for long been given – members of town councils, decurions, and those from whom the provincial assembly was composed. Such men had a vested interest in the maintenance of a 'Romanised' style of life, without the pressing obligations for public duty which had been imposed upon them by the Roman administration.

Our main sources for the period are three, and these have been subject to much critical examination in recent years. There is first the historical account given by Gildas and followed by Bede – a version of fifth-century British history which has had a great influence on the interpretation of the progress of Saxon dominance of England, and which remains our most valuable source. Our second source is a collection of various documents attributed to Nennius, a ninth-century Welsh collator of a 'History of the Britons'. Third, there is evidence from the *Anglo-Saxon Chronicle* itself, which was probably compiled in the form in which we now have it in the later ninth century.

Of these sources, the one compiled nearest to the date with which it was concerned, is the work of Gildas *About the Ruin and Conquest of Britain*.[18] The work itself is a religious homily, whose main purpose was to castigate a number of contemporary rulers for the religious and moral state of western Britain, where Gildas seems to have lived as a monk. Only a portion of the work is historical, and this is a section describing affairs in Britain up to Gildas' own day, which appears to have been in the middle of the sixth century.[19] Gildas was born at the end of the fifth century, and his historical account relies in its earliest stages on half-remembered historical facts which are clearly false. Yet despite this, we might expect Gildas's record of events closer to his time, and particularly those in the past recent enough to remain in older mens' memories, to be reported more accurately. Gildas's account is so important because of the use to which later historians including Bede have put it, that a brief summary of what he says is necessary here. His chronological framework, and in particular his identification of Magnus Maximus, the British usurper emperor of 383–8, as the first independent ruler of Britain, had a profound effect on later Welsh writings.[20]

Gildas's account of this period begins after the overthrow of Maximus in 388 with repeated invasions by Picts and Scots, and three appeals from an already independent Britain to Roman authorities to give assistance. The historical value of this account of repeated appeals is vitiated by the fact that after the first, the British were told to build a turf wall to keep the invaders out, and after the second they were instructed to build a stone wall. These appeals sound suspiciously like a made-up story to explain the phenomenon of the turf-built Antonine Wall between Clyde and Forth in Scotland, and then the construction of the stone wall between the Tyne and the Solway (Hadrian's Wall). It is no more than a piece of fiction, and fiction, at that, with a distinct northern bias, for it omits any reference to the British usurper Constantine III, although the same source which gave Gildas the name of Maximus must also have mentioned the later usurper.[21] However, the story of Constantine and his Continental involvement did not at this point suit Gildas's 'northern' theme, and so it was conveniently omitted. The third appeal, however, after the third raid, was made to a Roman general 'Agitius', who was unable to help.

There followed a famine, and the Britons finally repelled their enemies by themselves. There was then a period of prosperity and plenty, followed by reports that old enemies were once again threatening. The threat apparently did not materialise, and Britain was struck by a plague, after which there was again trouble from Picts and Scots. The members of the council and the 'proud tyrant' invited the Saxons to help them defend themselves against this danger, and three boatloads of warriors arrived, soon to be followed by others. For some time these arrivals were kept in control by payment, but eventually they rebelled, gained the mastery of the island and destroyed its civilisation. Some Britons fled the country, but others remained, under their leader Ambrosius Aurelianus, to resist the Saxon advance. After a long struggle, the Britons finally gained a decisive victory at the battle of Badon, putting a halt to Saxon expansion at least for the whole of Gildas's lifetime.

This account is the one which Bede, writing in the early eighth century, took over and skilfully adapted to form part of his *Ecclesiastical History of the English People*,[22] and it was from his reading and use of this account by Gildas that Bede produced his date of AD 447–9 for the coming of the Saxons, a date which has been the single most off-putting fixed point in fifth-century history, and which now must surely be seen to have been falsely calculated.[23] Bede has seized on the only datable event in the whole of Gildas's narrative – the third appeal of the Britons at the beginning of the story, addressed to Agitius, and then followed Gildas's narrative line from that point. Bede has gone slightly further than this, for Agitius (Aegidius) was a Roman commander in Gaul during the years 457–62, and Gildas describes him as consul for the third time. So far as we know, Aegidius was never consul, and so, acting on similar information, Bede has amended the name of the Roman commander to Aetius, a man whom he knew to have been consul for the third time in 447. Thus Bede has fixed the arrival of the Saxons at the invitation of the council and a man named Vortigern – Bede's further interpretation of the 'proud tyrant' of Gildas – on his only available date.

There is no way of knowing, however, that Gildas's only

documentary fragment, the appeal to Aegidius or Aetius, is correctly placed within his own narrative. From its context, at the end of two other clearly fictional appeals, its positioning is suspect, and it may well belong at some other point within Gildas's otherwise seemingly uninterrupted narrative framework. It has even been plausibly suggested that the story of the three appeals (Gildas's northern tales) should really be understood to be happening contemporaneously with the history which follows the appeal to Aetius.[24] The framework of the story after this appeal, however, is our best source for the sequence of fifth-century events, beginning with the overthrow of the Romans, a brief interregnum of British aggression against invaders, and culminating in the battle of Badon. Gildas wrote without reference to written sources, but he will have collated tales gathered from people whose fathers and grandfathers had long and personal memories of the various stages of the struggle against the Saxons as it developed during the course of the fifth century. Even if we cannot provide accurate dates for the various elements of the story, there is no reason to disbelieve the general pattern it portrays.

Our second source, Nennius' *History of the Britons*, was probably not by Nennius at all, and its preface, which records that it is no more than a heaped-up mass of documents from various sources, is probably spurious.[25] The central part of the work is about fifth- and sixth-century Britain, and consists of material from several different source documents, including little of unequivocal historical value. The intention of this writer of the *History of the Britons* was to provide a set of synchronised dates for fifth- and sixth-century events, his conclusions as often as not coloured by the political climate of the ninth-century Wales in which he lived, and also by the need to substantiate by this documentary history the descent and royal claims of his ruler Merfyn, king of Gwynedd. Thus although there may be tales about personalities who belong to the fifth century, and some of the sources which the *History* uses may contain a grain or two of truth, the whole compilation is essentially

145

suspect, particularly in its attempts to provide fixed dates for events such as the *adventus Saxonum*, 'the arrival of the Saxons'.

The third source, the *Anglo-Saxon Chronicle* itself, has scant reference to the earliest period of Saxon arrival within Britain. It was possibly compiled on the orders of Alfred the Great, and is thus a late ninth-century collection of sources for Saxon history, much of the earliest parts of which will be derived, not from written histories, but from heroic poetry of an oral, not written, tradition.[26] The dates given to the events in the *Chronicle* are based on entries added, long after the events themselves, to a table of dates for computing the date of Easter, and thus are not a contemporary independent record. The source material, however, is independent of Gildas and Bede, but the compilations within the *Anglo-Saxon Chronicle* may again give no more than the rough order of events, with no secure dating. The *Chronicle* is mainly concerned with the growth of the Saxon kingdom of Wessex in the sixth and later centuries, but touches briefly on the beginnings of the kingdom of Hengest in Kent and of that of Aelle in Sussex.

These sources are not the only ones for the study of the documentary history of fifth-century Britain, but they are the only records which seek to present anything like a narrative thread of events, from its own point of view. Other writers, particularly those on the Continent, could afford to view Britain more dispassionately, and such mention as they make is perhaps more likely to be reliable than insular British sources themselves.[27] These mentions occur in such reliable witnesses as the life of St Germanus, written towards the end of the fifth century, which describes the saint's two visits to Britain mentioned earlier, or in two Gallic chronicles purporting to have been written in the years 452 and 511, which record that Britain had fallen under the power of the Saxons in 441–2. By this they must mean not all of Britain, but merely that part which was most closely linked to Gaul, the south-eastern portion. The reliable dates for events in fifth-century Britain, therefore, are not many, but some attempt must be made to make a synthesis of what our inadequate and sometimes suspect historical sources tell us.

The starting point must again be 408 or 410, when the Britons had expelled Roman control, and when the Britons turned on the barbarians who were oppressing her. One of the Pelagian tracts linked with the name of Fastidius, a British bishop, describes in exultant tones the downfall of the former wicked rulers and the transference of power, seemingly in a violent fashion, to a new set of masters, who were counselled by the writer to use their power and wealth wisely.[28] The letter of Honorius in 410 was addressed, not to any Roman official, but to the cities of Britain, suggesting that the Roman administrative machine had been repla_ed by a council drawn from the cities themselves, successor to the old provincial council. But there are suggestions that already this was not capable of keeping complete control: success against barbarian invaders (one of the Gallic chronographers records a raid in 410–11) had thrown up military leaders who, in the time-honoured 'Roman' tradition, might demand a say in government. Procopius, a later historian from the Greek half of the empire, records that Britain was from now onwards ruled by 'tyrants',[29] a fragment of information which receives striking confirmation from Gildas's 'proud tyrant' who was the man who led the council to invite the Saxons to assist in their struggle against the Picts.

As the traditional Roman government of Britain had been that of a number of city-states, overseen by provincial or diocesan governors, there is no reason to suppose that what replaced this in the vacuum created by the withdrawal or overthrow of the men who had filled the topmost posts was substantially different. Such a situation, of course, might well produce its natural leaders: Germanus, visiting Verulamium in the 440s, was met by Elafus, described as the chief man of the area, and the actual overthrow of unpopular leaders or even of hated Roman administrators might be accompanied by the sort of bloodshed seemingly hinted at in Fastidius' *On the Christian Life* mentioned above (p. 139). Gildas, too, records that after the British had turned on the barbarians and driven them homewards, there came a period during which 'kings' were appointed and just as easily dethroned. One searches in vain for some indication of the main arena of political power at this date: was it still Britain-wide, with a council of chiefs, or did the various *civitates* seize a larger measure of independence and in effect create small city-states?

One of the leading figures of this transitional period seems to be Gildas's 'proud tyrant', a man who, by Gildas's account, came closest to wielding more than local power. Bede identified him as Vortigern – a Celtic name which itself means 'high king', much the same as 'proud tyrant', a phrase Gildas may have used to damn the memory of a man of whose actions he found it hard to approve. More information about Vortigern is forthcoming from Nennius's *History of the Britons*, which incorporates many otherwise unsubstantiated details about his life, including his relationships with Hengest, leader of the Kentish Saxons, and with the bishop Germanus. If one relies on all these details, an elaborate picture of Vortigern's life, activities and political career can be built up to suggest that he was born around AD 360, and that he died at some time after the late 430s, when Ambrosius Aurelianus led a successful British opposition to him.[30] Dates artificially computed in the portion of 'Nennius' known as the 'Nennius Chronographer' fix on the year 428 as the date of the Saxon arrival in Britain, and assert that this was the fourth year of Vortigern's rule. Such exactness, however, comes from a combination of various late classical date-tables and by reading more into the account of Gildas (which 'Nennius' evidently had to hand) than was justified. These dates, on the face of it reasonable, have no historical value, and one certainly cannot rely on all the details from Nennius to complete this rounded picture.[31]

Despite this, and despite Gildas's disapproval of Vortigern, which seems to have led Welsh sources to attempt to suppress and discredit his memory, his name has survived, in forms which are recognisably old enough to have originally belonged to the fifth century.[32] By the time of the ninth-century compilations he was due for rehabilitation, since his very age and his proximity to the established Welsh hero, Magnus Maximus, earned him respectability, and a place in at least two of the king lists of Welsh dynasties. But what of his historicity? The preservation of his name, the stories seemingly independent, but still romantic, which link him with Hengest and Horsa, the earliest Saxon arrivals in Kent, and the possibility that Gildas really did name him suggest that he was a real fifth-century figure, one of the shadowy local potentates who held some power in the earlier part of fifth-century Britain, and one who had some part in the fateful invitation of the Saxons to Britain.

One event which demonstrates the volatile nature of events in early fifth-century Britain comes within the story of St Germanus' visit. Into the narrative which portrays the peaceful arrival of Germanus, there came a joint raid by Saxons and Picts.[33] This threw the Britons into a panic, but Germanus, who had been a soldier in his youth, was able to provide just the positive military poise they needed to resist the onslaught. He led a waiting army out to battle, and gained a significant victory simply by using a new war-cry of 'Alleluia'. Such a story, however, which displays the conventional pictures both of the strong 'holy man' and of a miraculous victory through trust in the providence of God, may not be founded in historical fact.

The very invitation to Germanus, and the existence in 429 of well-dressed and presumably well-heeled Britons to whom the doctrinal issues of Pelagianism as against orthodox Christianity were of importance, spotlights two further points. One is that Christianity was a lively force; the other that some contact, at least within the ecclesiastical organisation, was maintained with Gaul. That this contact extended also to the intellectual life of civilised society need not be doubted, but it is the fifth-century church in Britain which exhibits influence from Gallic Christianity, not so much in the wealth or the size of its churches or other cult-buildings, but in the acceptance of Gallic institutions, notably the growth of monasticism. The ascetic Christian

149

41 The Pillar of Eliseg, near Valle Crucis Abbey, Llangollen, Clwyd. The stone is a portion of a ninth-century high cross which bore a long, now largely obliterated, inscription in honour of Eliseg, chief of the house of Powys, and set up by his great grandson, Cyngen. The text links this Welsh royal house with Gwrtheyrn (Vortigern) and (Magnus) Maximus, and even mentions Germanus as having blessed Gwrtheyrn. Its position, in the Vale of the River Dee, may very well be near the site of Germanus' 'alleluia' victory

life had claimed many converts during the course of the fourth century on the Continent, and the introduction of monasticism into Britain was not long delayed. This seems to have been connected with strongly missionary activity at the same time, suggesting that the Christian faith was strong and flourishing. The earliest monastery of which we know is that of 'Candida Casa' – Whithorn in southern Scotland, founded by St Ninian, probably at the very end of the fourth century – but there is also evidence for fourth-century missionary activity in Ireland even before the missions of bishop Palladius (sent by pope Celestine to Ireland in 431) or Patrick some ten years later.

150

Patrick himself was born probably in the north of England about AD 410. As a teenager he had been captured in an Irish raid, but escaped, later to return to Ireland as bishop to minister to already thriving Christian communities. His own writings provide some of the most reliable evidence for the progress of Irish Christianity, and for the growth of study to be found in the newly founded Irish monasteries, which took a lively interest in the furtherance not only of Christian teachings, but also grammar – Patrick himself was criticised in some places for his inadequate education. That such study was continued in mainland monasteries too can be seen from the elaborate Latin of the sixth-century monk, Gildas, whose classical erudition earned him the nickname 'the wise'. Another vexed question keenly studied in monasteries was that of the date of Easter. The calculation of this was of prime importance: changes in the methods of calculating Easter adopted by the Roman church in 455 were accepted by the Celtic church, but later 'orthodox' alterations were not adopted in Britain, and it was only much later, at the Synod of Whitby in 664, that the two methods, Roman and Celtic, of calculating the date of the most important Christian festival was reconciled.

The influence of Christianity, not only on fifth-century Ireland, but on areas of southern Scotland, will have taken some of the impetus out of Pictish and Irish raiding. Patrick himself was able to castigate one of the more bloodthirsty of the southern Scottish kings, Coroticus, who was clearly nominally a Christian, but yet had not allowed his acceptance of the Gospel to curtail the activities of his war-bands. Patrick's main weapon against such men was excommunication, and one he used unhesitatingly. No such influence, however, was to wield any power in keeping the eastern invaders at bay, and it is during the first few decades of the fifth century in particular that the historical sources seem to place the arrival of the pagan Saxons.

Though various later writers sought to place the *adventus Saxonum* as a single event in a specific year, the likelihood is that their arrival took place over a longer timespan, but in a fashion closely mirrored by our sources.[34] Gildas speaks of a time of prosperity after the first British onslaught against the barbarians, and this was possibly the period when a major power struggle went on among men jostling for political position in the British *civitates*. There was even a rumour that old enemies might come back – this has been variously interpreted and it has even been suggested that there was in fact renewed Roman intervention in part of Britain.[35] The evidence for this, however, is circumstantial and relies mainly on an interpretation of the *Notitia Dignitatum* which surmises that information about Britain would not have been retained within its pages (or files) unless there had been some intention to intervene again in the affairs of the island. Though this may have been the intention, no such intervention can be said to have actually taken place.

The threat of 'old enemies' passed, and this was followed by a plague, which in the crowded cities of the Roman world might find many ready victims. We may be reasonably certain, despite Gildas's sermonising overtones which saw it as the wrath of God, that such a plague actually occurred, and was widespread enough to be special and remembered. The problem is to relate a British outbreak of disease, by matching symptoms and likely distribution with other plagues of the fifth century of which continential sources speak. A serious outbreak, lasting from 443–5, seems to have affected much of the Mediterranean world, but there is no evidence that Britain was one of the areas which fell victim. Nor is there evidence to show that the incidence of plague left the country a weakened and ready prey once again to barbarian raiders.[36]

The pattern of events which Gildas records as the arrival of Saxons in Britain is one which was repeated in many other parts of the Roman world. The local populace, hard-pressed by enemies on one side, enlist their enemies on the other as allies or paid mercenaries, and successfully resist the attack, leaving themselves with the problem of how to rid themselves of their barbarian helpers. The only date on which we might still hang at least part of this episode is that given by the Gallic chroniclers of 441–2 for the period at which 'Britain passed into Saxon power', which suggests, if it can be believed, not merely Saxon assistance to the hard-pressed Britons, but the date at which Saxons in some numbers started to settle in parts of the island – possibly the period of the revolt from their British employers. This occurred, according to Gildas, 'a long time' after the initial invitation by the proud tyrant and the council, during which period the initial Saxon force had been kept quiet on an adequate supply of *annona*, the technical Latin term for 'troops' rations'.

If Vortigern really was the British leader (in whatever sense) who enabled the 'Saxon Wolves', as Gildas terms them, to fasten their claws into the eastern part of the island, then any immediate success he may have bought by this move gained him no lasting credit. One of the entries in the Nennius Chronographer, recorded there as some twelve years after (the beginning of) the 'reign' of Vortigern, is the battle of Wallop, where two Britons, Vitolinus and Ambrosius, were said to be in conflict. Now the dating of this battle is suspect, but it preserves at least the memory that there was some internal conflict between rival British leaders at this date: both men have Roman-style names. It may not be such a false assumption that the conflict was between the successors to Vortigern – the pro-Saxon party – and those who favoured the expulsion of the Saxons. Ambrosius turns up again later in Gildas's account as the leader of the fight against the Saxons, so it is fair to assume that he was on the pro-Briton (and possibly even pro-Roman) party. If he won the battle at Wallop, perhaps the Saxons felt that the time was right to assert themselves, their British support dwindling, and the party which desired their removal now in power. This would provide a neat context for their rebellion and revolt against the British – possibly occurring in 441–2, as the Gallic chronicler records.

So much is speculation, but not an unreasonable one for the possible course of events. Vortigern, who had originally invited the Saxons to Britain in the 420s, was now discredited. His successor Vitolinus was locked in battle with Ambrosius who wished to see tighter control over the Saxons. The battle was settled in Ambrosius' favour. At this the

Saxons were enraged, and took up arms about 440 against the British. A gradual growth of Saxon pressure throughout the island follows and eventually a migration of some of the British to lands over the sea takes place. A jarring note in this suggested pattern is the fact that towards the end of his life, in the 440s, bishop Germanus once again visited Britain, to combat the same heresies as he had done in 429.[37] This time there was no Saxon attack, and no sign of Saxon assault. All apears normal: but we do not know the area of Britain to which he came, and it must perforce have been a well-Christianised area of the island, away from pagan Saxon influence.

The migration of Britons mentioned by Gildas gives another fixed point which may allow dating. Not long after the mid-fifth century, the arrival of a number of British families is attested in Armorica (Brittany).[38] These men brought their own bishops, Mansuetus and Riocatus, with them. The former attended the council at Tours in 461, and the latter is mentioned by bishop Sidonius Apollinaris. Their king, whom they also brought with them, was Riothamus. Continental sources relate that the Britons were invited into Gaul to help fight against the Visigoths by the emperor Anthemius (467–72). Such a migration to Brittany does not sound like that of men fleeing from the Saxons in their homelands. Attractive though it is, therefore, to link Gildas's migration of men pushed out of Britain by the Saxon advance with the known arrival of Britons in Gaul around 470, we cannot effectively reconcile the two. That a migration of Britons to Brittany in Gaul was gradually taking place and continued to take place throughout the later fifth and sixth centuries can also be established and Gildas's story may be no more than the cumulative memory of this.

Following Gildas's account further, we learn that British resistance to this Saxon advance was effectively organised by Ambrosius Aurelianus, and a long series of battles with success on both sides culminated in a siege at Mons Badonicus (Mount Badon), in which the Anglo-Saxons were halted – a decisive enough victory to ensure almost complete peace during Gildas's lifetime. Ambrosius is described by Gildas as a 'modest man', and a *dux* – a war leader (though one cannot help perhaps gaining some overtones of the Roman military title 'Duke'). He was also 'almost the last of the Romans', and his parents had 'worn the purple' and had been killed in the Saxon invasions. The exact import of all the information we are here given about Ambrosius is hard to divine: the fact that his parents had 'worn the purple' might be taken to mean that they were imperial rulers of a united Britain at some stage in the years after 410, but this is hard to substantiate. We do not know how even the local rulers would have styled themselves in these years, and the surviving sources show that there was a wide range of titles in use, derived at various stages from Roman originals. Germanus, on his visit in 428–9, met a man 'of tribunician power' – a title which harks back to one of the earliest titles ever assumed by Roman emperors, and other sources throw up names and titles which echo Roman titles in the same way – 'Magistrat(us)', 'sacerdos' or 'protector'. Thus, to have 'worn the purple' may have meant no more than the family was one of the ruling nobility.[39]

It is time to look briefly at the Saxon side of the story, as related by the *Anglo-Saxon Chronicle*. This, as we have seen,[40] was compiled from information excerpted from poetry which celebrated the martial events of the heroes of the past, and even though its dates are unreliable, it gives a general pattern of Saxon progress under three headings – in Kent, Sussex and Hampshire (the growth of the kingdom of Wessex). The earliest settlement is recorded as that of Kent, by Hengest and Horsa, who were first invited there by Wyrtgeorn (Vortigern) and who at first co-operated with the Britons, but later fought against them. Hengest and Horsa are said to have fought against Vortigern: Horsa lost his life, but Hengest won the battle and the kingdom, the prelude to a series of battles at unidentified sites through which the Saxons expanded their territory and inflicted losses on the British.

A separate but interwoven tradition records the arrival of Aelle and his three sons in Sussex, an account which includes the record of a siege of 'Andredescester' – the fort

155

42 The walls and main gate of the Roman 'Saxon Shore' fort of Pevensey, probably the site of the battle at Andredescester where a massacre of the Britons by the Saxons took place

of Andread, and the slaying of all the Britons within it. The Roman name for one of the forts of the Saxon Shore, Pevensey, is Anderida, a name which seems to be remembered in this tale. This suggests that one of the heroic tales about Aelle and his son Cissa involved their sack and capture of Pevensey, a walled Roman stronghold, but at a date well into the fifth century, when the defenders were no longer Roman soldiers but Britons.

The third strand of Anglo-Saxon tradition records the arrival of Cerdic and Cynric, followed closely by Port, in the area of the Isle of Wight and Portsmouth. Here too, there was great slaughter of the Britons, with one of the noblest of them falling in a battle against Port.[41] Once again a sequence of battles against the Britons leads to Saxon land-taking. Of the three strands of tradition, the Kentish begins according to the *Chronicle* in 449, that of Sussex in 471, and that of Wessex in 495. If we assume that there was good reason for ths spacing of these dates from the traditions recorded in the ninth-century collation of the *Chronicle* and that the first of them relies on the mistaken date of 449 given by Bede for the 'coming of the Saxons', it should be possible to assign more correct relative dates to these three separate views of

156

Saxon arrival, having determined the date at which Vortigern first invited the Saxons to Kent. It would fit relatively well within the fifth-century pattern if this happened in the years around AD 430. This as a rough guideline would push the arrival of Aelle to Sussex forward to 450, and that of Cerdic and Port to around 475.

The Saxon chroniclers tell of no Saxon defeats, though there are battles recorded for which no claim of victory is made. Yet Gildas suggests that despite the Saxon advance, battle honours were equally shared between the time of Ambrosius' resistance and the siege of Mount Badon – another battle apparently not mentioned by the *Anglo-Saxon Chronicle*. It is not clear at Badon who was being besieged by whom, nor where 'Mount Badon' itself lay,[42] but it must have marked the limit of Saxon expansion at the very end of the fifth century. The dating comes from Gildas, who says in a very contorted way that he was born in the year that Badon was fought.[43] This was 43 years from the time of writing his *De Excidio* which was written during the currency of a number of Welsh and west-British kings, and can be quite firmly dated therefore to the early 540s. Badon therefore came at the very end of the fifth century, and marked the beginning of a time of comparative peace which Gildas himself had witnessed.

It is fair to assume that Ambrosius was no longer the leader of the Britons by this time: if he had been current in the 430s to be a young rival to Vortigern, and leading the opposition to him which either resulted in or sprang from the Saxon revolt of *c*. 440, he cannot still have been an active force by *c*. 500. Modern speculation has alighted on one figure as the leader of the Britons at this period, his existence at best shadowy and ill-documented, but a name which inspired early medieval historians to a frenzy of romantic storytelling. This figure is Arthur. Not mentioned by Gildas, not even claimed as the founder of any later Welsh dynasty, unsung in any but much later poetic and romantic sources, Arthur's existence, still less his position as one of the greatest war-leaders of his day, is still a matter for dispute.

What is not in dispute, however, is that by about AD 500, Saxon advances had been substantial, and the foundations laid for further expansion and consolidation to occur shortly after the period of peace of which Gildas speaks. Even though our sources for fifth-century Britain are imprecise, awkward to use, and in many ways misleading, the blurred picture which remains, as ever more stringent modern criticism of the sources themselves displays more of their unreliability, is that of a land torn with political and military conflict. The canvas is broad, the lines are often indistinct, but some of the main elements of the composition can be made out.

5 The arrival of the Anglo-Saxons

In view of the ambiguity and unreliability of the literary sources for the period, we must turn for further information to another source – that of the study of remains of the incoming Anglo-Saxons and their contemporary Britons. The main concentration of Anglo-Saxon finds from excavations and in museum collections consists of pottery urns and metalwork ornaments – brooches, bracelets and the like – which come from the cremation and inhumation cemeteries of these peoples. It is only in the last fifty years or so that excavators have begun to recognise 'pagan Anglo-Saxon' settlement sites, as well as cemeteries, and the greatest source of information is still the burial remains rather than material from excavated Anglo-Saxon villages. There are greater or lesser degrees of decoration on burial urns which contained the cremated remains of the dead. Cemeteries reveal that people were originally laid out for interment fully clothed and often fully armed, with belts, brooches and weaponry. Females were buried wearing necklaces, rings or bracelets. Such inhumations are occasionally accompanied by pottery, metal or glass vessels, perhaps the containers for a final ritual meal for the dead person. Settlement sites, on the other hand, produce a mass of evidence for the industrial and farming processes of the Anglo-Saxons, as well as a wide range of domestic hand-made pottery-types, normally plainer vessels than the decorated funerary urns.

To assign a precise fifth-century date to such objects is the task of the archaeologist, whose method depends mainly on their association with Roman literature or with objects like coins, with their dates and mint-marks.[1] No Anglo-Saxon artefact bears on it a date-stamp which can be read off, and there are few areas within Britain where early Anglo-Saxon material is in a close enough relationship with Roman finds for their dates to be clearly assessed. It is by their association with better-dated Roman material in the German homelands that early Anglo-Saxon pots and brooches can be dated. The method depends on establishing a valid parallel between the British pottery under consideration and decoratively similar vessels which can be dated by association with other groups of material in Germany. It is important always, however, to be aware that to arrive at a date by this method is imprecise: there can be uncertainties about the validity of the parallel (how close a copy of the German vessel does the English one have to be?), or about the relative dates within the life-spans of two vessels which give a 'linked' date.[2] A group of linked observations of this nature provides the basis for a typological study of the development of pottery, glass and metalwork, their form and decoration. Data from each new relationship between excavated material must be used to refine our assessment of the connections between objects and so to tighten the dating network.

Classification of the wide range of this material has provided the rough definition of a framework of dates for pottery, metalwork, glassware, and other finds (for example, bone combs), not only by stylistic decoration, which may have affinities with Roman or German objects, but also by chance association of various types of material within excavated sites. The dating of material by consideration of its style of decoration alone is particularly difficult. Few scholars would attempt to press any particular stylistic trait into a date range much more constricted than a rough 'generation' or so. There is a large body of material, therefore, which cannot with ease be assigned any closer date than a round half-century or so. In general, one can distinguish between types of pottery and metalwork currently in use during the first or second half of the fifth century, or the first half of the sixth, but any closer dating than this might well be misleading. A slightly closer dating for certain classes of

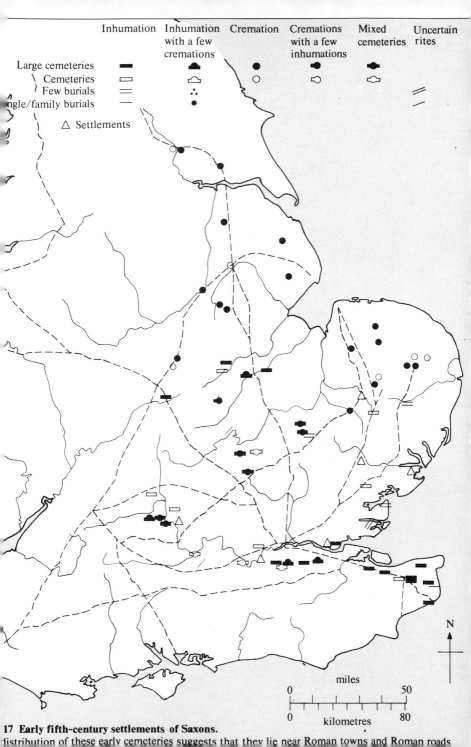

17 Early fifth-century settlements of Saxons.
distribution of these early cemeteries suggests that they lie near Roman towns and Roman roads

metalwork may be possible with the identification of an overlapping phase of material, current from *c*. 380–420.[3]

The areas of eastern England to receive the earliest incoming German nations were parts of Kent, the Thames Valley, East Anglia, Lincolnshire and the Wolds of Yorkshire north of the Humber.[4] Some broad distinctions between the types of finds, and perhaps more important, the types of burial rite from the various areas give some clue as to the peoples' basic origin. Bede, writing in the eighth century, says that the Jutes came to Kent and the Isle of Wight, the Saxons to Essex, Sussex and Wessex, and the Angles to East Anglia, Mercia and eventually to Northumbria.[5] This was no more than an educated man's guess from the names of the areas in the eighth century.[6] In reality, the settlement of Jutes, Saxons and Angles was more complex than this. In the general area from Norfolk to York almost all the cemeteries contain cremations only: in an area round the Thames, there are inhumations only, whereas in an area of the southern and eastern midlands, from Oxfordshire to Cambridgeshire, the burial rites are largely mixed. Among the distinctive types of brooches, the cruciform brooch seems to have belonged to the Anglian and Jutish peoples, and the saucer brooch was more characteristic of the mixed Angles and Saxons of the German homelands. Evidence from these, together with the practice of cremation or inhumation, suggests that the Jutes were more prevalent in the Kentish and Thames-side areas, the Angles in the northern parts, and the Saxons or Anglo-Saxons in the central area. There were, however, at an early stage in the Saxon influx, no hard and fast boundaries between the distinctive German tribes or nations, and some mingling of the basic cultural differences may already have been occurring.[7]

Of the settlement sites of these incoming Saxons, only a few have been identified and excavated with any degree of thoroughness. One of the best known, the subject of a notable series of excavations in recent years is the site at Mucking, near Stanford-le-Hope, in Essex.[8] The site occupies a gravel terrace with a commanding position on the north bank of the river Thames. An area of gravel under

43 Aerial view of the crop-mark sites at Mucking, Essex. The dominant features showing in this view of the gravel terrace before excavation are the circular ditches of the Iron Age fort, and, overlappig it, a rectangular Roman ditched enclosure. The majority of the small dark dots, however, represent features of the Saxon period, and are the sites of sunken-floored huts. The two Saxon cemeteries were found to the right, just off the picture

extraction was found to be rich in crop-marks, which have since been shown to belong to a range of features of widely differing dates. Of particular interest for the late Roman and Saxon periods are the field systems which were probably the outlying portions of a Romano-British villa which may have lain closer to the river on richer alluvial soils. The Saxon huts, whose layout bears little relationship to the

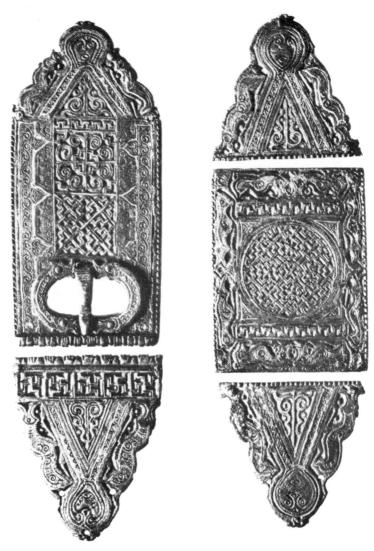

44 A fine set of late Roman belt-fittings from the Mucking cemetery. Found in a grave, these belonged to a mercenery soldier of late fourth- or early fifth-century date. The decoration on the plates bridges the gap between the late Roman and the barbarian world: the central roundel on the left plate is typically Roman, the four heads at the pointed ends typically Germanic

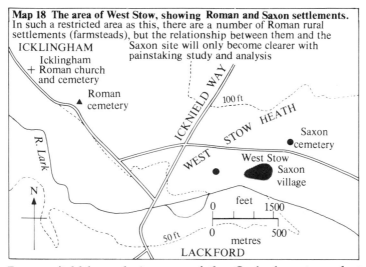

Map 18 The area of West Stow, showing Roman and Saxon settlements.
In such a restricted area as this, there are a number of Roman rural
settlements (farmsteads), but the relationship between them and the
Saxon site will only become clearer with painstaking study and analysis

Roman field-boundaries, are of the *Grubenhaus* type, but
there is one large timber hall certainly of Saxon date. Two
cemeteries have been located, perhaps serving separate
communities: these contain graves of fifth- to seventh-
century date. A number of factors suggest, however, that
the sometimes richly furnished graves belong to a more
prestigious community elsewhere – possibly on the better
agricultural land nearer the Thames – and that the remains
so far discovered at Mucking are merely those on the fringe
of a larger and more important settlement.[9] The earliest
finds from the site clearly identified as Saxon are pottery of
early fifth-century types; but some of the graves of Saxon
warriors contain military metalwork commonly categorised
as 'late Roman' types, which might be worn by German
mercenary soldiers of that period. Despite this, there is little
apparent overlap between the Roman and Saxon settlement: wheel-made pottery is largely absent from Saxon
levels and features, and Saxon huts lie over silted-up
Roman ditches. One of the cemeteries lies almost totally
bounded by one of the Roman fields, but the boundary was
probably used because it was still visible rather than as a
conscious continuity on the site.

Another site which dates from early within the period

165

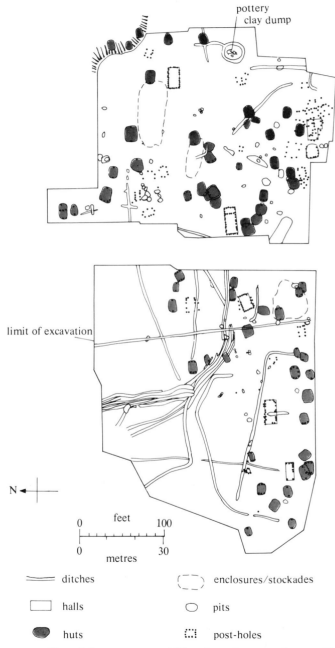

pottery
clay dump

limit of excavation

N

feet
0   100

0   30
metres

══ ditches   ⌐ ⌐ enclosures/stockades

▭ halls   ◯ pits

⬤ huts   ⠿ post-holes

Figure 12 Plan of the excavation of West Stow Saxon settlement. The settlement has at least five post-built halls, a pottery working area, enclosure ditches and several small huts – *Grubenhäuser*

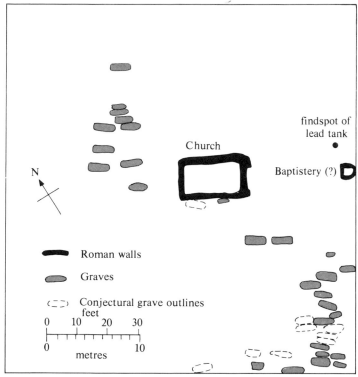

findspot of
lead tank
•

Church

Baptistery (?)

N

Roman walls

Graves

Conjectural grave outlines

feet
0   10   20   30

0   10
metres

Figure 13 Plan of the church and cemetery at Icklingham, Suffolk. The church, a small rectangular building at the centre of the site, is surrounded by graves orientated east-west. The small D-shaped building east of the church was probably a baptistery. Fragments of a lead tank similar to the one shown in Figure 3 were found nearby

during which the Saxons were arriving in Britain, is that of West Stow, near Bury St Edmunds in Suffolk.[10] Here since 1965 the almost complete excavation of a Saxon village has taken place, revealing a sequence of post-built halls, and smaller sunken huts of two distinctive types, stretching from the early years of the fifth century until the middle of the seventh. The completeness of the excavation has established that the Saxon village lay on the fringes of a more extensive Roman settlement some distance to the west. Substantial amounts of Roman pottery and coin finds at the Saxon village, however, suggest that there was some contact and overlap between the two communities.

The nearby Romano-British site at Icklingham includes a group of buildings which have most plausibly been identified as a church complex.[11] The church itself is a small rectangular building aligned east-west, surrounded by a cemetery of at least forty-five inhumations, one of which lay in a stone coffin. East of the church and apart from it lay a small D-shaped building with internal plasterwork on the walls. Near this building was found a pewter tank which bore a Christian chi-rho symbol, one of a total of three such tanks reported at various dates from the area. This building was probably a baptistery, or may have been a memorial shrine to one of the saints. The church area seems to have served the Icklingham Romano-British community from AD 350 until at least 400, and possibly nearer 420. The end of its use was marked by the deposition of a hoard of coins dating up to Honorius (395). The buildings had been deliberately dismantled, and the complex came to a rapid and intentional end. A connection between the end of this Romano-British church-site and the establishment of the pagan Saxon village in the area cannot yet be deduced. The most important point to make is that without detailed work on the relationship between Roman sites and newly formed Saxon ones in similar areas, progress will scarcely be made.

The organisation of the Saxon village at West Stow, as far as can be determined, was loose-knit. By contrast with some village sites in the Germanic homelands (p. 63), there is no sign that the settlers brought with them a ready-made hierarchy of chiefs and subjects. Only the sunken huts which are subsidiary to the main timber halls contain much dating evidence, but it appears that the earliest village consisted of some half-dozen family units, no one of which was pre-eminent over the others. These people began their British life as peasant farmers, presumably at little more than subsistence economy levels. The pottery they used was strongly typical of wares from the German homelands, but as time progressed, the settlement grew and became more prosperous, so that a distinctive style of pottery evolved. By the late sixth century West Stow was probably the manufacturing centre for a particular potter, whose wares, distinguished by their characteristic stamped decoration, have been found widely spread over an arc of Suffolk and Cambridgeshire.[12] The clear long-term continuity of Anglo-Saxon life on this site, from small, apparently fairly humble, beginnings of the years around 400, until about 650 at least, shows that the Anglo-Saxon settlement of places within eastern Britain was not a transient one. Even though the land they occupied was perhaps marginal to the Romano-British pattern of settlement, and lay at the boundaries of Roman communities, yet it formed a surprisingly stable basis for permanent habitation.

Few other early Anglo-Saxon villages have been excavated in anything like the same detail as those of Mucking and West Stow. Those sites which have been examined in any thoroughness, like Bishopstone near Newhaven (Sussex),[13] or Heybridge near Colchester (Essex),[14] suggest that the pattern of West Stow may well be repeated in other parts of the country, and further work, chance finds and aerial photography should begin to reveal the presence of other settlements of this nature in eastern England.

Still the best indication of the spread of Saxon culture within England therefore must be the distribution of the cemeteries, which must bear some relationship to the areas of settlement of the incoming Saxons. By and large, we run into the most difficult problems of dating the objects from the graves or cremations, for it is not easy stylistically to date many Anglo-Saxon funerary objects to a date c. 400 rather than one c. 450, and a potential date-range spanning this period would be of the greatest importance in assessing how much contact the settling Anglo-Saxon nations had with the established Romano-British community.

We have seen how the historical sources suggest, most plausibly, that the earliest Saxons to have arrived came as mercenary soldiers, but that their arrival in this capacity did not happen until well into the fifth century – possibly around 425–30 (p. 152). The most relevant question for the archaeological material in recent years has been how far the pottery and metalwork finds of the earliest Saxon arrivals appear to meet this date. From a wide-ranging study of

(a)

(b)

45 (a) and (b) Two of the early Saxon pots from the cemetery found near the Roman town of Caistor-by-Norwich. Both styles of decoration have some affinities with pottery of fourth-century date found in cemeteries in the Saxon homelands in Germany

pagan Anglo-Saxon pottery, Dr J. N. L. Myres has separated out five phases of Saxon penetration into Britain – categories which he would still doubtless wish to refine, but which in broad outline can be here summarised.[15] The initial phase might be expected to be the presence of groups of Saxons or Germanic barbarians within Britain at a time when Britain was still part of the Roman Empire, followed by a transitional phase in the years following the withdrawal of Roman military support during which the barbarian presence grew and consolidated. The third phase, that of the invasion of larger numbers of Anglo-

Saxon and other barbarians, is familiar from the literary record, and probably occurred in the latter part of the fifth century. The fourth phase is represented by the recovery of the Britons about AD 500, and their resistance to Saxon invasion until *c.* 550, when the Anglo-Saxon kingdoms finally began to take their historic form and to expand.

In his original distinction of these five phases, Dr Myres dated the first of them between 360 and 410, thus suggesting that there were groups of Saxons within the Roman province of Britain. The best example of an early Saxon cemetery is that of Caistor-by-Norwich (Norfolk).[16] Here a cemetery outside the defended circuit of the Roman town of Venta Icenorum contains one or two Saxon urns which might be dated as early as AD 300, but a greater number which could be assigned to the latter part of the fourth century. Such an early dating is uncomfortable for most scholars, who would not wish to place too much reliance on the early dating of comparative Germanic material.[17] Though it is undeniable that one or two of the pots in the Caistor cemetery appear on stylistic grounds to belong to the fourth, rather than the fifth century, these may be no more than antique survivals within a cemetery where the majority of articles found can be dated around AD 400 if not later.

The view that settlement of Saxons within Roman Britain would mean 'protectorates' with visible boundaries may be an entirely wrong one. If the process of infiltration of Saxons into the Roman world was happening, such men would want not a style of life to which they were accustomed, but a 'Romanised' existence, and they might well in the world of late Roman Britain have been accepted as immigrants, and develop a lifestyle fairly nearly indistinguishable from that of provincial Romano-Britons. Such men as were able to infiltrate this would scarcely be the leaders of war-bands, who would be regarded with grave suspicion, but craftsmen useful to society, mercenaries or recruitment material for the late Roman army. One cavalry unit of 'Saxons' – recruited, one presumes from among the tribe – is listed in the *Notitia* in Egypt,[18] but there surely must have been others, individuals or groups within the late Roman army as a whole, and indistinguishable from it. They would not necessarily retain their tribal warriors' dress, but be fitted out with normal late Roman equipment. Similarly, craftsmen who gained entry to the Roman world would ply their trade in producing goods for the Roman market, possibly with 'barbarised' decoration, but there would be no call within the empire for really 'Saxon-style' pots or metalwork.

On the Continent we are on surer ground in the search for barbarian settlers, for within areas of north-eastern Gaul a number of late Roman cemeteries have been found containing the bodies of men buried in full military uniform, including the distinctive types of chip-carved buckles and attachments for the *cingulum*, the sword-belt which was the mark of military as well as state civilian service. Such cemeteries lay near towns or in the countryside areas, in close association with re-used and redefended Iron Age hill-forts. The men buried in these cemeteries, to judge from their form of inhumation, regarded themselves as soldiers, yet they were stationed (with their womenfolk) in areas where they were unlikely to see continuous military action. Their strategic job was defence in depth, behind the troops of the frontier; but no less important a duty was the cultivation of the surrounding land. Such men were barbarian tribesmen with a veneer of civilisation, who, in return for land within Rome's provincial boundaries, performed this valuable double service – the natural one for the free Germanic peoples – of farmer and warrior.

It has often been considered that these apparently tribal groups constitute the military units classed as *'Laeti'* and *'Sarmatae'* in the *Notitia Dignitatum*, which details such men in this particular area.[19] But this is unlikely to be the case, for to warrant inclusion within the army lists, the units of *laeti* will have been formed under commissioned officers with a full-time military role. The men buried in their rich uniforms in the north Gallic cemeteries are more likely to be Germanic federates – tribesmen granted their land by treaty with the Roman state, and so occupying the most

46 A reconstruction of the set of late Roman metalwork found at Dorchester-on-Thames, Oxon., attached to a modern leather belt to show how once the equipment was worn

privileged status they could attain within the empire short of Roman citizenship itself. They were probably Franks, recruited originally in the latter half of the fourth century from free Germany.[20] Pride in their military status led their chiefs to insist upon burial in uniform, a practice which spread to the German homelands and to other Germanic soldiers within the late Roman army as a whole. These cemeteries belong to family or tribal groups of Germans whose individual style of dress marks them out as both wealthy and as of high military rank, whose control extends over hill-top fortresses, villas, rural estates, and even over sizeable Roman settlements.

Though some types of metalwork normally to be dated in the decades after 400 have appeared in Britain, there is as yet very little from the period 330–400 that can be specifically classified as Germanic. Military belt-buckles from several of the regional arms factories producing the belt-trappings were signs of military rank and service.[21] Most frontier provinces will have had their own individual styles of production according to the skill of the craftsmen employed within their factories, but such equipment is not necessarily a sign of status as *laeti* or federates. More particularly, there is a complete absence within Britain of the simple early Saxon cross-bow brooches, and of early forms of the 'short-armed' brooches (*Stützarmfibeln*), which suggests that as late as AD 400, there was yet no significant

(a)

(b)

47 Early Saxon vessels from (a) Mitcham, Surrey and (b) Mucking, Essex. The vessel with carination and pedestal base can be paralleled by fourth-century material from Anglian homelands in Germany (see Plate 14, p. 65)

Saxon presence in the province.[22] None of the early Anglo-Saxon cemetery groups has many more than one or two 'antique' pieces of Germanic metalwork which can be unequivocally dated before *c*. 420, the earliest British finds in general being equal-arm brooches and composite disc-brooches. There is thus little to suggest that before that date Saxons were within Britain as 'federate' troops, wearing their own uniforms and bringing with them their own chiefs and tribal organisation.

There has not been such determined excavation on late Roman cemeteries belonging to *civitates*, forts or settlements

48 Pottery vessel of 'Romano-Saxon' type from London Museum, found in the City of London. The overall shape of the vessel and its fabric suggest that it was made in the kilns at Much Hadham (Herts.). The shape and style is Roman, but the embossed decoration is in the so-called 'Saxon' style

in Britain as there has been on the Continent, so the British and Continental material cannot by and large be compared. However, it must surely be significant that so far no British cemetery of this period has been proved indisputably to contain early federate burials, though some individual graves do undoubtedly relate to Saxon military personnel. One of the best examples is a nineteenth-century find within the ramparts of the Iron Age fort near the Roman town of Dorchester (Oxon.), where the inhumation burials of a man in full uniform (and probably with his weapons though these were thrown away as useless ironwork) and of a woman were discovered.[23] The date range for these graves is in the years around AD 400, and is perhaps the best indication of Germanic settlement within the Roman province of Britain towards the turn of the fifth century.

The evidence of the metalwork accords well with that of the pottery finds. One of the earliest of Continental forms to be found in any numbers in Britain is a type of globular urn decorated with horizontal grooves on the shoulders and diagonal slashed strokes below, forming pendant triangles or a chevron pattern.[24] Continental examples of this type are dated independently, by association with the metalwork discussed above, to the fourth century and into the very early years of the fifth. Another type found in Britain is the derivative of the pedestal carinated bowl, of which examples have been found at West Stow, Mucking and early cemeteries of the south.[25] Apart from the pottery from the cemetery at Caistor-by-Norwich, there are few early Anglo-Saxon vessels within Britain dating much before 400, and the main influx should certainly be considered as later.

One type of pottery regularly discovered on late Roman levels, particularly in the eastern part of England, is distinctive enough to be stylistically linked with the decorative motifs and forms of Saxon vessels, and for this reason it has normally been named 'Romano-Saxon' ware.[26] Such pots are of normal Roman fabric and manufacture, but bear decorations such as pressed-out bosses or clusters of stamped designs which are also a hallmark of later Saxon ceramic design, and occasionally echo remarkably closely the general shape and appearance of Saxon pots. Though vessels bearing such designs are nowhere very common, they appear to have been produced, perhaps at one or two localised Romano-British pottery sites, throughout much of the fourth century. A coin-hoard of AD 350–2 was found deposited in a jar of this type at Water Newton, but the majority of known examples were probably deposited at a later date than this.

It is doubtful whether this pottery is of significance in determining the presence of Saxon settlers in fourth-century Britain. The ornamentation, with bosses, dimples and stamps, is not in itself foreign to Roman Britain, for these motifs occur in a variety of local wares which preserved something of a tradition of pottery craftsmanship independent from that of Rome. Even if 'Romano-Saxon' pottery bears the influence of Saxon designs upon Roman pottery – a factor hard to demonstrate without a clear link between decoration on pottery from the Anglo-Saxon German homelands and the British material – it is going beyond the evidence to suggest that such pottery might have been made for the use of exclusively Saxon communities within Britain.

Perhaps the best case for Anglo-Saxon overlap in the last decades of Roman Britain is provided by the locations of the Anglo-Saxon cemeteries themselves, and their relationship with Roman roads and settlements. The two cemeteries which lay within 300 metres of the walled *civitas* of Caistor-by-Norwich (p. 171) have a starting date at least as early as the fifth century, and there were early cemeteries round the walled towns of Cambridge and Great Chesterford, and probably near Colchester. Saxon burials took place near the walled Roman towns of Leicester, Great Casterton, Ancaster, Lincoln and York, as well as near Dorchester-on-Thames. Some Saxon cemeteries also lay on or near strategic points along Roman roads. Although this relationship can be shown to exist, its historical interpretation is by no means as easily fathomed. A similar number of early cemeteries appear to have little or no relationship with Roman towns (or even roads), such as those in Kent, in the west Suffolk and west Norfolk areas, and those on the Lincolnshire Wolds.[27] The interpretation of those cemeteries which lie in the immediate vicinity of Roman towns depends heavily upon the rather equivocal dating of their contents. If they belonged to 'federate' Saxons, there should be a clear relationship between an Anglo-Saxon and a Romano-British cemetery showing that both were in use at the same time. We also need a clear idea of the date at which members of the Romano-British population lived within the towns, and also to question whether they could still have been resident at a date contemporaneous with the earliest of Anglo-Saxon material from the cemeteries.

It will be difficult to prove a significant overlap between

Romano-British town-dwellers and incoming Anglo-Saxon settlers except in localised areas where the overall pattern of Saxon and Roman settlement is well-defined and studied. The area where such a relationship appears to be promising is in the region of West Stow, Lackford and Icklingham, mentioned above (pp. 167f), where there is a Roman village and church site, as well as the early Saxon village and cemetery. From excavations within the walled area at Caistor-by-Norwich there was no direct evidence of Saxon pottery or other artefacts despite the close proximity of the two cemeteries with grave-goods in an early Saxon style. The only finds which might suggest federates are the belt-buckles and equipment typical of an 'official' presence.[28] We meet once more the problem of having to assume what would be counted as evidence of Saxon 'federate' settlement at Caistor: such men would surely have lived in 'Roman-style' buildings provided for them, and might have reverted to their own native tradition only for the burial rite. One would, however, have expected more intermingling of contemporary Roman and pagan Saxon objects within the cemetery: some Roman pots were used as grave-goods and cremation vessels, but these appear on the whole to be much earlier pots found elsewhere and re-used in this fashion.[29]

Present evidence, therefore, does not establish what was the relationship between these Anglo-Saxon cemeteries and the Roman towns, settlements and roads. Certainly one cannot assume that early cemeteries of this character belong to groups of 'federates' garrisoned in the towns to protect them, unless one asks whether there was anyone with sufficient authority and financial resource to pay for this service, and perhaps more fundamentally, whether the towns contained anything or anyone worth protecting. There is clear evidence within the walls of some Roman *civitates* of fifth-century Saxon settlement in 'native' style. For instance early huts with sunken floors containing a distinctive form of Anglo-Frisian pottery have been found at Canterbury.[30] These huts were built above the debris of levelled Roman buildings and occupied (so far as is known)

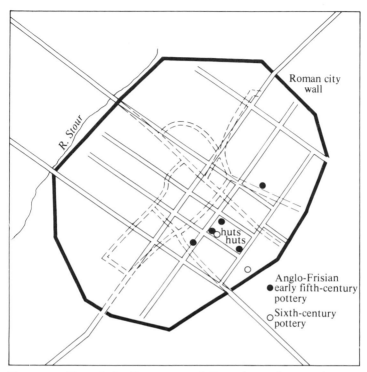

Figure 14 Plan of the Roman city of Canterbury, showing the sites where huts of early Saxon or Anglian style have been discovered

only a single *insula* of the city, but are to be dated only around the mid-fifth century. Such areas of Roman Canterbury as have been excavated show a fairly normal pattern of houses and buildings, some continuing in use until at least the end of the fourth century, though others appear to have fallen down by then. The Saxon huts, concentrated in the years around AD 450 within a single *insula* of the city, do not necessarily show that a Romano-British controlling authority gave them restricted space for settlement within the city. It may have been the most convenient area, where buildings had already fallen or been levelled.

Similar discoveries have been made at Colchester.[31] Here, in Lion Walk, two Saxon huts whose floors were sunk through the latest of the Roman levels were built in the fifth century. One of these huts leant against the substantial ruins of a Roman building, but the other cut through a Roman mosaic floor. It appears that the area of Colchester in which these huts stood lay derelict from about AD 300 onwards, but the pottery which dates them suggests a date no earlier than the fifth century for their occupation, and as yet there is no discovery of Saxon pottery in otherwise purely late Roman rubbish pits. This suggests that there was not necessarily any overlap between the two communities.

The present archaeological record therefore cannot be used to determine whether Anglo-Saxon occupation in and around the Roman towns of the east took place when those towns were still inhabited by Romans, still less whether the Saxon settlers were brought in by some official to perform a specific military function. By itself, archaeological evidence on such topics is almost always ambiguous, partly because there are few sites which have seen wide-scale enough excavation to form a complete picture of the development of settlement either within the Romano-British period or within the Anglo-Saxon period (let alone between them), and partly because of the immense problems of proving that separate portions of the same town were in contemporary occupation by Romano-Britons and Pagan Saxons.

That there was some overlap between incoming Saxons and Romano-Britons can be seen, not from the towns as yet, but from more rural sites, such as that of Kelvedon, in Essex.[32] This was a small settlement near Colchester on the main road to London and appears never to have been walled. Little of the actual township has been explored, and the main evidence for Roman-Saxon overlap comes from the Roman cemetery, lying south-west of the inhabited area. Late Roman inhumation graves here contained grave-goods which do not diverge from the late Roman norm – bronze trinkets, iron keys, earrings, glass vessels and some pottery. Mixed with the earth shovelled over and around the bodies, in some cases within the coffins, were abraded sherds of pagan Saxon pottery of fifth-century type. This is incontrovertible evidence for the presence of Saxon pottery at the time of these 'late Roman' burials, and arouses questions not only about an overlap period between Romans and Saxons, but also about how long into the fifth century the local population of a relatively undistinguished small Roman community would continue to bury its dead in Roman style, surrounded by objects of daily use which are typologically no different from finds of fourth-century date. We should not expect the burial rite to change – it would be most surprising if this happened. Perhaps, therefore, our search for overlap between Romans and Saxons should take the form, not of seeing how early we can justifiably push the beginnings of Saxon settlement, but how late we can assess what appear at face value to be normal 'fourth-century' Roman finds.

Evidence for Anglo-Saxon settlement on other rural Roman sites, such as villas, must also be examined. In general it is difficult to show what relationship Roman villas in eastern England had with Saxon invaders. At Barton Court, near Abingdon (Berks.), the villa was apparently deliberately dismantled in the last quarter of the fourth century, the building material being meticulously taken away. Not until the late fifth or sixth century, was this followed by Saxon settlement and burial on the villa site. Moreover this villa site cannot be closely linked with the known large early Saxon cemetery near the Roman town of Abingdon.[33] Elsewhere, particularly in Kent, the pattern is similar. In the valleys of the Kentish rivers flowing into the Thames there are several Roman villas, and the correspondence between Anglo-Saxon settlement and villa sites is uneven. At Eccles, for example, on the Medway, the Anglo-Saxons arrived only in the seventh century, with burials taking place within the (by then derelict) remains of the Roman villa.[34] Near the known early Saxon cemetery at Orpington (Kent) there lay another Roman villa, and on the site of a nearby villa at Keston there is a timber hall and two sunken-floored huts, from one of which came a comb datable to the early fifth century. Once again

49 Aerial view of Chalton Anglo-Saxon village. As at West Stow (Figure 12), the settlement contained post-built timber halls and small huts. The halls are visible in this view, as groups of excavated wall-trenches. The position of this site, on the hill slopes of Hampshire, well away from the present village, suggests that it was an early Saxon site at the edge of the settlement which was later superseded

the evidence is insufficient to show a temporal overlap on these sites between the phases of Roman and Anglo-Saxon settlement.[35]

A rather more detailed study of the process of Anglo-Saxon ingress into Sussex has suggested that the areas taken by the new settlers were precisely those left vacant or under-used by the Romano-British population.[36] This pattern is beginning to be underlined by fragmentary evidence from other parts of Britain, for there are many indications that the earliest Saxon arrivals settled on the fringes of Roman villa outfield systems, or on marginal land between two neighbourhoods. Whether this means Roman 'control' of Saxon settlement in an organised sense, or whether it means that the Romano-Britons, already in command of the best of the agricultural land, were not likely to be easily shaken off by a handful of incoming settlers, is a matter for debate. It is more likely that the known Saxon villages were placed on marginal land because incoming numbers were relatively few, and that they lived under the tenurial control of the existing landowners. In places they may have established a communal *modus vivendi*. The difference between the late Roman and early Saxon rural settlement pattern might not therefore be so very great.[37] It is worth remembering, however, that the known and excavated Saxon sites like West Stow, Mucking, and the somewhat later village of Chalton (Hants.),[38] are 'failed' sites. Better evidence for continuity from Roman community to Saxon village may lie buried deep underneath modern towns and villages where present-day occupation obscures and has possibly obliterated many of the archaeological traces of this chain.

One of the earliest studies which sought to deal in any way with this problem examined the small Gloucestershire village of Withington.[39] Though, from its position, it cannot really have been overtaken by the Saxon westward advance through Britain until the second half of the sixth century, none the less a consideration of the evidence may show the sort of process which had already been happening elsewhere in the east. Much of the present-day boundary of the parish of Withington derives in an unbroken continuity from an estate given to a nunnery by Ethelred, king of Mercia, in the late seventh century. It is likely that the land so granted was already in the form of an estate, and may conceivably have been even then of respectable antiquity. During the Roman period there had been a single large villa within Withington, whose estate boundary, judging from natural boundaries and the positioning of other villas, may well have been something similar to the present parish limits. The villa estate therefore may have formed the land given away to the nunnery in the seventh century.

It is one thing to suggest that land boundaries remained constant from late Roman times (say from AD 450) until about 700, the time of the transfer of the estate recorded in the early charter; but it is quite another thing to claim that of the Roman sites within the area, the villa itself went into decay during the fifth century, and the largest of the three humbler peasant settlements grew in importance as the new centre until it formed the nucleus of the seventh-century estate and the present-day village of Withington. This may be a valid reflection of the ways in which society developed from the end of the Roman period onwards: in the case of Withington there is no proof, but the more examples which are found of late Roman territorial boundaries surviving into mid- and late Saxon times, the more some such hypothesis gains credibility.

It is becoming increasingly possible to argue that the extent of Saxon settlement in the seventh and eighth centuries was as widespread as that recorded in the great land survey of Domesday Book compiled in the late eleventh century.[40] There has been a tendency to regard Domesday Book as recording the early stages of the growth of English life in Britain, and the understanding that Domesday is not as complete a gazetteer as it has sometimes been regarded suggests that many of the names of places not mentioned there, but occurring in later sources, did actually exist in the late Saxon period and earlier. As in the case of Withington, early charters preserve within them the evidence that in the seventh and eighth centuries land was already parcelled out in occasionally remarkably large and well-developed estates.[41] A series of studies of areas of Wessex has suggested that many of the present parish boundaries in Wiltshire were fixed at a date before the digging of the Wansdyke – itself not precisely dated, but probably of the late sixth century or the seventh century.[42] The inference is clear: modern ecclesiastical (and civil, where these are on the same line) parish boundaries may represent basic divisions in land holding which can date to AD 550 or thereabouts. It is hard to see how such early boundaries were fixed if they do not relate in some way to the parcelling of land by Roman or earlier landholders. The legal processes, however, which allowed ownership of such land to pass from Roman to Saxon remain shrouded in mystery.

At the excavations in the deserted medieval village of Wharram Percy, in the eastern part of Yorkshire, it was found that the boundary of the village in the heyday of its life in the tenth and fourteenth centuries was on the line of early Roman field ditches.[43] This is not likely to reflect continuity of habitation: the Roman boundaries may still have been visible and usable at the date of Saxon occupation of the site after the Roman period.

Area studies which show the relationship of Roman and Saxon settlement sites continue to throw up new facets of their distribution. In various disparate parts of England, it is becoming increasingly clear that Saxons were coming to live on and claim a share of the same lands as the Roman population – whether in a way that may imply a certain overlap between the two peoples, as in Northamptonshire,[44] or in the East Riding of Yorkshire,[45] or in some more complex fashion which may imply a rather more proprietary claim on the part of the British native and a less self-assured claim by the immigrant Saxons or Angles. The fact that Saxons chose to settle in areas where there had been (and possibly still was) a substantial rural population is significant. Here was the best agricultural land: in these areas the countryside had long since been brought under the control of man. Thus the acceptance of ready-made boundaries which partitioned this land into convenient areas was a natural and desirable step.

The evidence of place-name study can also be used to illuminate more of the relationship between Romano-British and Saxon in the early periods of the occupation. One indisputable factor of the Anglo-Saxon arrival in Britain was the eventual complete change of the language of England from Latin or British Celtic to the early Anglo-Saxon tongue which has since become English. As a measure of the spread of this development, one has only to look, for example, at the map of river-names prepared by Professor Jackson,[46] which shows clearly four contrasted zones of Saxon influence on the names. The areas from east to west have an increasing number of Celtic names which survive, until in Wales, Cornwall and other portions of the Celtic west, the rivers are called virtually by Celtic names alone. Such a map gives a rough estimate of the influence of the various stages of Saxon advance across the country.

A factor which can scarcely be stressed too strongly is the

Map 19 The rivers marked in black on this map of England and Wales have retained their British-Celtic (pre-Roman) names. Those in grey are of English nomenclature. There is a clear progression from east to west of the degree of influence which the incoming English had on river-names. All rivers in Wales and Cornwall retain their Celtic names

miles
0   50
0   80
kilometres

very radical change which came over place-names in the fifth to seventh centuries. The number of places which have preserved a Roman name, or even the number of places which have a French name dating from the conquest by the Normans in 1066 is very few. The basic stock of names, spoken by the people who worked the land, will have scarcely changed during either of those conquests by foreign military powers.[47] Seen against such a comparison, the success of English both as a spoken language and as a medium for naming places suggests a far more radical and remarkable influence on the part of the incoming English, over a period of time. At this level, we cannot be certain how much of the Anglo-Saxon naming of places was a straight translation, or even in some cases, a rough transliteration of the old British name into the new language.[48]

One aspect of the early relationship between Roman and Saxon is illustrated by the identification and topographical study of the layering of the earliest of Saxon place-names. These are not, as has previously been supposed, those ending in -*ing*; current opinion suggests that such forms belong more to the phases of expansion and consolidation of settlement in the seventh century. The earliest Saxon names are those which describe either natural features of the terrain, or, more interestingly, those which appear to contain a Latin element. The most useful of these is the element *wic*-, deriving from the Latin term *vicus*. This was the description originally applied to all settlements in Britain which were not Roman towns or cities, and implied a certain legal status for the community. Among the earliest of the Anglo-Saxon place-names appears to be the name *Wicham*, which might be translated as 'the village (*hām*) by the *vicus* (*wic*)'.[49] Of the present places bearing names derived from this compound – for example Wycomb near Andoversford (Glos.), Wickham Market (Suffolk), Wickham Hill (Braughing, Herts.) – several are known to apply to sites near substantial Roman remains, and the majority – there are about thirty – lie on or near Roman roads. The three sites mentioned are spectacular cases, for the name in each instance applies to the site of a fully-fledged

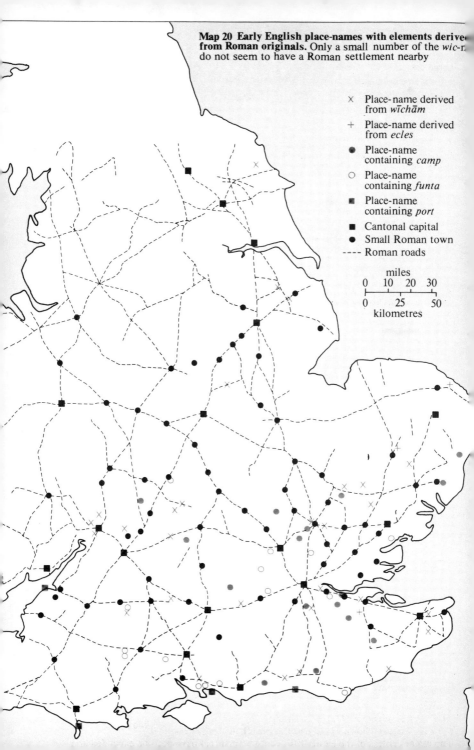

Map 20 Early English place-names with elements derived from Roman originals. Only a small number of the *wic*-names do not seem to have a Roman settlement nearby

×	Place-name derived from *wīchām*
+	Place-name derived from *ecles*
◕	Place-name containing *camp*
○	Place-name containing *funta*
◪	Place-name containing *port*
■	Cantonal capital
●	Small Roman town
----	Roman roads

miles
0   10   20   30

0   25   50
kilometres

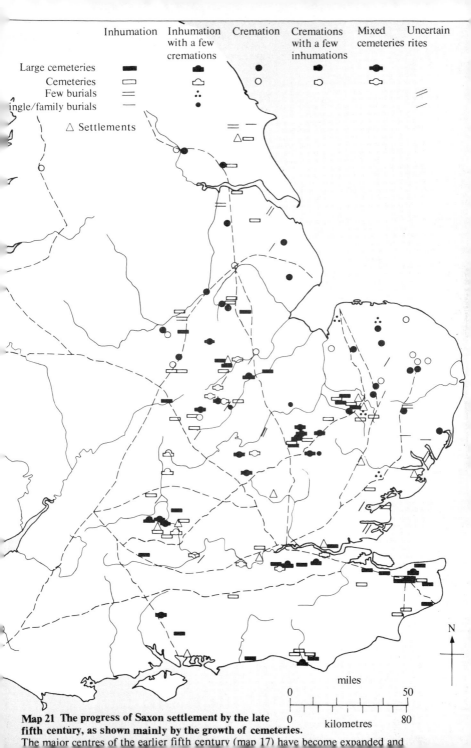

	Inhumation	Inhumation with a few cremations	Cremation	Cremations with a few inhumations	Mixed cemeteries	Uncertain rites
Large cemeteries	▬	◆	●	◗	◖	
Cemeteries	▭	◇	○	◖	◖	
Few burials	≡	∴				⫽
ingle/family burials	—	●				

△ Settlements

miles
0   50

kilometres
0   80

N

**Map 21 The progress of Saxon settlement by the late
fifth century, as shown mainly by the growth of cemeteries.**
The major centres of the earlier fifth century (map 17) have become expanded and

Romano-British town, and seems to substantiate the view that the name sprang up by derivation from the Roman settlements, as if the early Anglo-Saxons described their village as 'the one by the Roman *vicus*'. Other Latin words possibly borrowed by Saxons when the names for their communities were being formed were *camp-* (open plain), *funta-* (fountain), *port-* (harbour) and *eccles-* (church). The distribution of place-names containing these elements and their relationship to Roman establishments throws light on the character of Saxon settlement.

The areas of Anglo-Saxon occupation in the first half of the fifth century are relatively well defined by the rough distribution of the early cemeteries in what one may term as quite restricted areas of eastern Britain. The discovery of small areas of concentrated settlement is not so surprising, for Saxon immigrants will not necessarily have become immediately integrated with the indigenous population, though there is reason to suppose that at the lowest levels – those of subsistence farming for example – there must have been some contact. Any agricultural community needs seed-corn, and it is unlikely that incoming Saxons brought theirs with them. In so far as one can assume a general pattern to this process, the Saxons were accepted, but restricted to marginal land (in the areas where we have the evidence). This may be a sign of deliberate official control, but need not necessarily be so interpreted: it could be attributed to a far more fundamental protective spirit on the part of the established population, who jealously refused the immigrants the use of the best lands, while affording them some grudging recognition.

6 Continuity of settlement

In the preceding chapter, the evidence for the arrival of the Anglo-Saxons within Britain was examined. There is evidence for Saxon presence within some of the easternmost Romano-British cities in the first half of the fifth century, including Caistor-by-Norwich, Canterbury and Colchester. Other Roman cities in the same area where the evidence is less complete are Winchester, Chichester, Leicester, York and Lincoln, and these also may have received early settlers. In these places such evidence as there is – and it must be stressed that it is relatively fragmentary – suggests some continuity of settlement between native Romano-Britons and Anglo-Saxons.

Much of the tenor of recent work on the period has attempted to emphasise this continuity between the Roman and Anglo-Saxon periods. It is relatively easy to display an almost unbroken sequence of Roman town, Saxon settlement and mid- and later Saxon town, resulting in the formation of the medieval and modern places.[1] Even if there were periods of neglect in some of the eastern towns, such as at Colchester or Leicester, it is a fair assumption that *someone* lived within the derelict ruins. The survival of places like Canterbury, Colchester, Leicester and Lincoln as major cities, although they were nearest to the Saxon settlers of the fifth century, is far from accidental. Roman cities, linked by their road network and the focus, in Roman times, for commerce and administration over a wide area, were still remembered, and still formed natural centres for settlement. [2]

This in no way invalidates the search for continuity between the two periods: it merely means that we must be clear

50 The 'Anglian' tower at York. This tower, built to plug a gap which had formed in the Roman defences, is certainly of very late or post-Roman date, and it may be dated as late as the eighth or ninth century

about what we mean by it and about what will count as evidence for it. The choice of a settlement site in Romano-British times might be the product of the same set of chance circumstances – favourable soils, good communications, or the like – which would lead Saxons also to choose the site. This sort of continuity, however, can scarcely be said to be deliberate. There are indications, as we have seen, that the earliest Saxon settlement was taking place on less favourable land on the edges of established properties. Thus the deliberate settlement of Saxons was being directed away from established sites in the best areas which would normally be chosen. 'Continuity', therefore, might here be interpreted as the deliberate lack of continuity on Roman sites on good land. Later, when Anglo-Saxon influence had grown sufficiently, and when intermarriage had blurred the racial distinctions, a shift back to the more favourable sites would be possible.

The collapse of the administrative structure of Roman Britain might, however, allow new settlers vacant space to infiltrate. A large amount of property in Britain, as in any other province, was owned by the state or the emperor.[3] After 410, to whom did this belong? Much of imperial property was composed of mining industries and other enterprises vital to the empire's economic stability. Were these just taken over by the *civitates* of Britain, or was there still a central authority which could deal with them?

One class of site of especial interest at this time is the military fort. After the withdrawal of Roman support for its British army, there can have been no further military interest in the now abandoned fort-sites. At the south-coast fort of Portchester, for example, there is some evidence for fifth-century Saxon settlement, but this is the only such site to have produced signs of Saxon settlement this early.[4] At Dover, also, within the walls of the late Roman shore-fort, sixth-century Saxon sunken huts have come to light. At Richborough, however, a church was established for a short-lived period within the abandoned fort in the early fifth century. This pattern of use was repeated in other parts of the empire, where bishops were glad to establish their congregations within the safety of the now abandoned fort walls.[5] Other sites, despite their defensive capabilities, were in the seventh century adjudged to be of no further use, for we find that kings were prepared to give them away to missionary saints for the foundation of their monasteries. Such was the case at Bradwell, Reculver and at Burgh Cas-

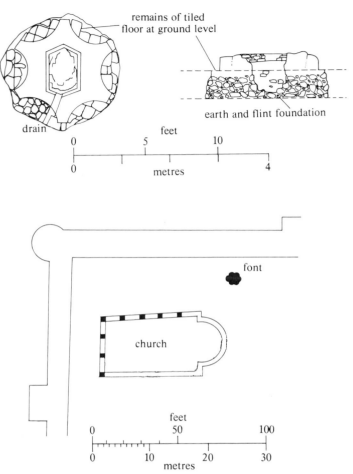

remains of tiled
floor at ground level

earth and flint foundation

drain

feet

0   5   10

0   metres   4

font

church

feet

0   50   100

0   10   20   30

metres

Figure 15   The baptistery and the probable position of the late Roman church at Richborough. The church, marked by a line of stone blocks acting as post supports, was removed by the early excavators. The font, probably in a separate building between the church and the fort wall, survives. It is a tiled hexagonal basin, with a facility to allow water to run off

tle.[6] The possession of these sites was regarded as important enough to remain the prerogative of the king within the
seventh century, and there may well have been cases, more
often in the west or in Wales, where the defended fort site
formed a convenient base for the establishment of a king's

194

51 The Saxon chapel of St Peter's, Bradwell-on-Sea, Essex. The site of Bradwell was given to the Saxon monk St Cedd (Chad) to found a missionary community of monks in 630. This chapel, though possibly not Cedd's original building, is formed of material from the Roman fort, and is of seventh-century date

court or that of a local chief.[7] The process by which such sites had reached the hands of seventh-century or earlier rulers is still obscure.

The problems posed by such considerations are worth examining also in relation to the western parts of Britain not immediately beset by the Saxon invaders. Here, Roman lifestyles and traditions perhaps stood a better chance of survival than in the east, for the people who withstood the Saxon advance of the later fifth century were descendents of men who had themselves been decurions and citizens of Roman Britain. A form of Roman lifestyle could therefore quite feasibly continue until well into the fifth century and possibly beyond.

When one begins to trace it in any detail, the evidence is surprisingly fragmentary, and the number of Roman cities where there is some attested archaeological evidence for continued 'Roman' life is few. Probably the best is St Albans (Verulamium), where in one *insula* as late as the later fourth

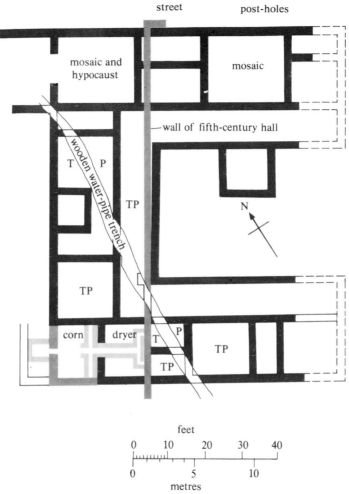

Figure 16 The late Roman building at Verulamium, St Albans (Herts.), showing the position of the wall of the fifth-century hall, and the line of the wooden water-pipe trench cutting it, and thus later than its demolition

century it appears that a large courtyard building containing a range of rooms, some with mosaic floors, was constructed after AD 370. This underwent alterations, including the addition of mosaics, some of which were patched up and therefore saw some considerable use. The building was then demolished to enable the construction of a large barn-like structure on the site. This too was eventually demolished, and a wooden water-pipe laid across its site, suggesting that by now, well into the fifth century, the town water-supply was still functioning.[8] This sort of evidence, admittedly from only a single *insula* of the Roman city, suggests that organised Roman life of a sort was still in full swing in the fifth century. St Germanus visited the shrine of St Alban in 428, and met a number of the well-dressed local inhabitants. The account of his visit given by his biographer has therefore received some partial confirmation by excavation, which provides a context within which a Christian community in fifth-century Britain may have maintained sufficient links with the Gallic church to call in one of the more illustrious bishops of the day to combat the problems of Pelagianism. Two buildings within Verulamium might be identified as Roman churches: one is a basilical building within one of the town *insulae*, and the other is a small apsidal chapel within the town cemetery outside the London gate.

Our assessment of the quality of fifth-century life in other Roman towns is hampered both by the lack of comprehensive excavation and also by a dearth of material to supply an exact date. Much of the precision of dating possible for the earlier Roman period comes from the use of coins as dating agents or by the use of common types of pottery which are themselves cross-dated by association with coins and by typological progression. Study and analysis of the main British producers of pottery in the fourth century is continually refining and narrowing down the dating which can be given to any particular layer or site. Most of the centres of pottery production were still operating in about AD 400, but were largely producing only a fairly standardised range of vessels whose characteristics and decorative forms had changed little for forty years. By 425, however, none of these main centres, Oxford, the Nene Valley, the New Forest, or the Yorkshire kilns of Crambeck, were any longer in production. Before this date, the whole British industry for producing Roman pottery had suffered a dramatic collapse in common with a more general recession which hit the

197

flourishing Mediterranean industries. For much of the fifth century, therefore, there are scarcely any new forms of British-made pottery to provide distinctive evidence of deposits of that date. Even the Roman pottery produced in the first quarter of the fifth century is mainly in the same shapes and forms as the pottery of the second half of the fourth and this makes it difficult to substantiate a claim based on pottery evidence alone that certain layers belong to fifth-century occupation.

Nor are the coins very much help. There was no functioning mint in Britain after 325, and all the coinage used to pay the military forces had to come into the province from one of the main western mints in Italy or Gaul. Already by the early fifth century the supply of new coin to Britain was beginning to dry up. The latest known gold coins are those of Constantine III (the British usurper) and Honorius while the last silver issue which reached Britain in any numbers was that from Milan minted around AD 400. Bronze coinage is even worse represented, for the latest issues reported from Britain are generally those of Theodosius minted in 395. This pattern of coin supply strongly suggests that the numbers of troops garrisoned in Britain at this stage were both being neglected and rapidly dwindling. The main reason for the supply of coin to a province was to pay the soldiers, and a fairly continuous supply of new coinage would normally be necessary to provide the salaries for a large garrison. Such a supply was clearly not forthcoming for Britain in the early years of the fifth century because the coinage could not be brought from Italy itself, thus forcing the authorities to rely on recycling such coinage as was already in circulation. This gave the impression – possibly to the military themselves – that there was a certain amount of forced neglect of the troops stationed there. At all events, the fact that virtually no coinage of the fifth century, and certainly none after the gold coins of Constantius III (407–11), were entering Britain provides another difficulty for the archaeologist: the most obvious tool for dating is absent.

There remains the problem, however, of the length of

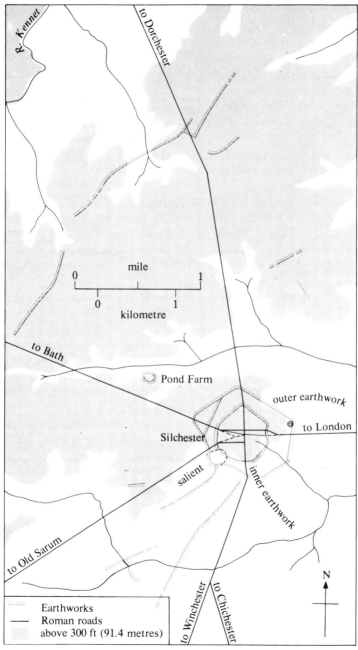

Figure 17 The Silchester dyke system. The most substantial portion of this defensive system, possibly to fend off fifth-century Saxon attacks from the Thames Valley area, is Grim's Bank, which runs across the north-western quadrant of the town of Silchester some 3 km from its boundaries. This earthwork still stands some 3 m high in places

time for which objects, including coins, normally considered to be of fourth-century date may have been in use in the fifth century. Because of the shortage of supply of coin, its use had probably been dwindling over the last decades of the fourth century, and in all probability it was no longer used after about AD 430 at the latest. This implies that there was a return to a barter system for trading.[9] Although pottery production on an organised scale seems to have come to an end, there are also some more local wares which may have been produced in the fifth century, including grass- and shell-tempered vessels. Though there is a strong likelihood that the 'late Roman' pottery types known to us, including those of more local manufacture, continued in use into the fifth century, it is difficult to argue this in any particular case since there is scarcely any recoverable object which would clinch so late a dating.

In other Roman towns in the western part of Britain, there are a number of indications of their continuing life after the end of the fourth century. At Silchester, for example, the excavations early in this century recovered large numbers of late Roman coins, mostly in a very worn state, suggesting that coinage may still have been used there for some time. Although it lies close to the Thames Valley area where Saxon settlement was probably taking place in the early decades of the fifth century, there is no trace at Silchester of such settlement round the city itself. A dyke system, lying some 3 km from the city centre, cordons off the north-western quadrant, stretching between the two main routes to the city from this direction, and controlling the road to Dorchester-on-Thames, part of this early Saxon enclave. This dyke therefore may have been intended to delimit the city's territory and to control access to the city from the directions from which Saxons might approach, for its position suggests that the construction of this barrier dates from the late fourth or the early fifth century. Various dates within the sub-Roman period have been suggested for this ditch system, but since it controls the northern road rather than the western one (towards Bath) it was probably constructed at a period when the main threat lay to the north (i.e. 420–50) rather than a time when the Saxons were expanding westwards (before the battle at Badon about 500).[10]

Further west, at Cirencester, the picture is more one of gradual Roman decay. By a Saxon tradition, the cities of Bath, Cirencester and Gloucester passed into Saxon control after the battle of Dyrham, for which the traditional date is AD 577. This followed on the westward spread of Saxon influence after the temporary halt during the first half of the sixth century. There is no sign, however, that the cities which the Saxons took over at this date were flourishing centres. Cirencester's street-surface off the main road (Ermine Street) was so ground down, probably by the passage of vehicles, that a roadside ditch and portico became quite choked with debris. The overall impression is of continuing life, but for how long? A further ditch cut to act as a drain for a later road surface was found to be filled with organic matter, as if it had grown choked with weeds, thus suggesting that the roads were not in such heavy use. In addition one such ditch contained a human skeleton, a vivid portrayal of a time when a human body could be left disregarded at the roadside.[11] Though the onset of a plague might be seen as a plausible general context for such a find, and for the neglect of the city area which this evidence seems to show, it cannot necessarily be linked to any of the historically attested (and therefore dated) incidences of plague in the post-Roman world.

There is some similar evidence for neglect and decay at Exeter and also at Gloucester. At Exeter the *palaestra* (exercise-hall) of the baths was growing grass and weeds by the end of the fourth century but structural periods which date after AD 400 have been recognised in other parts of the city.[12] The city lies in an area where memorial gravestones of Celtic Christian style are found: the majority of these date from the mid- or late-fifth century and suggest the missionary activity and colonisation of western and even Irish Celts at that time, one of two waves of such Irish and western settlement which took place in the south-west. The other, shown by the distribution of similar memorial stones in west Cornwall and the Scillies, reached those areas in the sixth century.[13] At Gloucester, although portions of the town may have been subject to flooding (as was also the case at York), the defences were refurbished, possibly at a date late in the fourth century, and in all probability occupation continued until well into the first half of the fifth.

Several of the villas, not only those in the west, have provided evidence for occupation into the fifth century, and some were undergoing repairs and improvements in the last years of the fourth, suggesting that their owners foresaw no sign of the impending catastrophe. Within Somerset, however, occupation of a villa within the second half of the fifth century has been claimed for only two sites, those of Star villa and Butcombe, on the basis of the rather tentative dating of hand-made pottery found there.[14] Elsewhere the majority of villa buildings seem to have gone into a decline, though the estates which belonged to them were probably still in use. The cessation of occupation of the sites of the villa buildings suggests more a transfer of ownership. There was certainly some revival of Romano-Celtic paganism in the hill-top temples of the south-west, and this religious revival, in a small way symptomatic of the old Celtic traditions to which the native population seem naturally to have reverted, may have lasted some time into the fifth century. A number of enigmatic single-celled buildings placed on or near the sites of these temples after their demolition may represent a fifth century 'conversion' of the sites to Christianity.[15]

In this area by the second half of the fifth century the lifestyle of the towns, villas and farms owed its origins to the Roman traditions, but it was beginning more and more to incorporate elements of pre-Roman traditions. Some of the towns, including Ilchester and Bath, may still have been occupied, but new centres of power were beginning to be set up with the reoccupation of the sites of former hill-forts like Cadbury Congresbury and South Cadbury. At both these sites some refortification was carried out, at South Cadbury with a new timberwork defence in association with a flat-topped bank which encircled the whole site.

52 The hill-fort of South Cadbury from the air. Excavations at the gateway revealed that there had been a refortification of the site after *c.* 400, and before *c.* 575. Evidence was found for a timber gate-tower linked to a timber-framed, stone-lined rampart erected on top of the decayed innermost Iron Age defences. A large post-built hall, measuring 19 by 10 m with bowed ends and straight sides, was thought to be contemporary with this refortification

Much the same was found at Cadbury Congresbury, except that there was an added fortification along a completely new line, including a freshly dug ditch and entrance. Within the defences of both sites, dated from pottery, there were timber buildings, some of them, as at South Cadbury, of considerable size and pretension.[16]

Such refortification (or new fortification) is not confined to Somerset alone, for a number of sites in the West Country and in Wales have produced similar evidence, from those like High Peak, near Bidmouth (Devon), which appears to have been fortified in the fifth or sixth century for the first time, to those like Castle Dore (Cornwall), Dinas Powys (S. Glam.), or even as far east as Cissbury (Sussex), which made use of the pre-existing Iron Age or earlier defences.[17] A possible antecedent for this sort of defensive move on the part of an embattled local population or their leaders can be seen at Cirencester, where excavations in the amphitheatre

53 The prehistoric fortification of Castle Dore, Cornwall. On the basis of small-scale excavations it has been claimed that this site was refortified in the fifth or sixth century. Fragmentary traces of two timber buildings – usually identified as post-built halls – were found within the defended area. The dating of these is uncertain, but scraps of pottery found with them are probably of immediate post-Roman date

of the Roman town suggest that there was some very late Roman occupation of the site. It seems to have been used as a bastion of considerable defence: one at least of the entrances was blocked and traces of substantial timber buildings were located inside, on the flat arena floor. The date of this development has yet to be defined, but it could even be contemporary with the late fifth century and later refurbishing of defences round western hill-forts.[18]

Developments of this sort are not necessarily all contemporary, nor can they be assumed in each locality to be the products of the same sets of circumstances. Defended sites may be seen as the strongholds of local chieftains – leaders of war-bands who sought a defensible site away from the Roman towns from which to carry the fight either against the Irish or the advancing Saxons. Alternatively these hill-forts might be seen as one of the elements of a communal defence – a strong-point into which the populace could flee in times of danger. The apparent association of cemeteries (often containing burials with no grave goods and nothing to give a secure dating) with some hill-top sites might suggest a little more permanency of occupation than this, but might always belong to some nearby and as yet unidentified 'sub-Roman' site.[19]

If we are to accept that the establishment of these fortified sites presages the emergence of a ruler (and even one who might be of more than local significance, as has been claimed for 'Arthur' at South Cadbury[20]) then we must recognise that somehow the structure of society had thrown up a ruling element. This might come either from within its own ranks, or be imported, possibly from Ireland, where in the fourth century a number of petty kings began to establish territorial authority within firmly constricted bounds. By the time of Gildas, the fact of kingship was accepted, for his diatribe condemns five western kings in the 540s for failing to rule in a proper fashion. At no stage does Gildas suggest that kingship in itself is wrong, or that these kings' positions were those of usurpers. In the same way that in the Anglo-Saxon homelands one family within a village community seems to have been able to establish a privileged position and to maintain it over several generations (pp. 60–3)), so in western Britain ruling families might emerge to challenge whatever political authority the community council might still have. In a society under threat, and therefore dependent upon military prowess for its survival, the war-leader more easily establishes a position of absolute power. In this way, too, the men who came to the fore were re-establishing something of an Iron Age Celtic power-structure, in which a ruling nobility was recognised as pre-eminent. Such men may well have been the sons of decurions of the Roman period – a line probably in fairly direct succession from those now remote pre-Roman Iron Age chiefs.

Even though this may have been the background of men who came to power as local rulers, any authority they held was still in a loose way based on Roman forms of authoritative terminology. Such Latin terms as *sacerdos* (priest) and *magistrat(us)* (magistrate), occur on Celtic tombstones of the fifth century,[21] and the life of St Germanus records that the saint met a man 'of tribunician power'[22] who asked him to restore his daughter's sight. We have already seen the recollection of the title 'Protector' both in some of the Welsh genealogies and on the memorial stone of Vortepor, an Irish chieftain in South Wales (p. 84). None of these Latin terms is used precisely in its Roman sense. Continual usage may however have gained them some technical precision of meaning though it is more likely that they were 'honorific' titles, which did no more than claim for their holders some undefined link with the now past Roman authoritative structure.

What of the social structure beneath such rulers, whose rise to positions of power must have come about during the course of the fifth century? Between such men and the peasant farmers – a class present throughout the Iron Age, Roman and post-Roman periods – there was a kind of middle class of 'landed gentry'. In Dumnonia, the Cornish peninsula, where a separate Celtic kingdom was now beginning to emerge, such people lived in the 'rounds' – a type of defended farmstead-cum-homestead similar to the 'raths' of Ireland.[23] Such sites were in use throughout the whole of the Roman period in this area, which never really saw a full 'Romanisation'. The Roman villa is scarcely known in the region, and recent excavations have shown that there was continuity of occupation on some 'rounds' into the fifth and possibly the sixth century as well.[24] The settlements of this class of populace are not so easily pinpointed within other areas of the Celtic west. The enclosed homestead settlements of fourth- and early fifth-century Wales may have been the homes of their social equivalents there, but in the Romanised parts of the south-west, traces of such people ought to be discovered on the site of Roman villas or in the entourage of the war-leaders.[25]

The crystallisation of society into such classes is possibly easiest to follow for the emerging kingdom of Dumnonia, where Roman influence had not been as deeply felt as in areas further east, but the emergence of separate kingdoms

54 Aerial view of the settlement at Chysauster, at the western tip of Cornwall. Though not known to have been surrounded by a ditch, this settlement is not unlike a Cornish 'round' and was probably occupied during at least the second to fourth centuries AD

in the Celtic west – and particularly those of Wales – may well have been formed in this way from an infra-structure which underlay the whole of society during the Roman period. How far a parallel development might have begun or established itself in more Romanised areas like modern-day Gloucester and Somerset is impossible to tell. Further Saxon advances after the mid-sixth century swamped the area and converted what may have been other emerging Celto-Roman kingdoms into portions of the rapidly growing Saxon kingdom of Wessex.

Something of the enigma posed by these Roman towns in the west and the problems involved in the interpretation of the excavated remains can be seen from Wroxeter, near Shrewsbury, the *civitas* capital of the tribe of the Cornovii. The latest of a long series of excavations on the site of the great *basilica* which adjoined the public baths have revealed an enigmatic series of structures cut into and formed out of the rubble of demolished portions of the *basilica* itself.[26] The excavators defined some thirty buildings built into the ruins of this great hall, their presence suggested by little more than platforms of graded rubble which acted as foundation for timber-built structures above. Subtle and minute differ-

207

ences in the composition of this rubble show the change between one building and the next.

The first building to be discovered was a bow-sided wattle-and-daub building, somewhat similar to a Germanic long-house, which lay in an area just east of the baths *basilica*, but which was aligned on a north-south street of the Roman town. One end of this building (which was itself the successor to two similar structures on the site) had been cut away by a large pit or water cistern which had been probably used in the tanning process. There is thus an established sequence of buildings and periods of use for this site.

Within the area of the *basilica* itself, the main building has been identified (from the rubble platform) as a large timber-framed structure with a portico along its south front, and wings which projected slightly forward from the building line. This was linked to the main Watling Street through Wroxeter by a narrow extension to the west. This structure, occupying most of the nave of the earlier baths *basilica*, dominated the area, the rest of which was filled with a complex of buildings fronting onto the central yard to both south and north of the large building, and which leant against and incorporated parts of the *basilica* which still stood. Though their rubble platforms only survive, some of these buildings were evidently constructed in a pretentious architectural style, with columned porches, symmetrical façades, and other features which would align them with more orthodox stone-built 'classical' buildings. Possibly the most peculiar of all is a building which appears to possess a surrounding colonnade of massive post holes, its partial plan (much of it lies under the modern road) suggesting that it may have looked remarkably like a wooden-built version of a proper classical temple. Incorporated with the complex of buildings is also an area of booths which may have had a controlled access (again from Watling Street) and which seems to have been a covered precinct throughout its existence.

The very possibility that such a collection of timber buildings might be constructed on the site of a demolished *basilica* in the centre of the Roman city of Wroxeter throws a sub-

208

stantial amount of light on the later phases of the city's history. The evidence points to a decline in city life, but one tempered in very great measure by the sophistication of the timber buildings which sprang up in the place of the masonry ones. The date at which the baths *basilica* went out of use seems to have been about AD 350. This complex of buildings therefore dates from after that period, a date confirmed by the discovery of a coin of *c*. 367 found built into one of the rubble platforms. A wide range of Roman pottery characterises finds from these latest layers, including not only the commoner fourth-century wares, but also substantial amounts of shell-gritted fabrics.

Though a date reaching well into the fifth century can be claimed for this arrangement of timber buildings within the heart of Wroxeter, there is nothing within the excavated material which definitely suggests a date within the second half of the fifth century for any of the complex. The number of separately laid floor levels between the latest phases of the use of the baths *basilica* and the abandonment of the timber buildings (itself an orderly procedure, with the buildings apparently systematically dismantled) was surprisingly large in places, but small in others. This may signify a long life for the timber buildings.

The discovery of these buildings is a most significant advance of our knowledge of the later phases of one of the major Roman towns in Britain, but it still presents many problems. We do not know the purpose of this set of buildings. There is evidence to suggest it may either have been commercial or religious. Or was the whole complex of buildings, and particularly the large porticoed building in the centre the palace, an administrative centre for one of the fifth-century petty kings? Ironically, though skilled excavation has given us the possibility of knowing about these buildings, it will not give unequivocal evidence about the people who lived in and used them, nor will it necessarily be able accurately to date them. The Roman town itself was abandoned by about the end of the fifth century for the more easily defended site of Shrewsbury some few miles to the north-west, and one of the latest finds from the site of

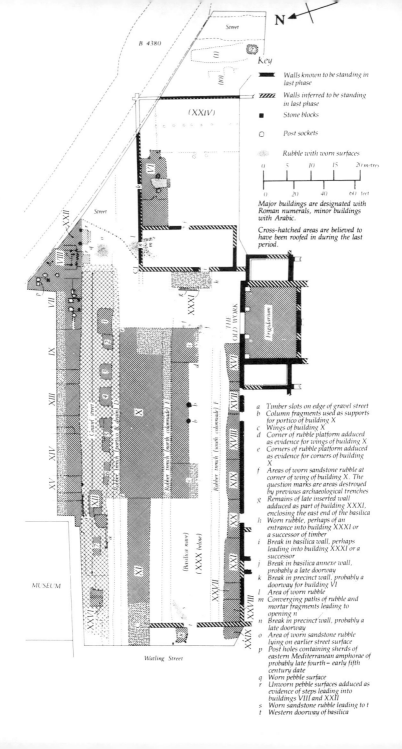

N

B 4380

Street

(1)

(10)

(XXIV)

VI

Street

XXXIII

VIII

XXXII

VII

IX

XIII

XIV

XV

XII

MUSEUM

Watling Street

Court Street

Robber trench (portico & drain) D

Robber trench (north sidewalk) E

Robber trench (south sidewalk) F

(Basilica nave)
(XXX below)

X

XI

XXXV

XXXVI

XXXI

CI

III
OLD WORK

frigidarium

XXV

XVII

XVIII

XIX

XXVII

XXVIII

XXIX

Key

— Walls known to be standing in
last phase

▨ Walls inferred to be standing
in last phase

■ Stone blocks

○ Post sockets

▒ Rubble with worn surfaces

0   5   10   15   20 metres

0   20   40   60 feet

Major buildings are designated with
Roman numerals, minor buildings
with Arabic.

Cross-hatched areas are believed to
have been roofed in during the last
period.

a   Timber slots on edge of gravel street
b   Column fragments used as supports
    for portico of building X
c   Wings of building X
d   Corner of rubble platform adduced
    as evidence for wings of building X
e   Corners of rubble platform adduced
    as evidence for corners of building
    X
f   Areas of worn sandstone rubble at
    corner of wing of building X. The
    question marks are areas destroyed
    by previous archaeological trenches
g   Remains of late inserted wall
    adduced as part of building XXXI,
    enclosing the east end of the basilica
h   Worn rubble, perhaps of an
    entrance into building XXXI or
    a successor of timber
i   Break in basilica wall, perhaps
    leading into building XXXI or a
    successor
j   Break in basilica annexe wall,
    probably a late doorway
k   Break in precinct wall, probably a
    doorway for building VI
l   Area of worn rubble
m   Converging paths of rubble and
    mortar fragments leading to
    opening n
n   Break in precinct wall, probably a
    late doorway
o   Area of worn sandstone rubble
    lying on earlier street surface
p   Post holes containing sherds of
    eastern Mediterranean amphorae of
    probably late fourth – early fifth
    century date
q   Worn pebble surface
r   Unworn pebble surfaces adduced as
    evidence of steps leading into
    buildings VIII and XXII
s   Worn sandstone rubble leading to t
t   Western doorway of basilica

the Roman city is the tombstone of an Irish chieftain, dating possibly to the turn of the sixth century. Despite the temptation to link these buildings at the heart of the Roman town with an emerging 'sub-Roman' power base, it is still possible that they were built within the Roman period, and that they represent the latest phases of public or institutional use of the central areas of this important Roman site. Our overall knowledge of late Roman timber buildings is quite slight, and such structures as these may have been the norm at other places too – within the forts of the 'Saxon Shore', for example, where there are few stone buildings, but timber buildings of some sophistication may well have existed. It is important to remember too that construction in timber was the traditional British building-method, carried through into the sub-Roman period. [27]

One of the most obvious points of continuity between the late Roman period and the Celtic successors is that provided by Christianity. The number of finds which suggest the presence of at least areas of Christianity within late Roman Britain is now considerable, including not only the 'portable' objects such as finger-rings, bone ornaments or belt-buckles bearing some Christian symbolism, but also, and more importantly, buildings and more immovable objects which show evidence of adherence on the part of their owner to the Christian faith. [28] Among such sites are not only the churches in Romano-British cities like Silchester or Verulamium, but house-churches within Roman villas, such as that at Lullingstone or the similar rooms at Frampton or Hinton St Mary which contain mosaics depicting Christian figures or allegories. The church with its sur-

Figure 18 (*opposite*) The latest phase of buildings found on the site of the baths *basilica* at Wroxeter, Salop. The bow-sided building is at the top of the plan (no. 1), and the other buildings whose plans have been recovered from the spread of rubble on which they were built are all defined by cross-hatching. By far the largest is the winged building X which appears to have faced south. The row of buildings XVI-XXIX leant in the main against standing portions of the baths *basilica*, whose walls are shown in solid black. A covered street or pedestrian precinct (possibly a market area) lay behind the large building X, and this incorporates a building with a monumental entrance VII, and the building which may be a 'classical' style temple in wood, no. VIII

Map 22 'Christian objects in Roman Brita
The map shows, in the main, the non-mov
objects which testify to some permanency
Christian belief or occupancy

⚲	Bishoprics
+	Churches
▪	Lead 'baptismal' ta
▬	Cemeteries contain possibly Christian
●	Mosaics or inscribed slabs
⌷	Tombstones
×	Martyrdoms
■	Cantonal capitals
●	Small Roman tow
---	Roman roads

miles
0   50
0   80
kilometres

Carlisle

York

Lincoln

Chesterton

Icklingham

Caerwent

Cirencester

St Albans

London

Silchester

Lullingstone

Dorchester

rounding cemetery at Icklingham has already been mentioned (p. 168), and the finds of such 'Christian' objects as lead tanks for baptismal purposes (of which there were three at Icklingham) may suggest that where these have been found, for example at the settlement of Ashton, near Oundle (Northants.),[29] a Christian community may have flourished. The relatively recent and spectacular find of silver treasure within the Roman town at Water Newton has been plausibly interpreted as the church plate of one of the richer Christian communities.[30] The Mildenhall treasure, equally, if not more spectacular, may have been, in origin, the same sort of thing. One may mention also the identification of Christian cemeteries as a fruitful source of information. The best known is that lying outside Dorchester (Dorset) at Poundbury, where several seasons of excavations have taken place. Work at the site has revealed that the cemetery of more than 4,000 burials grew apparently out of the private graveyard belonging to a courtyard house in the suburbs of the Roman town, and expanded to include several burials in lead-lined and stone coffins. Some burials were 'plaster' burials – a method in which the attempt was made to preserve the body by encasing it in plaster. Several small rectangular mausolea have been found, one of them at least decorated with wall-paintings which depict a group of male figures. The centre of the cemetery is occupied by the burial of a man and two children within a burnt wooden structure: these were evidently people of importance, but the ritual connected with their burial is unfathomable. By current estimates this cemetery fell into disuse by the end of the fourth century.[31] The presence of this cemetery at Dorchester enhances the view that the city may have harboured one of the stronger pockets of Christian believers in the fourth century – a view given added support by the fact that the firm of mosaicists which was able to produce the Christian pavements of Frampton and Hinton St Mary was also operating from the town.

What is the connection, however, between these outward forms of Christianity and the forms which persisted into the fifth century? A common pattern for the growth of a Christ-

ian centre was from the site of a *martyrium* or memorial chapel within the cemetery outside a Roman town. A *martyrium* was normally a small simple building, constructed to protect and commemorate the last resting place of a Christian martyr (as, for example that of St Peter on the site of the Vatican hill outside Rome). British martyrs were still remembered into the fifth century and beyond – for example St Alban, whose shrine was visited by Germanus in 429, or the men named Aaron and Julius of Caerwent who were mentioned by Gildas. There are few candidates for the sequence of Roman *martyrium* to fifth-century and later church within Britain. One of these is St Alban's itself, where the Abbey lies outside the Roman town of Verulamium and could lie on the site of the memorial chapel to St Alban. Another possible candidate is the small ruined church of Stone-by-Faversham in Kent, which incorporates within its structure a rectangular Roman building which may have been an early Christian *martyrium* near to, if not actually within, a Roman cemetery on Watling Street.[32]

Our search for a church building which might have remained in use into the fifth century is hampered by a lack of knowledge of the scale of building for which to look.

Opposite
55 (*top*) The hoard, mainly of silver, found at Chesterton, Cambs. Of the thirty or so pieces, nine are silver vessels – jugs, bowls, a cup and a strainer. Many bear the chi-rho monogram, and two jugs and one of the small plaques bear longer inscriptions, all of them apparently Christian dedications. While it seems reasonably certain that this group of silver (and some gold) plate belonged to a Christian community, the reason for its burial and concealment as a group in antiquity is not clear: it may have been buried to escape looting or persecution. Whatever the reason, it was clearly never reclaimed
56 (*centre*) The head of Christ, from the Hinton St Mary mosaic pavement. The figure, flanked by pomegranates, has characteristics (the cleft chin, for example) which link it with the figures on mosaics from Frampton (see also Plate 11)
57 (*bottom*) Wall-paintings from one of the Poundbury mausolea. This fragment, unique in Roman Britain, shows the upper part of a group of men (possibly *decuriones?*) with their staffs, depicted on the interior of the mausoleum walls. Their significance is hard to determine, but they suggest that the person buried here was of some considerable importance and influence

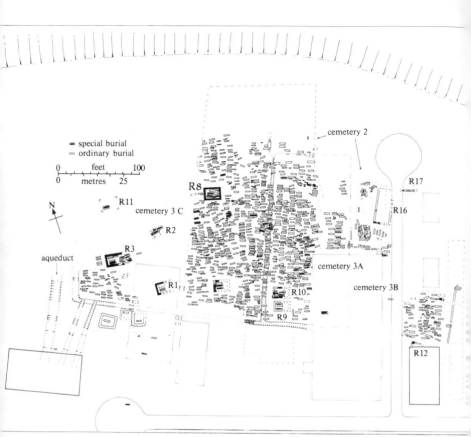

Figure 19 Plan of the cemetery of Poundbury, Dorset, showing the boundary ditches and the graves orientated east-west. The mausolea are marked in black squares: the wall painting (Plate 57) came from the mausoleum here marked as R8

Reliable sources record that there were British bishops in the fourth century, and such bishops, one may presume, were based on 'cathedral' churches within the major British *civitates*, if not within all of them. What would such an episcopal church look like? Could it conceivably be as small or as ill-furnished as the Silchester church, which appears to have had no baptistery? Or are we to search for a somewhat grander version of a house-church?[33] In other parts of the Roman world during the fourth century great basilical

216

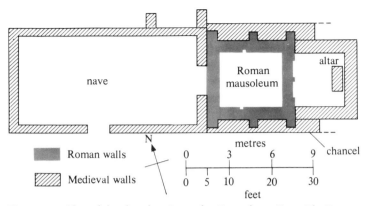

Figure 20 Plan of the church at Stone-by-Faversham, Kent. The Roman building, most distinctive within the medieval structure by its tile courses, forms part of the chancel of the church

churches were built, and at Trier, Ravenna, Aquileia and other major centres, there were grand episcopal churches with a double nave. It is possible that such a building may be discovered within Roman Britain – at London or one of the other provincial capitals – but the episcopal church in Britain was probably a much humbler affair, reflecting more nearly the reduced state of the faithful. Small wonder that at the council of Rimini in 359 British bishops faced with the opulence of their continental colleagues readily claimed the subsistence which the state offered.[34]

The amount of contact between the Christian community in Britain and the Christian communities in Gaul during the first half of the fifth century has already been touched on (p. 146). A number of Gallic bishops, not only Germanus, had cause to be active in Britain during the last years of the fourth and the early years of the fifth centuries, and the very strength of the Pelagianism which had laid hold of Britain at this date suggests that not only was it voluble, but that it was also widespread. Gradually, however, the contact through Gaul with the Roman church was severed, and the British church of the fifth century was left to rebuild on the foundations of a monasticism brought to the islands at the time of the greatest Gallic contact. Two aspects of fifth-century Christianity emphasise the break with a more

217

58 Two of the early Christian funerary stones from southern Scotland. The *Te Dominum* stone from Whithorn (a) is perhaps of mid-fifth-century date, and is the earliest of the Scottish stones of this type. The *sacerdotes* stone (b) from Kirkmadrine is a little later in date. Both stones represent an attempt to continue the tradition of Roman, and in particular Roman Christian, burial practice

218

59 The handle-mount from the bucket found in a well at Mountsorrel in the Charnwood Forest, Leics. Though it dates from *c.* AD 300, the date at which the well was filled up, the ox-head portrayed on the mount has much in common with the artistic style of animal heads produced by Celtic craftsmen of the first century BC

immediate Christian tradition from within Britain. One is the appearance of the early Christian memorial stones, whose layout and design is loosely based, not on the Roman tombstone, but on the normal pattern for a Roman milestone. The other main distinction is the lapse of the tradition for stone building of churches. When the Continental tradition once again began to influence the western church, it found its first expression in the construction of timber churches alone.[35]

This reversion to more traditional Celtic forms of construction in the fifth and later centuries (not until the eighth century in Ireland does one find the first tentative buildings in stone) is symptomatic of the limited measure to which Roman achievements with stone carving or building had

60 The bronze cauldron from Loveden Hill, Lincs. The cauldron is of fourth-century date, but the design on the cauldron mount, like that from the Mountsorrel bucket (Plate 59), has strong affinities with pre-Roman Iron Age artistic styles

been transmitted to the Celtic substratum of the population during the period of Roman occupation. The 'Romanness' of Celtic Christianity was transmitted through contacts maintained with the south-west, where sixth-century Mediterranean pottery has been found at several sites, suggesting flourishing trade contact at that date. Only rarely does a recognisably Celtic motif break through the Roman veneer of Roman Britain and appear on a stone carving.

Such decorative motifs are more readily seen on later Roman styles of metalwork, in particular the remarkably Celtic-looking decorative roundels which appear on bronze fourth- (and possibly fifth-) century bucket and bowl mounts.[36] Throughout the Roman period in Britain, in all forms of craftsmanship, there is something of a Celtic undercurrent which occasionally breaks the surface, with the recurrence of a specific motif or technique. Such native traits would be readily incorporated within the Romano-British culture, accepted as just one of many elements which made up the cosmopolitan nature of the later Romano-British world.

Given this rejection, if it can be said to be a conscious one, of certain Roman traditions which were foreign to the Celts, it is interesting to look with closer attention to the ways in which Rome's presence had unconsciously made itself felt over the preceding centuries. The Celtic language, which remained firmly embedded within the usage of the native population, contains many loan-words derived from Latin. Neither the date nor the method of absorption of such words can easily be ascertained. A remarkably wide range of Latin terms for various aspects of agricultural, administrative, religious and intellectual activity have found their way into the Celtic tongue. There are even terms derived from the Latin for parts of the body, or for such important animals as the horse. This should not be taken to mean that there was no respectable British word for 'cheek', 'arm' or 'horse'. The arrival of such words rather signifies some administrative or social level at which some aspect of these particular features was important enough to plant the Latin term into the spoken British vocabulary. [37]

Early Welsh charters, like those of early Anglo-Saxon England, carry within them some indications that the estates which emerged in the post-Roman period in south-east Wales in particular are basically of late Roman origin. Though the number of villas in this area in Roman times is not known to have been great, there is a more or less closely knit relationship between later estates and Roman settlements of various types, including villas, small settlements, and possibly even forts. Several factors within the charters combine to stress the continuity of these land boundaries: they include the use of Latin terminology for measurement, and the very mechanism of writing the charters themselves, both of which are probably derived straight from late Roman originals. More complex is the fact that in the earliest period (in these cases the sixth century onwards) the king only records the transfer of land. This may mean that only he was allowed to do this, and thus provides another link with late Roman practice which on the whole did not permit of alienation of land. It is interesting, however, that in many cases people other than the man to whom the land was being granted had some claim or rights over portions of it: there were thus in several cases rights of occupancy, established by the sixth century, which were by then shrouded in a respectable enough antiquity – originating in Roman times? – to ensure that they were recognised as a legal right within early charters. [38]

Such forms of institutional and social continuity as these present a fruitful field of study for the historian, and even though a direct line of continuity in an unbroken sequence is difficult to prove from the Roman period, they are beginning to show that within both post-Roman, Celtic and Anglo-Saxon society there was probably an inherent orderliness from a very early period, later expressed by the complexity and depth of tenth- and eleventh-century social structure. This will include not only patterns of land-tenure and the continuity of estate and land parcelling, but also such things as the beginnings of lordship, which may have evolved from a common origin, or the very recognition of kingship itself. [39]

In one sense, therefore, a parallel might be drawn between Celt and Saxon within fifth-century Britain. Both peoples were part of the same European root-stock, and both had had their lives and lifestyles coloured and enhanced to a greater or lesser degree by the presence of Rome over the last few centuries. On both, Rome had acted as a stimulus for development in different ways. For those within the empire she had provided luxury goods, a sound economy, a

222

more than local *raison d'être*. For those outside she had provided a ready market for a two-way trade in consumer goods, and the inspiration to new heights of craftsmanship. Little of this, however, was ultimately lasting for either: with the removal of Rome's continuing influence and presence, the underlying Celts and Saxons reached once again their own levels of society – a level necessarily enhanced by the traditions which Rome had left behind, but one which was germane to the underlying root-stock of both Celt and Saxon. At the lowest peasant levels, the subsistence farmers of both types of economy will have had everything in common. There would be small difference to the landsman whether the Lord of the Manor was a Roman tax-collector, a Celtic war-lord, or a Saxon chieftain. Higher up the social scale, too, seen in the desire for a basic orderliness of society and in the evolution of kingship, there is a broad similarity between the Celts and their Saxon adversaries which did much to override the struggles for power which continued through the fifth and sixth centuries.

How much, then, of Roman Britain survived the trauma of the fifth century? The dramatic collapse of the Roman administrative machinery, so sudden that it must have taken most people by complete surprise, left in its wake a people unprepared on the whole and inexperienced in facing the problems of self-government and self-defence. The story of how they adapted themselves to the emergency is still obscure in many details, but, despite conscious efforts to maintain a certain standard of Romanised life into the fifth century, the structure of the society which evolved was something which combined elements of native Celtic and Roman institutions. Whether because of hostile pressure which forced a less elaborate and expansive lifestyle than the Roman model, or because of the lack of expertise among both Celts and Saxons, the material culture of Rome gradually faded from Britain. The administrative legacy of Rome, imparted over three centuries and more of structural organisation of Romano-British society, did not fade so easily, and acted in part as the basis for the new structures which grew in its place.

The best of later Roman Britain

The late Roman period

Many Roman sites were occupied throughout the Roman period, so it is by no means always easy to pick those for a visit which are specifically 'late Roman' (i.e. dating between AD 250 and 400). In looking at Roman towns and villas in particular, it will not always be easy to wear 'late Roman blinkers', but I have here attempted to single out some of the major museums and monuments, classified by type.

Town or city defences
York, the Multangular tower and the riverside wall of the fortress
Lincoln, the 'lower Colonia' and the west gate
Canterbury, Kent
Caerwent, Gwent, added bastions
London, added bastions

Town life
The Museum of London
Corinium Museum, Cirencester, Glos.
Jewry Wall Museum, Leicester
Verulamium Museum, St Alban's, Herts.

Roman military sites
Piercebridge Roman Fort, Durham
Lancaster Roman Fort (the Wery Wall)
Caer Gybi, Holyhead, Gwynedd
Cardiff Castle, surrounding walls
Scarborough Signal Station, N. Yorks.
Burgh Castle, Norfolk
Richborough, Kent
Dover, Kent, Painted House Museum
Pevensey, Sussex
Portchester Castle, Hants.

Roman villas and mosaics

Bignor villa, Sussex
Chedworth villa, Glos.
Lullingstone villa, Kent
Kingston-on-Hull Museum (mosaics from Rudston, Horkstow and Brantingham)
Corinium Museum, Cirencester, Glos. (mosaics from Cirencester and region)
The British Museum (mosaic from Hinton St Mary, Dorset)
Dorchester Museum (mosaics from Dorchester and region)

Romano-Celtic temples

Lydney Park, Glos.
Maiden Castle, Dorset
Jordan's Hill, Dorset

Native settlements

Milking Gap, near Housesteads, Northumberland
Din Lligwy, Angelsey, Gwynedd
Chysauster village, Cornwall
Carn Euny village, Cornwall

The immediate post-Roman period

The remains of the Anglo-Saxon period in Britain consist in the main of museum collections of finds and pottery from excavated Anglo-Saxon cemeteries. Very few sites of early settlement retain anything visible from the period. The most important is the West Stow Archaeological Centre, near Bury St Edmunds, Suffolk, where the site of the village now bears reconstructed huts.

Collections of Anglo-Saxon pottery

The Yorkshire Museum, York
Kingston-upon-Hull Museum, Humberside
The City and County Museum, Lincoln
Jewry Wall Museum, Leicester
Cambridge University Museum of Archaeology and Ethnography
Ipswich Museum, Suffolk
Norwich Castle Museum
Winchester Museum, Hants.
The Barbican House Museum, Lewes, Sussex
Worthing Museum, Sussex

Reused hill-forts

South Cadbury, Somerset
Castle Dore, Cornwall

The Breiddin, Powys
Dinas Powys, Gwent
High Down, Sussex

Dark Age Earthworks (not securely dated)
Bokerley Dyke, Wilts.
The Wansdyke, Wilts.
The Silchester Dykes (Grim's Ditch, Padworth, Berks.)

Notes

Chapter one The provinces of Britain

1   *Pan. Lat.* VI (VII), 9.
2   *Pan. Lat.* VIII (V), 8, 11.
3   J. C. Mann, 'The administration of Roman Britain',
    Antiquity xxxv (1961), 316f.
4   Frere, 1974, 241.
5   Jones, 1964, 396f.
6   These governors are Alypius of Antioch, A.M. XXII, 3, 3;
    and Crysanthus, *Socrates* VII, 12. See Jones, 1964, 389 and
    n. 47; J. P. Migne, *Patrologia Graeca* (Paris, 1857), lxvii,
    33f.
7   Twenty-eight is the figure given by Gildas, 3, for the
    number of *civitates* within Britain. His figure may well
    have been derived from a late Roman administrative list,
    similar to the *Notitia Galliarum* which survives to give
    details about Gaul at a comparable period. Gildas's figure
    is discussed by C. E. Stevens, 'Gildas Sapiens', *EHR* 206
    (1937), 193f., and also C. E. Stevens, 'The *Notitia Digni-
    tatum* in England', in Bartholomew and Goodburn, 1976,
    211f. Such a list was possibly of ecclesiastical origin,
    and may not therefore accurately reflect the current
    administrative divisions either of the Gallic or the British
    diocese; see A. L. F. Rivet, 'The *Notitia Galliarum*, some
    questions', in Bartholomew and Goodburn,
    1976, 119f.
8   For the life of Melania the Younger, see *Vita Melaniae*, with
    references to it in Jones, 1964, 721.
9   Examples of notable men banished to Britain in the fourth
    century: Bishop Instantius and the Spaniard Tiberianus,
    Sulpicius Severus, *Dialogus* III, 141f. See also A.M.
    XXVIII, 3, 4 for Valentinus, and A.M. XXVIII, 1, 21 for
    Frontinus.
10 D. J. Smith, 'The mosaic pavements', in A. L. F. Rivet
    (ed.), *The Roman Villa in Britain* (London, 1969), 95f.

11 The gist of the allusion is that if Juno had seen Jupiter carrying Europa off across the seas as depicted in the mosaic design, she would have had some justification in raising the storm described in Book 1 of Virgil's *Aeneid* (where Juno is trying to prevent Aeneas, Venus's favourite, from reaching Italy to found Rome).

12 On the transport of corn from Britain across to the Rhine, A.M. XVIII, 2, 3; Zosimus, iii, 5.

13 The British *thesaurus* in the *Notitia*, *ND*, Occ. XI, 37.

14 J. C. Mann, '*Duces* and *Comites* in the fourth century', in Johnston, 1977, 11f.

15 J. C. Mann, 'What was the *Notitia* for?', in Bartholomew and Goodburn, 1976, 1f., Jones, 1964, Appendix II (pp. 1417f.). See also Chapter 3 of the present work, n. 25 and the references there.

16 *ND*, Occ. XXIII, XXVIII, XXIX, and XL.

17 J. P. Wild, 'The *Gynaecea*', in Bartholomew and Goodburn, 1976, 57f.

18 Frere, 1974, 317.

19 Martial, xiv, 99; A.M. XXIII, 6, 88.

20 The emperor Probus encouraged the cultivation of the vine in Britain, *SHA, Vita Probi* 18, 8. See Frere, 1974, 331.

21 The literature on the Roman pottery industries of Britain is becoming most extensive. The most recent studies to have appeared are A. Detsicas (ed.), *Current Research in Romano-British Coarse Pottery*, CBA Research Report 10 (1973), and J. Dore and K. Greene (eds), *Roman Pottery Studies in Britain and Beyond*, *BAR* Supp. 30 (1977). Two recent monographs on particular production areas are C. J. Young, *The Roman Pottery Industry of the Oxford Region, BAR* 43 (1977), and M. G. Fulford, *New Forest Roman Pottery*, *BAR* 17 (1975).

22 Jones, 1964, 736, 745, 998f and 1012f.

23 Jones, 1964, 732f.

24 See further Chapter 6 of the present work, pp. 166–73, and also J. M. C. Toynbee, 'Pagan Motifs and Practices in Christian Art and Ritual in Britain', in Barley and Hanson, 1968, 177f.

25 M. J. T. Lewis, *Temples in Roman Britain* (Cambridge, 1966), and D. R. Wilson, 'Romano-Celtic temple architecture', *JBAA* 38 (1975), 3f.

26 Frere, 1974, 297f.

27 Ausonius, *Parentalia*, vii, 1–6.

28 Macmullen, 1967, 119f.

29 A. Alföldi, 'The moral barrier on Rhine and Danube', in *Roman Frontier Studies* (Durham, 1949), 1f.

30 Zosimus, I, 68.
31 Sextus Aurelius Victor, Epitome, *De Caesaribus*, 41, 2.
32 On one aspect of this, see C. E. Stevens, 'The social and economic aspects of rural settlement', in A. C. Thomas, 1966, 108f.
33 Jackson, 1953, 97f; see also J. C. Mann, 'Spoken Latin in Britain as evidenced by inscriptions', *Britannia* ii (1971), 218f.; E. B. Hamp, 'Social gradience in British spoken Latin', *Britannia* vi (1975), 150f.; and D. Green, 'Some linguistic evidence relating to the British church', in Barley and Hanson, 1968, 75f.

Chapter two The enemies of Roman Britain

1 On the Nydam Ships, see B. Greenhill, *Archaeology of the Boat* (London, 1976), 178f.
2 On Feddersen Wierde, see the interim excavation reports on the site published by the excavator, W. Haarnagel, in *Germania* xxxiv (1956), 126f.; xxxv (1957), 275; xxxix (1961), 42f.; xli (1973), 280f.
3 On Wijster: W. A. Van Es, 'Wijster, a native village beyond the Roman frontier', *Palaeohistoria* xi (1967), 29f.
4 On Fochteloo: A. E. Van Giffen, 'Ausgrabungen zu Fochteloo in den Jahren 1935 und 1938', *Germania* xxxvi (1958), 51f.
5 W. H. Zimmermann, 'A Roman Iron-Age and Early Migration settlement at Flögeln, Kr. Wesermunde, Lower Saxony', in Rowley, 1974, 56f.
6 W. A. Van Es, 'Paddepoel, excavations of frustrated terps, 200 BC–AD 250', *Palaeohistoria* xiv (1968), 187f.
7 On Ezinge, M. Todd, 1975, 98f.; A. E. Van Giffen, 'Der Warf in Ezinge, Provinz Groningen, Holland, und seine westgermanische Häuse', *Germania* xx (1936), 40f.
8 Myres, 1969, p. 42f. The best known of these cemeteries are Westerwanna, Mahndorf, Galgenburg-bei-Cuxhaven, Altenwalde, Quelkhorn and Wehden.
9 On Anglian Pottery: see Todd, 1975, 80f.
10 On Thorsbjerg: C. Engelhardt, *Thorsbjerg Mosefund* (Copenhagen, 1863); Todd, 1975, 187f.
11 On Vimose and Esbjøl: C. Engelhardt, *Vimose Fundet* (Copenhagen, 1869); M. Ørsnes, 'The weapon find in Esbjøl Mose at Haderslev', *Acta Archaeologica* xxxiv (1963), 232; Todd, 1975, 192f.
12 A.M. XXVII, 8, 5. In general, see F. T. Wainwright, *The Problem of the Picts* (Edinburgh, 1953); I. Henderson, *The Picts* (London, 1967).

13 E. W. Mackie, 'The origin and development of the broch and wheelhouse building cultures of the Scottish Iron Age', *Proceedings of the Prehistoric Society*, 31 (1965), 93f.

14 In general on this period, see L. R. Laing, *The Archaeology of Celtic Britain and Ireland, 400–1100* (London, 1975), chapter 2.

15 G. Jobey, 'Homesteads and settlements of the frontier area', in Thomas, 1966, 1f.

16 G. Jobey, 'Traprain Law, a reassessment', in D. Harding, *Hillforts* (London, 1976), 191f.

17 A. O. Curle, *The Treasure of Traprain* (Glasgow, 1923).

18 A. S. Robertson, 'Roman finds from native sites in Scotland', *Britannia* i (1970), 198f.

19 *ND*, Or. ix, 29; Occ. v, 197 and 200.

20 On the Coleraine Hoard: H. Mattingley, and J. W. E. Pearce, 'The Coleraine Hoard', *Antiquity* xi (1937), 39f. On the Balline Hoard, see S. P. O Ríordáin, 'Roman material in Ireland', *PRIA*, 51 (1947), 35f.

21 For the hoard from Gross Bodungen (and a list of all other similar finds) see W. Grünhagen, 'Der Schatzfund von Gross Bödungen', *Römisch-Germanisch Forschungen* 21 (Berlin, 1954), 58f.

22 For discussion of ring-forts, M. J. O'Kelly, 'Problems of Irish ring-forts', in D. Moore (ed.), *The Irish Sea Province in Archaeology and History* (Cardiff, 1970), 50–4.

23 On Freestone Hill: B. Raftery, 'Freestone Hill, Co. Kilkenny: an Iron Age hill-fort and Bronze Age cairn', *PRIA* 68 (1969), 1f.

24 S. P. Ó Ríordáin, *Antiquities of the Irish Countryside* (London, 1953), 15f.

25 S. P. Ó Ríordáin, *Tara: The Monuments on the Hill* (Dundalk, 1964); E. E. Evans, *Prehistoric and Early Christian Ireland* (London, 1966), 174.

26 H. O'N. Hencken, 'Lagore crannog, an Irish royal residence of the 7th and 10th centuries AD', *PRIA* 53 (1950), 1f.

27 G. J. Wainwright, 'Walesland Rath', *Britannia* ii (1971), 48f.; G. J. Wainwright, *Coygan Camp* (Cardiff, 1967).

28 On Irish settlement in Wales, see Alcock, 1973, 122f.; L. Alcock, *Dinas Powys* (Cardiff, 1963), 58f.; M. Richards, 'The Irish settlements in south-west Wales', *Journal of the Royal Society of Antiquaries of Ireland*, 90 (1960), 139f.

29 C. Thomas, 'Irish colonists in south-western Britain', *World Archaeology* 5 (1973), 5f.

30 W. F. Nicholaisen, 'Scottish placenames', *Scottish Studies* ix (1965), 91f.

31 M. Miller, 'Date-guessing and pedigrees', *Studia Celtica*
    x–xi (1975–6), 96f.
32 D. M. Dumville, 'Sub-Roman Britain', *History* 62 (1977),182.
33 R. White, *BBCS*, forthcoming.
34 A. H. A. Hogg, *RCHM Caernarvonshire, passim*. M. Miller,
    'The foundation-legend of Gwynedd in the Latin texts',
    BBCS xxvii (1978), 515f.
35 See n. 28 above.
36 For discussion of this genealogy, J. W. James, 'Harleian
    MS. 3859', *BBCS* xxii (1969), 143.
37 Zosimus, i, 68.
38 A.M. XXIX, 4, 7.
39 M. J. Swanton, 'An early Alemannic brooch from York-
    shire', *Ant.J* xlvii (1967), 43f., with note by J. N. L. Myres,
    pp. 49–50.

Chapter three Defence against the barbarians

1   On British coin-hoards, see A. S. Robertson, 'The numis-
    matic evidence of Romano-British coin hoards', in
    R. G. Carson and C. H. V. Sutherland, *Essays in Roman
    Coinage presented to Harold Mattingley* (Oxford, 1956), 262f.;
    A. S. Robertson, 'Romano-British coin-hoards', in J. Casey
    and R. Reece, *Coins and the Archaeologist* (*BAR* 4, 1974),
    12f. For Continental material, see H. Koethe, 'Zur
    Geschichte Galliens in letzten Drittel des 3 Jahrhunderts',
    Berichten der Römisch-Germanisch Kommission 32
    (1942), 199f.
2   A. H. M. Jones, 'Inflation under the Roman empire', *Econ.
    HR* v (1953), 293f., reprinted in P. A. Brunt (ed.), *The
    Roman Economy* (Oxford, 1974), 187f., especially pp. 224f.
    For a view of fourth-century inflation within Britain, see
    A. Ravetz, 'The fourth-century inflation and Romano-
    British coin-finds', *Numismatic Chronicle* vii, vol. 4 (1964),
    201f.
3   On the Gallic empire, see J. F. Drinkwater, 'Coin-hoards
    and the chronology of the Gallic Empire', *Britannia* v
    (1974), 293f. A succinct summary of the history of the
    Gallic empire has not been published in English recently.
    On Proculus and Bonosus, see Frere, 1974, 216.
4   M. Todd, *The Walls of Rome* (London, 1978); I. A. Rich-
    mond, *The City Walls of Imperial Rome* (Oxford, 1931).
5   *SHA, Probus* 13, 5–7; Julian, *Convivium*, 314b; Zosimus, i,67.
6   For the type of walls now constructed, see R. M. Butler,
    'Late Roman town walls in Gaul', *Arch. J* cxvi (1959), 25f.
7   For fuller discussion, see S. Johnson, 'Late Roman fortifi-
    cations and the *limes*', in Johnston, 1977, 63f.

8   See Johnson, 1976, for further detail on this and on much
     of the following passage.
9   I. A. Richmond, 'A new building-inscription from the
     Saxon-Shore fort of Reculver, Kent', *Ant. J* xli (1961),
     224f.; R. P. Wright, *JRS* lv (1965), 220; J. C. Mann, 'The
     Reculver inscription – a note', in Johnston, 1977, 15.
10   Europius ix, 21; Aurelius Victor xxxix, 20.
11   *ND*, Occ., XXVIII.
12   Fuller discussion in S. Johnson, 'Channel commands in
     the *Notitia*', in Bartholomew and Goodburn, 1976, 81f.
13   Johnson, 1976, chapter 2, p. 23f. The literature on
     Carausius grows apace: see N. Shiel, *The Mints and Coin-
     age of Carausius and Allectus* (*BAR* 40, 1977), and P. J.
     Casey, 'Carausius and Allectus – rulers in Gaul?', *Britannia*
     viii (1977), 283f.
14   For fuller discussion of most of these points, see Johnson,
     1976.
15   P. Scott, *A Guide to Roman Piercebridge* (Durham, 1977); on
     Elslack, T. May, 'The Roman forts at Elslack', *YAJ* 21
     (1911), 113f.; and Newton Kyme, J. K. St Joseph, 'Air
     reconnaissance of southern Britain', *JRS* xliii (1953), 87 and
     xlvii (1957), 209.
16   Breeze and Dobson, 1976, 206f.; for Corbridge, see P.
     Salway, *The Frontier People of Roman Britain* (Cambridge,
     1965).
17   Breeze and Dobson, 1976, ch. 7.
18   *Pan. Lat* VIII (V) 11, 4.
19   *RIB* 1912.
20   *RIB* 1613.
21   J. J. Wilkes, 'Early fourth-century rebuilding in Hadrian's
     Wall forts', in Jarrett and Dobson, 1966, 114f.
22   On Bainbridge: *JRS* xlviii (1958), 135; xlix (1959), 108; li
     (1961), 167. On Brough-on-Noe: *Britannia* i (1970), 253. On
     Ilkley and Malton: *JRS* liii (1963), 129; B. R. Hartley, *Pro-
     ceedings of the Leeds Philosophical and Literary Society* xii (2),
     (1966), 23f.
23   G. Simpson, 'Roman Manchester and Templeborough', in
     Hawkes 1973, 69f.
24   On Binchester: B. Dobson and M. G. Jarrett, 'Excavations
     at Binchester, 1955', *TASDN* 11 (1958), 115f.; Lanchester:
     K. A. Steer, 'The Roman fort of Lanchester, a survey',
     TASDN, 7 (1936), 200f.
25   *ND*, Occ. XL. On the whole problem of this section of the
     Notitia, see Frere, 1974, 262f.; J. Gillam, 'Also along the line
     of the wall . . .', *TCWAS*, xlix (1949), 38f.; E. Birley, 'The
     Beaumont inscription, the *Notitia Dignitatum,* and the garri-

son of Hadrian's Wall', *TCWAS*, xxxix (1930), 190f.

26 G. Simpson, *loc. cit.* (n. 23).

27 *Britannia* vii (1976), 306f., viii (1977), 371f.

28 J. S. Wacher, 'Yorkshire towns in the fourth century', in R. M. Butler (ed.), *Soldier and Civilian in Roman Yorkshire*, (Leicester, 1971), 167f.

29 R. Birley, *Vindolanda* (London, 1977), 69f.

30 Macmullen, 1967, 126–7.

31 On this period on the Northern frontier, J. C. Mann, 'The northern frontier after AD 369', *Glasgow Archaeological Journal*, iii (1973), 36f.

32 J. C. Mann, *loc. cit.* (n. 31).

33 Zosimus, ii, 34.

34 Eusebius, *Vita Constantini*.

35 A. Dornier, 'Was there a coastal *limes* in western Britain in the fourth century?', *Roman Frontier Studies* (Tel Aviv, 1967), 25f.

36 K. M. Martin, 'A reassessment of the evidence for the *Comes Britanniarum* in the fourth century', *Latomus* 28 (1969), 408f.

37 Frere, 1974, 268f.

38 Johnson, 1976, 132f.

39 G. Boon, *Isca* (Cardiff, 1972), 65–6.

40 F. H. Thompson, *Roman Cheshire* (Chester, 1965), 28–9.

41 G. D. B. Jones, 'Roman Lancashire', *Arch. J* 127 (1970), 240f.

42 A. H. M. Jones, 'The date and value of the Verona List', *JRS* xliv (1954), 21f.

43 G. Webster, 'A Roman system of fortified posts along Watling Street, Britain', *Roman Frontier Studies* (Tel Aviv, 1967), 38f.

44 J. Mertens and Ch. Léva, 'Le fortin de Braives et le *Limes Belgicus*', in *Mélanges Piganiol*, II, 1063; H. von Petrikovits, *Das Römische Rheinland* (Köln, 1960), 83.

45 G. Webster, 'Small towns without defences', in Rodwell and Rowley, 1975, 53.

46 M. Todd, 'Margidunum and Ancaster', in Rodwell and Rowley, 1975, 211f.

47 *RIB* 235; see also M. Todd, 'The small towns of Roman Britain', *Britannia* i (1970), 123.

48 P. J. Fowler, 'Hillforts 400–700', in Jesson and Hill, 1971, 203f.

49 Julius Maternus, *De Errore Profanarum Religionum*, 37, 6; A.M. XX, 1, 1.

50 L. Langouet, 'The fourth-century Gallo-Roman site at Alet (St Malo)', in Johnston, 1977, 38f.

51 A.M. XXVIII, 3, 2.

52 A.M. XXX, 7, 3.

53 A.M. XX, 1, 2.

54 A.M. XXVII, 8, 1–3, 5–8. See also R. S. O. Tomlin, 'The date of the "Barbarian Conspiracy"', *Britannia* v (1974),303f.

55 Frere, 1974, 291; the passages are A.M. XXVIII, 3, 2 and 3, 7.

56 *Britannia* iii (1972), 302.

57 On this type of metalwork, S. C. Hawkes and G. Dunning, 'Soldiers and settlers in Britain, fourth to fifth century', *Med. Arch.* v (1961), 1f.; S. C. Hawkes, 'Some recent finds of late Roman buckles', *Britannia* v (1974), 386f.; Böhme, 1974.

58 The Winchester Cemetery is that at Lankhills: see Giles Clarke's interim reports in M. Biddle, 'Excavations at Winchester, 1969', *Ant. J* 1 (1970), 278f., and M. Biddle, 'Excavations at Winchester, 1970', *Ant. J* lii (1972), 94f. For a further comment on this metalwork, see C. J. Simpson, 'Belt-buckles and strap-ends of the later Roman empire', *Britannia* vii (1976), 192f.

59 R. S. O. Tomlin, '*Notitia Dignitatum omnium, tam civilium quam militarium*', in Bartholomew and Goodburn, 1976, 189f.

60 Bowes: *JRS* lvii (1968), 179; Ilkley and Bainbridge, see n. 22 above.

61 J. G. F. Hind, 'The British provinces of Orcades and Valentia', *Historia* 24 (1975), 101f.

62 J. G. F. Hind, *loc. cit.* (n. 61).

63 J. C. Mann, *loc. cit.* (n. 31).

64 See F. J. Haverfield, 'Notes on the Roman coast defences of Britain, especially in Yorkshire', *JRS* ii (1912), 210f.; W. Hornsby and J. D. Laverick, 'The Roman signal station at Goldsborough, Whitby', *Arch. J* lxxxix (1932), 203.

65 *RIB* 721. See C. E. Stevens, 'The British sections of the *Notitia Dignitatum*', *Arch. J* xcvii (1940), 151f.

66 T. W. Potter, 'The Biglands milefortlet, Cumbria', *Britannia* viii (1977), 183.

67 J. S. Wacher, *Brough-on-Humber* (Society of Antiquaries Research Report, 25, 1969), 25f.

68 Prosper Tiro, *Chronicon Gratiani*, iv.

69 S. Johnson, 'Channel commands in the *Notitia*', in Bartholomew and Goodburn, 1975, 81f.

70 S. Johnson, 'Late Roman defences and the *limes*', in Johnston, 1977, 63f.

71 Vegetius, *De Re Militari*, iv, 37.

72 M. Miller, 'Stilicho's Pictish war', *Britannia* vi (1976), 141f.

73 Claudian, *De Bello Getico*, xxvi, 416f.

Chapter four History of the Anglo-Saxon invasion

1   The sources and the historical episode are fully discussed
in two articles by E. A. Thompson, 'Zosimus on the end
of Roman Britain', *Antiquity* xxx (1956), 163f., and 'Britain
AD 406–410', *Britannia* viii (1977), 303f.

2   Zosimus, vi, 2, 1–2, following Olympiodorus. See also
Orosius vii, 40, 4.

3   Prosper Tiro, *Chronicon Gratiani* 1230.

4   Zosimus, vi, 2, 2; vi, 3, 1.

5   Olympiodorus, Frag. 12; Zosimus, vi, 1, 2; vi, 3, 2–3.

6   Zosimus, vi, 5, 2.

7   Gallic Chronicler of the year 452 (*Chronica Minora*, 1, 654).

8   Zosimus, vi, 5, 2.

9   E. A. Thompson, 'Britain AD 406–410', *Britannia* viii
(1977), 311–13.

10 Gallic Chronicler of the year 452, 117, 119; Merobaudes,
Panegyric, ii, 8.

11 The depression of the times is most obviously seen in the
sermons of such men as bishop Maximinus of Turin.
There were, however, some notable exceptions: The
African bishop Synesius and the later bishop Severinus in
Noricum (Austria) were more active characters who were
prepared to carry the fight to the barbarians. Within
Britain, bishop Germanus of Auxerre led an army at
Easter 429 to battle against a combined force of Saxons
and Picts (see below p. 116).

12 J. Ferguson, *Pelagius* (Cambridge, 1956); R. F. Evans, *Pelagius* (London, 1968); J. R. Morris, 'Pelagian Literature',
Journal of Theological Studies, 16 (1965), 26f.

13 J. R. Morris, *loc. cit.* (n. 12). Fastidius' *De Vita Christiana* is
published in J. P. Migne, *Patrologia Latina* (Paris, 1878–90),
40, 1031.

14 J. N. L. Myres, 'Pelagius and the End of Roman Rule in
Britain', *JRS*, 1 (1960), 21f.

15 W. Liebeschuetz, 'Did the Pelagian movement have social
aims?', *Historia*, xii (1963), 227f.; W. Liebschuetz, 'Pelagian
evidence in the last period of Roman Britain', *Latomus*,
xxvi (1967), 436f.

16 On Synesius (n. 11) see J. C. Pando, *The Life and Times of
Synesius of Cyrene*, (Washington, 1940); on Severinus, see
S. S. Frere, 'The end of towns in Roman Britain', in J. S.
Wacher, 1966, 98f. The life of Severinus by Eugippius is
edited (and translated into German) in R. Noll, *Das Leben
des Heiligen Severin* (Berlin, 1963).

17 Constantine, *Vita Sancti Germani*, III, 14.

18 Gildas, *De Excidio et Conquestu Britanniae*.

19 J. R. Morris, 'Dark Age Dates', in Jarrett and Dobson, 1966, 150–1; Alcock, 1973, 22–4.
20 A general survey of this source material will be found in most of the latest works on the period. See Alcock, 1973, 99f.; Morris, 1973, 35f., and 44f.; Morris, 1973 (n. 19), 151f. Caution is advised in the use of all these sources by D. M. Dumville, 'Sub-Roman Britain', *History* 62, no. 205 (June 1977), 173f.
21 On the view that this portion of Gildas's writings constitute a 'Northern History', see Dumville, *loc. cit.* (n. 20) p. 180; see also M. Miller, 'Bede's use of Gildas', *EHR*, 90 (1975), 241f.
22 M. Miller, *loc. cit.*
23 See J. N. L. Myres, 'The *Adventus Saxonum*', in W. F. Grimes (ed.), *Aspects of Archaeology in Britain and Beyond* (London, 1951), 221f.; M. Miller, *loc. cit.* (n.21); Alcock, 1973, 91–2, 104–9.
24 Dumville, *loc. cit.* (n. 20) 180.
25 D. M. Dumville, 'Nennius and the *Historia Brittonum*', *Studia Celtica* x–xi (1975–6), 78f.; and Dumville, 'Sub-Roman Britain', *loc. cit.* (n. 20).
26 Collingwood and Myres, 1937, 327–8.
27 J. Morris, *loc. cit.* in Jarrett and Dobson, 1966, 146.
28 Fastidius, *De Vita Christiana*, ch. 3.
29 Procopius, *De Bello Vandalico*, i, 2, 38.
30 J. H. Ward, 'Vortigern and the end of Roman Britain', *Britannia* iii (1972), 277f.
31 J. P. Kirby, 'Vortigern', *BBCS*, 23 (1968–70), 37f.
32 Dumville, *loc. cit.*, n. 20, 183f.
33 Constantine, *Vita Sancti Germani* III, 17.
34 See n. 23 above.
35 J. B. Bury, 'The *Notitia Dignitatum*', *JRS* x (1920), 131f.; J. H. Ward, 'The British sections of the *Notitia Dignitatum*: an alternative interpretation', *Britannia* iv (1973), 253.
36 M. Todd, 'Famosa Pestis and fifth-century Britain', *Britannia* viii (1977), 319f., in answer to J. S. Wacher, 1975, 411f.
37 Constantine, *Vita Sancti Germani*, V, 25f.
38 N. K. Chadwick, *Early Brittany* (Cardiff, 1969) 162f.; Morris, 1973, 88f, and Morris, *loc. cit.* in Jarrett and Dobson, 1966, 168.
39 Alcock, 1973, 121f., 238f.
40 See n. 26.
41 Morris, *loc. cit.* in Jarrett and Dobson, 1966, 169–70, claims that this battle is that celebrated on the British side as Llongborth by the 'Lament for Geraint'. He suggests that

Geraint may have been the British prince who was slain in that engagement.

42 Mount Badon has been claimed as near Bath (Alcock, 1973, 71) or at one of several places named 'Badbury' scattered round the country.

43 Gildas, *De Excidio*, 26.

Chapter five The arrival of the Anglo-Saxons

1 For an expanded version of how such material is dated, see J. Morris, reviewing Myres and Green, 1973, in *Med. Arch.* xviii (1974), 226f.; see also Morris, 1973, 30–3.

2 D. Kidd, reviewing J. N. L. Myres and W. H. Southern, *The Anglo-Saxon Cremation Cemetery at Sancton, East Yorkshire* (Hull, 1976), in *Med. Arch.* xx (1976), 202–4.

3 Identified by Böhme, 1974. For a summary of Böhme's main views and conclusions in English, see S. C. Hawkes, 'British antiquity 1974–5: Post-Roman and early Saxon', *Arch. J* 132 (1975), 333f.

4 Morris, 1973, ch. 15, especially p. 267–9; Myres, 1969, chs 5 and 6, pp. 62–99. Though the two authors differ over the precise dating for the Saxon arrival, there is broad agreement over the areas to which the Anglo-Saxons first came.

5 Bede, *Historia Ecclesiastica*, i, 15.

6 Collingwood and Myres, 1937, 337.

7 Morris, 1973, 270.

8 For interim reports on finds from Mucking, M. U. Jones, V. I. Evison and J. N. L. Myres, 'Crop-mark sites at Mucking, Essex', *Ant. J* xlviii (1968), 210f., M. U. Jones, 'Excavations at Mucking, Essex, a second interim report', *Ant. J* liv (1974), 183f. Numerous other articles have been produced about the site by its excavators W. T. and M. U. Jones: one of the more important from the Anglo-Saxon viewpoint is W. T. and M. U. Jones, 'The early Saxon landscape at Mucking, Essex', in Rowley, 1974, 20f.

9 S. C. Hawkes, 'British antiquity 1973–4, post-Roman and pagan Anglo-Saxon', *Arch. J* 131 (1974), 410.

10 Interim report by S. E. West, 'The Anglo-Saxon village of West Stow: an interim report of the excavations', *Med. Arch.* xiii (1969), 1f.; a further report also in *Curr. Arch.* 40 (September 1973), 151f.

11 S. E. West and J. Plouviez, 'The Romano-British site at Icklingham', *East Anglian Archaeology* 3 (1976), 63f.

12 The so-called Illington-Lackford potter: Myres, 1969, 132–3.

13 *Curr. Arch.* 53 (July 1976), 166f, and M. Bell and others, *Excavations at Bishopstone, Sussex Archaeological Collections*

115 (1977), 1–299, especially pp. 192f. See also *Med. Arch.* xii (1968), 161 and xiii (1969), 240.

14 *Med. Arch.* xvii (1973), 140.
15 Myres, 1969, 63–4.
16 Myres and Green, 1973.
17 For reviews of Myres and Green, see S. C. Hawkes, *Arch. J* 131 (1974), 412–13; D. M. Wilson, *JBAA* 37 (1974), 124–5; J. Morris, *Med. Arch.* xviii (1974), 225f.
18 *ND*, Or. XXXII, 37.
19 *ND*, Occ. XLII, 33–44, 64–70.
20 Böhme, 1974, 201f.
21 See Chapter 3, n. 57.
22 S. C. Hawkes, *loc. cit.* (n. 3), 334.
23 D. Brown, in Rowley, 1974, 16f.; see also Rowley, 1974, 42.
24 Myres, 1969, fig. 32 (p. 210).
25 Myres, 1969, fig. 37 (p. 220) and Pl. 2. For recent finds at West Stow, see n. 10. For Mucking: M. U. Jones, 'Saxon pottery from a hut at Mucking', *Berichten van de Rijksdienst voor Oudheidkundig Bodemonderzoek* 19 (1969), 145f. On the Mitcham pedestal carinated bowl and its associated finds, M. G. Welch with a note by J. N. L. Myres, 'Mitcham grave 205 and the chronology of applied brooches with floriate cross decoration', *Ant. J* lv (1975), 86f., and M. G. Welch, 'Liebenau inhumation grave II/196 and the dating of the Anglo-Saxon cemetery at Mitcham', *Med. Arch.* xx (1976), 134f.
26 Myres, 1969, 65f., and especially p. 77.
27 Myres and Green, 1973, 41–2 and fig. 64.
28 Myres and Green, 1973, 74f.
29 *Ibid.*, 74f.
30 On Canterbury: S. S. Frere, 'The end of towns in Roman Britain', in Wacher, 1966, 91f.
31 On Colchester: *Curr. Arch.* 43 (March 1974), 237f.
32 On Kelvedon: W. J. Rodwell, 'Trinovantian towns and their setting', in Rodwell and Rowley, 1975, 95. See also *Curr. Arch.* 48 (January 1975), 25f.
33 On Abingdon: D. Miles, 'Abingdon and region, early Anglo-Saxon settlement evidence', in Rowley, 1974, 36f.
34 On Eccles: S. C. Hawkes and A. P. Detsicas, 'Finds from the Anglo-Saxon cemetery at Eccles, Kent', *Ant. J* liii (1973), 281–6.
35 On Keston: B. J. Philp, *Excavations in West Kent 1960–1970* (Dover, 1973), 156f. Another villa in the same area with Anglo-Saxon remains is that of Darenth (*ibid.*, p. 155–6).
36 M. G. Welch, 'Late Romans and Saxons in Sussex', *Britannia* ii (1971), 232f.
37 C. C. Taylor, 'The Anglo-Saxon countryside', in Rowley, 1974, 5f.

38 B. W. Cunliffe, 'Saxon and medieval settlement patterns in the region of Chalton, Hampshire', *Med. Arch.* xvi (1972), 1f.

39 H. P. R. Finberg, *Roman and Saxon Withington, a Study in Continuity*, (Leicester, 1959).

40 P. Sawyer, 'Anglo-Saxon settlement, the documentary evidence', in Rowley, 1974, 108f.

41 *Ibid.*, 110f.

42 D. Bonney, 'Early boundaries in Wessex', in Fowler, 1972, 168f.; see also P. J. Fowler, 'Agriculture and rural settlement', in Wilson, 1976, 39f.

43 M. W. Beresford and J. G. Hurst, 'Wharram Percy: a case study in microtopography', in Sawyer, 1976, 141–4.

44 C. Taylor, *op. cit.* (n. 37), fn. 8.

45 M. L. Faull, 'Roman and Anglian settlement patterns in Yorkshire', *Northern History* ix (1974), 1–25.

46 Jackson, 1953, 220–3.

47 M. Gelling, 'The evidence of place-names', in Sawyer, 1976, 200f.

48 As in the case of York: the Latin *Eboracum*, meaning 'a yew-grove', had developed by the fifth century to *Evoróg*. It was later replaced by *Eoforwic*, whose English meaning would be 'bear-farm': this might seem an acceptable example of a completely new coining of a place-name, were it not for the fact that these antecedents are known. See M. Gelling, *loc. cit.* (n. 47), 201.

49 On this, see M. Gelling, 'English place-names derived from the compound *wichām*', *Med. Arch.* xi (1967), 87f.; and M. Gelling, 'Latin loan-words in Old English place-names', *Anglo-Saxon England* 6 (1973), 1f.

Chapter six Continuity of settlement

1 Wacher, 1975, 311f.

2 This sort of process can also be seen in areas of Germany abandoned by the Romans in AD 260. East of the river Rhine, the Roman towns of Ladenburg and Wimpfen formed the nucleus of native German settlement in the area. See K. Weidemann, 'Untersuchungen zur Siedlungsgeschichte des Landes zwischen Limes und Rhein vom Ende der Römerherrschaft bis zum frühen Mittelalter', *Jahrbuch der Römisch-Germanisch Zentralmuseum, Mainz*, 19 (1972), 99f.

3 J. Campbell, reviewing Morris, 1973, in *Studia Hibernica* 15 (1975), 177f.

4 B. W. Cunliffe, *Portchester II (Saxon)*, Research Report of the Society of Antiquaries, 33, 1976, 301.

5 P. D. C. Brown, 'The church at Richborough', *Britannia* ii (1971), 225.

6   S. E. Rigold, 'Litus Romanum', in Johnston, 1977, 70f.
7   Laing, 1977, 57f.
8   S. S. Frere, 'Excavations at Verulamium 1959', *Ant. J* xl (1950), 19.
9   J. P. C. Kent, 'From Roman Britain to Saxon England', in R. H. M. Dolley (ed.), *Anglo-Saxon Coins* (London, 1961), 1f.
10 G. C. Boon, *Silchester* (Newton Abbot, 1974), 78f.
11 Wacher, 1975, 313; J. S. Wacher, 'Cirencester 1962, third interim report', *Ant. J.* xliii (1963), 21.
12 Wacher, 1975, 334–5.
13 C. Thomas, 'Irish colonists in south-western Britain', *World Archaeology* 5 (1973), 5f.
14 P. J. Fowler, 'Somerset AD 400–700', in Fowler, 1972, 207f.
15 *Ibid.* 191f.; P. J. Fowler, 'Hillforts AD 400–700' in Jesson and Hill, 1971, 201f.
16 See n. 15. L. Alcock, *By South Cadbury, that is Camelot* (London, 1972).
17 P. J. Fowler, *loc. cit.* in Jesson and Hill, 1972, 201f.
18 Wacher, 1975, 313–14; Wacher, *loc. cit.*, *Ant. J* xliii (1963), 26; Wacher, 'Cirencester 1963, fourth interim report', *Ant. J* xliv (1964), 18.
19 P. J. Fowler, *loc. cit.* in Fowler, 1972, 199f.
20 L. Alcock, *By South Cadbury, that is Camelot* (n. 16), 11–23, 193–4.
21 V. E. Nash-Williams, *The Early Christian Monuments of Wales* (Cardiff, 1950).
22 Constantine, *Vita Sancti Germani*, III, 15. This is a clear throwback to two of Jesus's miracles (Matthew 8: 5f., and Mark 5: 22f.), including that of the healing of the centurion's servant. But the fact that Germanus is recorded as having met a man of 'tribunician rank' and not an exact parallel to the Gospel story may suggest that this detail was authentic.
23 C. Thomas, 'The end of the Roman South-west', in K. Branigan and P. J. Fowler, *The Romans in the South-West* (Newton Abbot, 1976), 198f.
24 H. and T. Miles, 'Interim report on excavations at Trethurgy, Cornwall', *Corn. Arch.* 12 (1973) 25f.; C. Saunders, 'The excavations at Grambla, Wendron, 1972', *Corn. Arch.* 11 (1972), 50f.
25 On Welsh farmstead settlements, see A. H. A. Hogg, *RCHM, Caernarvonshire* III, p. lxxxviif.
26 P. A. Barker, 'Excavations on the site of the Baths-basilica at Wroxeter', *Britannia* vi (1975), 106.
27 L. R. Laing, 'Timber halls in Dark Age Britain', *Transactions of the Dumfriesshire and Galloway Natural History and Antiquarian Society* 46 (1969), 110f.

28 C. Thomas, *The Early Christian Archaeology of Northern Britain* (Oxford, 1971), 10f.

29 C. Guy, 'The lead tank from Ashton', *Durobrivae* 5 (1977), 10f.

30 K. Painter, in *Wealth of the Roman World* (British Museum Exhibition Catalogue, 1977), 29.

31 C. J. S. Green, 'The significance of plaster burials', in R. M. Reece (ed.), *Burial in the Roman World* (CBA Research Report 22, 1976).

32 C. A. R. Radford, 'Christian Origins in Britain', *Med. Arch.* 15 (1971), 1f.

33 C. A. R. Radford, *loc. cit.* (n. 32).

34 W. H. C. Frend, 'The Christianisation of Roman Britain', in Barley and Hanson, 1968, 38f.

35 C. A. R. Radford, 'The Mediterranean sources of sculpture in stone among the insular Celts and the survival into the full Medieval age', in Laing, 1977, 113f.

36 D. R. Longley, *The Anglo-Saxon Connection* (*BAR* 22, 1975), 32; C. F. C. Hawkes, 'Bronze-workers, cauldrons and bucket-animals in Iron Age and Roman Britain', in W. F. Grimes, *Aspects of Archaeology in Britain and Beyond* (London, 1951), 177f.

37 Jackson, 1953, 97f; J. P. Wild, 'Borrowed names for borrowed things?', *Antiquity* 44 (1970), 125f.; J. P. Wild, 'Loanwords and Roman expansion in north-western Europe', *World Archaeology* 8 (1976), 57f.

38 W. Davies,'*Liber Landavensis*: its construction and credibility', *EHR* 347 (1973), 375f. I refer also to a communication by Dr Davies to a Conference on 'The End of Roman Britain' at Durham, April 1978.

39 See the discussion of this in J. Campbell, *loc. cit.* (n. 3), 181f.

Bibliography and abbreviations

Ancient authors and texts

A.M.   Ammianus Marcellinus, ed. J. C. Rolfe (Loeb edn, 1935–9).

Bede   *Ecclesiastical History*, ed. C. Plummer (Oxford, 1896), or ed. B. Colgrave and R. A. B. Mynors (Oxford, 1969).

Constantine   *Vita Sancti Germani (Life of St Germanus), Monumenta Germaniae Historica* VII (Berlin, 1920), 247f.

Gildas   *De Excidio et Conquestu Britanniae (On the Ruin and Conquest of Britain)*, ed. T. Mommsen, *Monumenta Germaniae Historica* III (1898), translated and reprinted by H. Williams, *Cymmrodorion*, Record Series 3, 1899.

ND   *Notitia Dignitatum*, ed. O. Seeck (Berlin, 1876).

Nennius   *Historia Brittonum (History of the Britons)*, ed. T. Mommsen, *Monumenta Germaniae Historica* III (Berlin, 1898).

Pan. Lat.   *Panegyrici Latini*, ed. R. A. B. Mynors (Oxford, 1964).

RIB   *The Roman Inscriptions of Britain*, ed. R. G. Collingwood and R. P. Wright (Oxford, 1965).

SHA   *Scriptores Historiae Augustae*, ed. D. Magie (Loeb edn, 1922–32).

Zosimus   *Historia Nova*, ed. L. Mendelssohn (Leipzig, 1887).

Periodical literature: abbreviations

Ant. J   *Antiquaries Journal*
Arch. J   *Archaeological Journal*
BAR   *British Archaeological Reports*
BBCS   *Bulletin of the Board of Celtic Studies*
CBA   Council for British Archaeology
Corn. Arch. *Cornish Archaeology*
Curr. Arch. *Current Archaeology*
Econ. HR   *Economic History Review*
EHR   *English Historical Review*
JBAA   *Journal of the British Archaeological Association*
JRS   *Journal of Roman Studies*

245

Med. Arch.	*Mediaeval Archaeology*
PRIA	*Proceedings of the Royal Irish Academy*
RCHM	*Royal Commission on Historical Monuments*
TASDN	*Transactions of the Architectural Society of Durham and Northumberland*
TCWAS	*Transactions of the Cumberland and Westmorland Archaeological Society*
YAJ	*Yorkshire Archaeological Journal*

Modern works

Alcock, 1973   L. Alcock, *Arthur's Britain* (Harmondsworth, 1973).

Barley and Hanson, 1968   M. W. Barley and R. P. C. Hanson (eds), *Christianity in Britain 300–700* (Leicester, 1968).

Bartholomew and Goodburn, 1976   P. Bartholomew and R. Goodburn (eds), *Aspects of the Notitia Dignitatum, BAR* S15, 1976.

Böhme, 1974   H. W. Böhme, *Germanische Grabfunde des 4 bis 5 Jahrhunderts zwischen unterer Elbe und Loire* (Munich, 1974).

Breeze and Dobson, 1976   D. J. Breeze and B. Dobson, *Hadrian's Wall* (Harmondsworth, 1976).

Collingwood and Myres, 1937   R. G. Collingwood and J. N. L. Myres, *Roman Britain and the English Settlements* (Oxford, 1937).

Fowler, 1972   P. J. Fowler (ed.), *Archaeology in the Landscape* (London, 1972).

Frere, 1974   S. S. Frere, *Britannia* (London, 1974).

Hawkes, 1973   C. F. C. Hawkes (ed.), *Greeks, Celts and Romans* (London, 1973).

Jackson, 1953   K. H. Jackson, *Language and History in Early Britain* (Edinburgh, 1953).

Jarrett and Dobson, 1966   M. G. Jarrett and B. Dobson (eds), *Britain and Rome* (Kendal, 1966).

Jesson and Hill, 1971   M. Jesson and D. Hill (eds), *The Iron Age and its Hill-Forts* (Southampton, 1971).

Johnson, 1976   S. Johnson, *The Roman Forts of the Saxon Shore* (London, 1976).

Johnston, 1977   D. E. Johnston (ed.), *The Saxon Shore*, CBA Research Report 18 (1977).

Jones, 1964   A. H. M. Jones, *The Later Roman Empire* (Oxford, 1964).

Laing, 1977   L. R. Laing (ed.), *Studies in Celtic Survival, BAR* 37 (1977).

Macmullen, 1967   R. Macmullen, *Soldier and Civilian in the Later Roman Empire* (Cambridge, Mass. 1964).

Morris, 1973   J. Morris, *The Age of Arthur* (London, 1973).

Myres, 1969   J. N. L. Myres, *Anglo-Saxon Pottery and the Settlement of England* (Oxford, 1969).

Myres and Green, 1973   J. N. L. Myres and B. Green, *The Anglo-Saxon Cemeteries of Caistor-by-Norwich and Markshall*, Society of Antiquaries Research Report 30 (1973).

Rodwell and Rowley, 1975   W. J. Rodwell and T. Rowley, *The Small Towns of Roman Britain*, BAR 15 (1975).

Rowley, 1974   T. Rowley (ed.), *Anglo-Saxon Settlement and the Landscape, BAR* 6 (1974).

Sawyer, 1976   P. H. Sawyer (ed.), *Medieval Settlement* (London, 1976).

Thomas, 1966   A. C. Thomas (ed.), *Rural Settlement in Roman Britain*, CBA Research Report 7 (1966).

Todd, 1975   M. Todd, *The Northern Barbarians* (London, 1975).

Wacher, 1966   J. S. Wacher (ed.), *The Civitas Capitals of Roman Britain* (Leicester, 1966).

Wacher, 1975   J. S. Wacher, *The Towns of Roman Britain* (London, 1975).

Wilson, 1976   D. M. Wilson (ed.), *The Archaeology of Anglo-Saxon England* (London, 1976).

Index

early Roman contact with, 8–10; fifth-century history, 134–40; language of, 52–5; Roman conquest of, 9; 'Romanization of', 10–11, 52 ff; sources for study, 11–13, 134–9

Britannia, 11; army of province, 36–9; Christianity, 43 ff; description of province, 13 ff; formation of province, 8–10; governors of, 13–16; trade within, 39–42

brochs, 71–2, 78

Brough-on-Humber (Humbs.), 25, 130

Brough-on-Noe (Derbys), 111

Burgh Castle (Norfolk), 192

Burgundians, 52, 90

Butcombe Down (Som.), 28, 30

Cadbury Congresbury (Som.), 203

Caerau, 89

Caerleon, 116

Caernarvon, 115–6

Caerwent, 57, 115, 124, 215

Caesar, Julius, 8

Caister-on-Sea (Norfolk), 99

Caistor (Lincs.), 130

Caistor-by-Norwich (Norfolk), 171, 176, 191

Caledonians, 77, 118, 121, 130

Cambridge, 177

Camerton (Som.), 40

Canterbury (Kent), 178, 191

Cantioris, 88

Carausius, 32, 113, 134; usurpation of, 102–7

Cardiff, 115

Cardurnock (Cumbria), 130

Carlisle (Cumbria), 13, 108, 112

Carmarthen, 58, 115

cashels, 79

Castle Dore (Cornwall), 203

Catsgore (Som.), settlement, 29

Catterick (N. Yorks.), 112

Cefn Graeanog (Gwynedd), 89

Celts, 79; Celtic art, 52, 220–1; Celtic language, 53 ff, 187–8, 221; construction techniques among, 208–11, 216–20

cemeteries: Anglo-Saxon, 169, 177–8, 180; Christian, 211–4; 'laetic', 172; Roman, 174

Cerdic and Cynric, 156

Chalton (Hants.), 183

Chelmsford (Essex), 96

Chester, 116

Chesterton–Water Newton (Cambs.), 17, 25, 176, 213

Christianity, 26, 45–7, 220; churches, 47, 168, 193, 197; church plate, 213–4; fifth-century evidence, 150–2, 209–19; mosaics, 26, 47; Pelagianism and, 149; treasure from Traprain Law, 75–7

Cirencester (Glos.), 13, 25, 201

Cissbury (Sussex), 203

civitas, 17, 33, 47, 48, 119, 124–6, 152, 174, 193

Claudian, 133

coins: Carausian, 103, 106; in hoards, 92, 176; lack of in fifth century, 198

Colchester (Essex), 9, 46 96, 99, 177, 180, 191

Coleraine Hoard, 79

Comes (Count), 37, 121, 130;